KU-479-200

Too You're Kind

A Brief History of Flattery

Richard Stengel

POCKET
B O O K S

LONDON · SYDNEY · NEW YORK · TOKYO · SINGAPORE · TORONTO

CAMDEN LIBRARIES

First published in the USA by Simon & Schuster Inc, 2000
First published in Great Britain by Simon & Schuster UK Ltd, 2001
This edition first published by Pocket Books, 2001
An imprint of Simon & Schuster UK Ltd
A Viacom Company

Copyright © Richard Stengel, 2000

This book is copyright under the Berne Convention
No reproduction without permission
® and © 1997 Simon & Schuster Inc. All rights reserved
Pocket Books & Design is a registered trademark of Simon & Schuster Inc

The right of Richard Stengel to be identified as the author of this work
has been asserted by him in accordance with sections 77 and 78 of the
Copyright, Designs and Patents Act, 1988

1 3 5 7 9 10 8 6 4 2

Simon & Schuster UK Ltd
Africa House
64-78 Kingsway
London WC2B 6AH

Simon & Schuster Australia
Sydney

A CIP catalogue record for this book is available from the British Library

ISBN 0-7434-1500-0

CAMDEN LIBRARIES	
38902093	BFS
-- DEC 2001	£6.99
177.3	PHI

Praise f

301110 **3890209 3**

'Flattery will get you nowher   case. In fact, as Richard Stengel magnificently demonstrates (do I overstate?), ingratiation has been a fundamental, perhaps an evolutionary aim of most social behaviour and polite speech . . . Stengel is able triumphantly to conclude (am I reaching too high?) flattery is more pervasively present than ever, although disguised and venally debased in these revitalizing times, in this age of irony'
The New York Times

'Mr Stengel has prepared an entertaining and at times surprisingly serious and disturbing meditation on flattery . . . Lively, analytically penetrating and theoretically sound'
New York Observer

'All of which should make it clear – especially you, gentle and quick-witted reader – that Stengel has written not merely a popular history of flattery but also a guide to its employment . . . If you must flatter – and there are times when flattery is clearly the wisest course – then by all means do it well'
Washington Post

'The book has many delights and charms . . . Reading this one wonders what fun Mr Stengel could have with other human habits of disposition, say calumny. But he is too good natured for that'
Washington Times

'taking us from ancient history to modern psychology, Stengel offers plenty of sage advice in his guide to brown-nosing through the ages'
Scotland on Sunday

'How ironic – a flatteringly solicited bit of flattery slapped on a book about flattery. But as *You're Too Kind* reminds us, it's important to distinguish between mere flattery and honest praise: this book is really smart and funny and wise'
Kurt Anderson, author of *Turn of the Century*

'Along with discovering democracy, the ancient Greeks were also wary of demagoguery – the flattering of the public. But there's no danger in praising *You're Too Kind* for what it is: a sly and surprisingly deep study of the courtier's art'
George Stephanopoulos, author of *All Too Human*

'A funny and informative chronology of kiss-upmanship . . . Surely any area of human behaviour so widespread, and so integral to our daily lives, deserves its own well-researched, thoughtful and often downright funny historical analysis. It's not mere flattery to state that Richard Stengel has delivered such a book. Readers – especially the supremely sophisticated – will enjoy it immensely'
Forbes FYI

'A genial, witty and engaging account (honestly!) of human foibles, relationships and social conventions . . . This is a work of insightful social criticism'
Publishers Weekly

'A witty, savvy guide to the age-old art of strategic sweet-talking'
Salon

'*You're Too Kind* hooked me from the first hello, and it's not because of the blatant flattery Stengel dishes out . . . This is wonderfully entertaining book'
Contentville

'An engaging and original book'
Chicago Tribune

'*You're Too Kind* is a learned and lucid examination of ass-kissing over the ages'
Washington Monthly

'A comprehensive, humorous, and insightful history of man's sycoph
behaviour . . . Highly readable'
Kirkus Reviews

For Mary—
"By heaven I think my love as rare as any
she belied with false compare."

Contents

You're Too Kind

Introduction

Pleasure to Be Deceived

Perfect, gentle reader: I will not begin this book with a tribute to your discernment, because a person of your obvious accomplishments would certainly be immune to such blandishments. You would surely see through such transparent puffery and reject it out of hand. Someone with as much self-assurance and insight as you would not want any soft soap and sycophancy, but rather candor and direct truth.

Well, nothing personal, dear reader, but I doubt it.

We like to think that the smarter a person is, the higher she ascends up the ladder of success, the less susceptible that individual is to flattery. In fact, the opposite seems to be the case. People of high self-esteem and accomplishment generally see the praise directed at them as shrewd judgment rather than flattery. While people with low self-esteem are much warier. *Yes, how bright young Smith is for seeing how brilliant I am.* "Self-love," said La Rochefoucauld, "is the greatest of all flatterers." People who do not suffer fools gladly, gladly suffer flatterers. (Ergo, flatterers are no fools.) I will simply flatter you, then, by not flattering you—which is perhaps the highest flattery of all.

When I told friends that I was working on a book about flattery, they would often pause for a moment, smile, and then say, in a theatrical tone, "What a brilliant idea! Yes, that'll be a fantastic book. You're just the person to do it." When this first happened, my initial reaction was to say to myself, *Hmm, they really seem to like the idea*—and then I caught on to the irony. That is why flattery works: We are all so very eager to believe what we want to believe.

That ironic tone is so often the cloak for all flattery, indeed all praise, these days. What we think of as flattery is usually delivered with an air of arch knowingness, a kind of self-consciousness that says, *We all know this is flattery, so don't consider me a weaselly little brownnose for saying it.* In fact, these days we struggle to invent new ways to praise people because the traditional methods are seen as a worn-out currency.

Much of *public* praise has become sly and ironic, delivered in quotation marks. The old late-night talk-show introductions, "a great entertainer and a great American," are now used only as a form of kitsch. Public praise has become that way because no one wants to be perceived as a smarmy suck-up. We still occasionally hear sincere seventies superlatives—"You're the best"; "You're the greatest"—on daytime TV talk shows. Those pat phrases are the continuing legacy of the various self-esteem movements of the past three decades. Those superlatives defined flattery downward. If everyone is "the best," of course, then no one is—or we all are.

Flattery, of late, has become more covert, better hidden. When I first started working as a magazine journalist in New York City in the early 1980s, the editor was a crusty, no-nonsense fellow who seemed allergic to phonies and impervious to small talk. My great fear was having to get in the elevator alone with him, for I knew I didn't have a clue as to what to say to him.

Not too long after I started work, there was a kind of get-acquainted session for new writers. I suspect it was the suggestion of some management consultant who urged the editor to try to make new employees feel more comfortable or some such thing. At the meeting the editor tried to be affable and he even gave us his rictus of a smile. Instead of talking about the magazine and its history, though, he fell back on discussing that week's events and his notion for a certain cover story. One of the young writers raised his hand and in the most earnest tone said, "I really think that's a brilliant idea. Your ideas are always so perceptive, so much ahead of the pack. So wise, really."

I looked around the room to see if people were smirking or rolling their eyes. They weren't. I looked at the editor to see if this gruff fellow who was famous for his bullshit detector was ready to kick the little toady in his sycophantic butt. No. In fact, the editor smiled softly. At the end of the meeting, he invited the writer to send him a memo with some cover suggestions. I was dumbfounded. This man was in fact an excellent editor, smart, hardheaded, with a good design sense. But this very obvious flattery penetrated his defenses like the proverbial knife through butter. "Everybody likes a compliment," said Abraham Lincoln.

I think today such straight-out flattery is rarer than it was back then. You don't see such fastball-over-the-center-of-the-plate flattery, but a slider that just nicks the corner. We are subtler about flattery. We are warier about being detected. Bystanders are more cynical. We don't want to seem too *earnest*. We are better versed in the wily arts of what sociologists call "impression management." Public flattery is less over-the-top, but people can still be fervently flattering in private as a kind of remedy for not being more effusive in public: *I could never say this at the staff meeting, but I wanted to tell you your suggestion was just superb.*

These days, we tend to think of all praise as flattery. We rarely bother trying to distinguish between the two. Praise seems to have become a subset of flattery. Flattery has never been a flattering idea, but now our slightly jaundiced, strategic view of it has tainted ordinary praise. What does it say about our culture that we don't make a distinction between praise and flattery, or that we look at all praise as flattery?

It has become a cliché to declare that we live in an ironic age. But what does that really mean? For one thing, we all have a looser, more skeptical relationship with the truth. We are all moral relativists these days. No one believes in the George Washington–cherry tree standard anymore—if they ever did. The Enlightenment idea of truth as a supreme value has gone by the wayside. Nothing is completely straight anymore. Nothing is unstrategic.

Irony always flourishes in ages when the idea of truth itself is relative. But pervasive irony engenders a kind of cynical moral lethargy. Ethical distinctions make us weary. Such fine differences are met either with a smirk or a shrug. We cloak ourselves in what Christopher Lasch called "protective shallowness." If all truth is relative, flattery is just another way of massaging it.

When I talk to someone I don't know very well, I no longer think, *Is this person telling me the truth?* I think, *How close to the truth is what he's telling me?* It is not that I think people these days are more deceptive; I think they are more self-aware, shrewder and more pragmatic about interpersonal relations. Our view of reality is more nuanced, and that is not a bad thing. These days, honest people try to stay as close to the truth as possible. Less honest folk stray as far from the truth as practical.

The root of the word "irony" is the Greek term *eiron,* which we translate as "dissembler." That is how we tend to think of flattery, as dissembling, a particular kind of manipulation of the truth. But flattery is different from dissembling because it is a stretching of the truth we rarely question. If someone tells me that she is a very insightful person, I wonder whether it can be true. If she tells me that I am a very insightful person, *Well, hmm, that's very perceptive of her.* In many ways, flattery works like a heat-seeking missile, only what the missile homes in on is our vanity. And vanity, as the sages tell us, is the most universal human trait. We all want to be liked. We all want to be appreciated. Flattery almost always hits its target because the target—you, me, everybody—rises up to meet it. We have no natural defense system against it. We don't doubt because we want to believe. As John Locke said, we all "find pleasure to be deceived." If it's a lie, it's a lie we don't care or want to question. "Lie to me," sings Sheryl Crow, "and I'll promise to believe."

*   *   *

A working rule of anthropology is that the most important thing to examine about a society is what it takes for granted. We take flattery for granted. We assume that it has always been with us and always will be. In this book, I'm not going to use the scientific principle of parsimony—that is, making only the most spartan assumptions when constructing an argument. I'm going to take a broader, more expansive view of flattery. There will be examples that will probably make you say, *Well, no, that's not flattery.* But I would rather err on the side of inclusiveness than exclusiveness.

Before I go any further, let me quickly posit a brief working definition. Flattery is strategic praise, praise with a purpose. It may be inflated or exaggerated or it may be accurate and truthful, but it is praise that seeks some result, whether it be increased liking or an office with a window. It is a kind of manipulation of reality that uses the enhancement of another for our own self-advantage. It can even be genuine praise.

I'm not going to spend much time talking about the everyday, obligatory forms of flattery that we use in what used to be known as polite society. Yes, we tell the hostess that the paella was delicious even though it tasted like glue. We tell the corporate lawyer that we enjoyed talking with him even though we found his conversation about the changing legal status of real estate investment trusts to be a mite tedious. There are also the vestigial limbs of flattery, rituals we no longer think about, like signing a letter "Yours sincerely." This type of flattery is something we do out of habit, the original desire to please having long since departed. And in the age of e-mail and cell phones, there is a new etiquette that drops these old terms as useless and tiresome.

Then there are the situations where flattery is mandatory: The bride is always beautiful. The deceased was always kind. If we go to someone's art opening, we are obliged to say something complimentary to the artist. If we visit someone with a new baby, it is incumbent upon us to say the infant is cute. In such situations, to say nothing is interpreted as a rudeness; the lack of praise will be conspicuous by its absence. We do it because we understand that flattery in such circumstances is the lubricant that makes civilization go. Without it, we will have, as sociologist Erving Goffman suggested, drawing-room chaos. Social stability depends on a certain amount of deception. "At every level," wrote the philosopher George Steiner, "the linguistic capacity to conceal, misinform, leave ambiguous, hypothesize, and invent is indispensable to the equilibrium of human consciousness and the development of man in society." We have to prepare a face to meet the faces that we meet.

There are many useful analogies for flattery. Flattery is a kind of propaganda in which the information is, as historian Daniel Boorstin said, "intentionally biased." Like propaganda, it is information that depends on an emotional appeal that we want to believe. Flattery is also a kind of mask, a mask that protects and enhances the flatterer in the guise of enhancing the person being flattered.

The sense of all these metaphors is that flattery is not quite what it seems, that there is a disjunction between appearance and reality. To use still another metaphor, it is the idea that flattery is forked, that it is double-edged, that it seems to be saying one thing while saying another. And the reason that it is double or forked is because it has something to hide. Its success depends on disguising any motive other than disinterested sincerity. Flattery at its core is language that advances self-interest while concealing it at the same time.

Beautiful Lies

It was Montaigne who wrote that the beauty of truth is that it has one face. "The reverse of truth," he says, "has a hundred thousand forms, and a field indefinite, without bound or limit."

Almost all definitions of lying describe flattery as well. Lying is generally defined as one person misleading another. Game theorists call lying "strategic misrepresentation." Whereas lying has traditionally been treated as a form of social deviance, flattery has been considered a part of social norms. At worst, it's a misdemeanor.

There are two primary ways to lie: by concealing or by falsifying. Flattery tends to be the latter rather than the former: We falsify or exaggerate the truth. (Though tactically omitting criticism when it is deserved is a kind of flattery.) Lying can be passive; flattery is usually active. While we think that there are signs that can reveal a lie, there is no *tell*—the sign in poker that someone is bluffing—for flattery. Liars often feel guilt about the deception; flatterers rarely do.

Whereas a lie can sometimes be detected *(No, sir, despite your testimony, I can conclusively prove that you were not home on the night of the twenty-seventh),* flattery usually cannot. Flattery tends to be subjective, lying objective. And the stakes are far lower. At worst, if you are caught flattering someone, you are at least displaying your deference. "What really flatters a man," said Bernard Shaw, "is that you think him worth flattering." Even if we see through it, we are hardly outraged. Usually, we just say thank you. "We love flattery," wrote Emerson, "even though we are not deceived by it, because it shows that we are of importance enough to be courted."

But all deception, like all flattery, is not equal. There are lies and there are *lies*. Even Montaigne noted that truth is an abstract ideal, not an everyday reality. "I do not want to deprive deceit of its proper place," he noted, "that would be a misunderstanding of the world." St. Augustine proposed that there were eight different categories of lies. I won't go through them all, except to say that they ranged in levels of seriousness from a lie against God's word that injures someone, to a lie that harms no one and may actually protect someone from harm. We generally call these latter "white lies." I would make a similar distinction among different types of flattery. There is flattery that actually seeks to harm and there is flattery, like telling a hospital patient he is looking healthier or a struggling student that she is improving, that is virtuous. Flattery, even at its worst, seems less reprehensible than simple, straightout lying.

Francis Bacon said there were two types of flattery—malicious and benign. Malicious flatterers are those who come to bury you while praising you. (Tacitus said the worst class of enemies are those who praise you.) Benign flattery is simply exaggerated praise without a specific motive. The sixteenth-century Italian writer Stefano Guazzo made a distinction between fawning and flattery, fawning being dissembling without any intent to harm.

The best analogy I have found for the difference between good and bad flattery comes not from literature but from the law, and it has to do with intent. In the case of the failed prosecution of former secretary of agriculture Mike Espy for accepting illegal gifts, the Supreme Court made an interesting distinction between gifts and gratuities or bribes. A gift, the court said, was something given for its own sake with no particular expectation of a return. A gratuity or a bribe was a gift in order to get something in return, it was the *quid* in the *quid pro quo*.

Flattery, I think, exists along the same continuum. It can be a gift given more or less for its own sake, with no expectation of a return, or it can be a bribe given in the hope of some benefit. The first is harmless and may even do some good; the latter is basically just strategic, and the goal can range from the mere desire to be liked to a more malign desire to hurt the person you are appearing to help.

If flattery is a bribe, it's almost always one we're ready to pocket. If flattery were a crime, the recipient would always be an unindicted co-conspirator. Bribed politicians usually have their gifts seized, but the receiver of flattery can't—or won't—return his illegal gains.

The aging lover in Shakespeare's Sonnet 138 perfectly understands this dynamic. It is a mutually fulfilling deception.

> *When my love swears that she is made of truth*
> *I do believe her, though I know she lies.*
> *That she might think me some untutored youth,*
> *Unlearned in the world's false subtleties.*
> *Thus vainly thinking that she thinks me young,*
> *Although she knows my days are past the best,*
> *Simply I credit her false-speaking tongue;*
> *On both sides thus is simple truth suppressed.*
> *But wherefore says she not she is unjust?*
> *And where say not I that I am old? . . .*
> *Therefore I lie with her, and she with me,*
> *And in our faults by lies we flattered be.*

Use It or Lose It

The issue about flattery, though, is not so much whether it is true or false—praise is subjective anyway—but whether or not it is *sincere*. In his famous lectures on "Sincerity and Authenticity," Lionel Trilling defined sincerity as a "congruence between avowal and actual feeling." We think of flattery as being precisely the opposite: that we are saying something we don't really feel. Something that is not genuine.

Trilling makes the point (which seems to be the theme of virtually every twentieth-century artist) that society compels a kind of insincerity, a parting of the ways between avowal and actual feeling. That the constraints of society do not let us be our true selves.

Trilling asserted this with some gravity, but to our twenty-first-century ears it sounds a little trite. To say that society forces us all to be insincere is today merely a truism. Some would call that an ironic view, but I think it is simply a practical one. We do not believe that there is a virtue in sincerity because sincerity is perceived not as truthfulness but a kind of simple-minded naiveté. Being sincere is regarded as showing all your cards up front—in other words, a losing strategy. Sincerity, even as a style, is seen as old-hat, creaky, *earnest*—the most dread word in the modern critical lexicon.

Flattery is not seen as *bad* or *wrong* because it is perceived as another tool for playing the game. Flattery is not bad because gamesmanship is not bad. Flattery is not bad because strategizing and calculating are not bad. Flattery is not bad in a world where twenty-three-year-old cyber-millionaires must read Sun-Tzu and Machiavelli. And, finally, flattery is not bad because there are no longer any consequences for outright false-hood, much less insincerity. Public lies are now treated as social misde-meanors, something between a parking ticket and drunk driving. Public liars are hardly even shamed anymore. The ubiquitous use of the word "spin" as a synonym for what we formerly would have called *lying* sug-gests that we're comfortable with the avoidance of outright falsehoods by using less obvious ones like obfuscation and indirection.

Today we think of flattery a little like Hegel did, who used the phrase the "heroism of flattery." By that he meant that the individual had come to rec-ognize the essential falseness of society and that he bravely understood that he must play along to get along. This, suggests Hegel, gave a person more not less freedom, and it also made him a more artful player of the game. Using flattery, then, becomes a little like Pascal's wager: You're only damned if you don't.

Another reason that flattery has lost its moral sting is that we no longer have an internal moral compass. We tend to form our opinion of ourselves based on others' opinion of us. The modern individual, as everyone from Rousseau to David Riesman has suggested, is obsessively concerned with how we are perceived. We have less faith in our own sense of ourselves than in how others see us. "The savage lives within himself," Rousseau wrote. "The social man knows how to live only in the opinion of others, and it is, so to speak, from their judgment alone that he draws the sentiment of his own being." *(Note to reviewers only:* But I well know that some wise, measured, and well-written opinions are more valuable than others.)

In a society where we live by the opinion of others, the stock of flattery should just go up and up. If we give disproportionate value to others' opin-ions, why wouldn't we give even more value to disproportionate praise? In a society where there is less personal or individual validation, flattery becomes more valuable. In that sense, we have a greater hunger for praise than ever before. It validates us to ourselves. It shores up our fragmented identities. And besides, it's really, really nice.

So we play the game. We do our best to seem sincere, both in the giving of compliments and in the receiving of them. ("You flatter me" is not an accusation of duplicity or strategic manipulation but an exclamation of false modesty.) Yet we're not very good at playing sincere anymore. That suit doesn't hang as well as it used to. Whether it is because we are self-conscious, or that we are more aware of duplicity, or just more hardheaded, I don't know, but we have seemingly lost the trick. As André Gide said, "We cannot both be sincere and seem so." But we still do our best to fake it.

The Golden Rule of Flattery

The Greeks were idealists. They believed that there was such a thing as absolute truth. Nature itself was the unembellished truth, and language was just our poor attempt to find a handsome container for it.

But truth is a concept to which nature is indifferent. In fact, according to evolutionary biologists, natural selection often favors deception. Certain edible snakes have evolved to resemble inedible ones so that they will not be eaten by their natural predators. It's been said that man is the only animal that lies, but according to the evolutionary biologist Robert Trivers, many species deceive each other as successful survival strategies. The better deceivers are the ones that get their genes into the next generation. "The conventional view," Trivers writes, "that natural selection favors nervous systems which produce ever more accurate images of the world must be a very naive view of mental evolution." Deception is in our genes.

Evolutionary biologists also posit another type of behavior that is adaptive: They call it reciprocal altruism. Trivers summarizes this idea as "one good turn deserves another." I would suggest, as I do in a subsequent chapter, that flattery is a subset of reciprocal altruism. Flattery is a kind of favor exchange. I praise you (one good turn) and you help me (another) and together we get our genes into the next generation—or our cyber-company to an initial public offering. It stands to reason that if I flatter you, and you are bigger and stronger than I am, and as a result you save me from that saber-toothed tiger, we both benefit and I still have a chance to keep my DNA in the evolutionary line. It was Darwin who first suggested that the love of approbation and the desire for praise are grounded in instinct.

If we look at flattery from a purely utilitarian perspective—that is, from the philosophical point of view that anything that boosts happiness is good and anything that detracts from it is bad—flattery is a good. When it works properly, flattery makes the subject of the flattery a little happier and it makes the flatterer a little happier. And that is true even when the *flatteree* is wise to the *flatterer*. (The flatterer is still happy because he doesn't know he's been discovered and the flatteree is happy because he at least knows he's worth flattering.)

John Stuart Mill said that Christ's golden rule—Do unto others as you would have them do unto you—is the essence of utilitarianism. The golden rule is really just a mutually rewarding exchange—which is what flattery is. In a modern study of ingratiation, which is what sociologists call flattery, the social scientist Edward Jones explains the golden rule of ingratiation: "We influence others to give us the things we want more than they do, by giving them the things they want more than we do." With flattery, both sides have a stake in allowing the deception to be believed. Both parties have something to gain by cooperating with the lie. According to game theory, the flattery exchange (I flatter you and you say Thank you) is the opposite of a zero-sum game (because no one loses) and the opposite of a perfect information system (because no one knows what is really going on). It's a transaction in which both parties come out ahead.

Flattery Maketh the New Man

Flattery is not immutable. It has not forever been the same. It has changed as humankind itself has changed. In telling this unorthodox history of flattery, I will also be charting the course of the slow transformation from a world of character to one of personality, the transformation over the centuries from a world where much was assumed and little was in doubt to one where little is assumed and much is in doubt; a world where truth and morality seemed clear, to one where they are fuzzy and relative.

Flattery once was more institutional than individual, more generic than personal. Flattery once was of roles, of offices, of archetypes—you flattered the king's office and his kingly attributes, you did not flatter his personal characteristics or abilities. That would have been unthinkable, not to mention impertinent. The rise of the individual during the Renaissance changed the nature of flattery. The transition from a world where people thought of themselves as serfs or cogs to a world where people felt themselves to be unique and individual meant that you tailored your flattery to the specific attributes of the person you aimed to please. Today, you no longer flatter the office, you flatter the man—or the woman—who holds it.

As societies themselves changed and became freer and more democratic, the perception of flattery shifted as well. Once societies were no longer so rigidly hierarchical, flattery lost its dangerous quality, its notion of trespassing against what was established and perceived as right. If whatever *is* is right, as Browning said, anything that changed what *is* must be wrong. But once social mobility became a good, flattery lost much of its sinful character. Flattery, in a sense, became just another tool of advancement, not as useful as a degree but more effective than a new tie.

In fact, as we shall see from the chapter on Renaissance courtesy literature, flattery became an instrument of social change. Dukes are born, not made, but flattery was a way to get the duke to give you land and turn you into a gentleman, even though you weren't born one. Later, flattery became an engine of democracy, for it helped people rise not according to their birth but because of their (perceived) merit. It helped open doors that had been closed before. We've come full circle, for in a democracy, if every man is a king, we are all courtiers as well.

America, the crucible of modern democracy, invented a new form of flattery. Forget the furbelowed affectations of Europe; American flattery was as spare and practical as the cotton gin. In America, as Emerson said, "the only sin is limitation." In the Old World, flattery was born of limits and died of mobility. In the New World it was precisely the opposite: Flattery rejected limitation and thrived on mobility. Flattery might get you anywhere. A shoeshine, a smile, and a compliment might be your ticket to the middle class. Just as America perfected mass production, it also commodified flattery. Now, on Mother's Day (another triumph of manufacturing) you can buy one of dozens of greeting cards telling dear old Mom how wonderful she is. And now, you have your choice of sincere ones or ironic ones.

What's the Harm?

I think we can all agree that giving praise where praise is due is an unalloyed good. The question is: What is the downside of giving praise where it is not due? In other words, is there a moral cost to flattery?

I suppose the downside of giving praise where it's not due is that it can render people incapable of self-criticism, and unfit them for weathering criticism of any kind. I've generally found that when people are not self-critical—or have a nonstop insecurity tape playing in their heads—they consider any criticism an attack. You see this often among politicians and movie stars. While they don't suspect flattery of having an ulterior motive, they do suspect criticism of one. People without the ability to criticize themselves are people who make the same mistakes over and over again and then refuse to take responsibility for them. That is a good description of the modern narcissist who merges lack of self-awareness and a high sense of entitlement—a very unattractive cocktail—and doesn't blame himself or herself for anything.

One could also argue that there is an economic or fairness cost to flattery. That is, if the less competent person gets the job by virtue of flattery over the more competent person. But is it unfair? I'm not so sure. First of all, it is not as common as one might think. Studies of ingratiation, as we shall see in a later chapter, show that flattery increases liking but not perceptions of competence. But yes, given equal competence between two competing people, the deft flatterer will likely get the job. One could argue that flattery is actually just another useful skill and that the person who does the hiring will unconsciously be rewarding it. And then, that new hire will use flattery to be successful in her new job, which will only make the boss look better. Nothing succeeds like successful flattery.

* * *

Francis Bacon, in making his distinction between malicious and benign flattery, notes that "some praise comes of good wishes and respects." As an example, he cites Pliny's phrase *"laudando praecipere"*—to teach by praising. To teach by praising is one of the foundations of civilization; we teach the values we esteem by reinforcing them in our children—and in ourselves. When my niece Amanda correctly spells "aardvark," I praise her. When my son, Gabriel, shares a toy with his friend, I praise him. Many studies over the years have confirmed that children who are told that the teacher thinks they're smart will do better on tests than they would have otherwise. Praise *does* make people better and smarter. "More people are flattered into virtue," wrote the English novelist Robert Smith Surtees, "than bullied out of vice." And if we sometimes use excessive or undeserved praise to encourage someone, that is not a crime.

As you've gathered by now, I've done a little sleight of hand and turned flattery into a subset of praise rather than of lying. One of the classic definitions of flattery is that it is "insincere praise." Well, that's still praise. The reason I have elided the two is that it seems to me that in our society these days there is not an overabundance of praise but a dearth of it. Yes, there is the absurd and shallow flattery of movie stars and celebrities. But I am not talking about undeserved praise, but praise where praise is due. Sometimes we must even praise the giving of praise to make sure that it is given where it is due.

In his poem on the death of William Butler Yeats, W. H. Auden praises the Irish poet not so much for writing well, or even for turning swords into plowshares, but for turning pain into a kind of gladness, for teaching us how to find something good where we could easily see only ill. It is a song of praise to praise itself.

> *Follow, poet, follow right*
> *To the bottom of the night,*
> *With your unconstraining voice*
> *Still persuade us to rejoice; . . .*

> *In the deserts of the heart*
> *Let the healing fountain start,*

In the prison of his days
Teach the free man how to praise.

Given the choice of living in a world without praise or one with too much, I would unhesitatingly choose the latter. What a joyless world a world without praise—or flattery—would be.

A Word or Two on the Etymology of Flattery

The origin of the word "flattery" isn't terribly clear. (It's what the *Oxford English Dictionary* snootily calls "of somewhat doubtful etymology.") The English verb "flatter" is believed to have come from the Old French word *flater,* which meant "to flatten down, smooth," or "to stroke with the hand, caress." "Flattery" is also thought to derive from the Provençal noun *flataria,* which means "the passing of the flat or palm of the hand over an object, a person, or an animal." The origins all suggest the action of stroking, smoothing, caressing.

What does seem clear is that there is a literal and a figurative connection between the action and the word. We use the word "stroke" to mean "flattering someone's ego." But look at all the other *touch*y metaphors for flattery: tickling someone's vanity, scratching or patting someone's back, caressing or massaging someone's ego, smoothing feathers. "To smooth" was a seventeenth-century term for using flattering or complimentary language. Caressing or stroking is certainly an ingratiating activity. Chimpanzees cannot say "I love your hair," but as we will see, they do stroke and groom each other all day long for strategic reasons. We touch someone when we are talking as a kind of physical flattery through a demonstration of extra warmth or intimacy. "The common touch" suggests a sympathetic caress from on high. The king's touch bestowed both favor and grace. Jesus' touch healed. Somewhere in the history of the word "flattery," the literal became figurative.

*   *   *

From the moment the word appeared anywhere, flattery had a negative connotation. The earliest definitions saw it as a deep moral failing, a way of upending the moral order. The ancient Greeks regarded it as an illicit technique that preyed on men's weaknesses and could disrupt the society. Satan, of course, was the Arch Flatterer, according to Milton. But it was Dante who gave flatterers the blackest name in all of history. He situated them in the eighth ring of hell, just one step up from the seventh, which was populated by tyrants, murderers, suicides, blasphemers, sodomites, and usurers. In Dante's cosmology, flatterers are worse than hypocrites, thieves, astrologers, and "sowers of scandal & schism."

> *This was the place we reached; the ditch beneath*
> *held people plunged in excrement that seemed*
> *as if it had been poured from human privies.*
> *And while my eyes searched that abysmal sight,*
> *I saw one with a head so smeared with shit,*
> *one could not see if he were lay or cleric.*
> *He howled: "Why do you stare more greedily*
> *at me than at the others who are filthy?"*
> *And I: "Because, if I remember right,*
> *I have seen you before, with your hair dry;*
> *and so I eye you more than all: you are*
> *Alessio Interminei of Lucca."*
> *Then he continued, pounding on his pate:*
> *"I am plunged here because of flatteries—*
> *of which my tongue had such sufficiency."*

Not a pretty picture.

Dante uses the Italian word *lusinghe* for flattery, but the more common Italian term is *adulazione,* which comes from the Latin root for flattery, *adululotor,* from which we get the word "adulation" or "to adulate," the meaning of which is to praise effusively or slavishly, to pay homage without thought. This is certainly part of our sense of flattery, but the English word "flattery" has no roots at all in the Latin. The idea is the same, the genesis different.

From early on, one of the senses of flattery is that it is somehow illegitimate, that it is deceptive, illicit. Truth is the gold standard, so flattery is alchemy. God's word is the truth, so deceptive language must come from the devil. It is close to the sin of idolatry. In the *Canterbury Tales,* Chaucer writes, "Flaterie is general wrongful preysing." The *OED*'s second and third definitions underline that same sense of both exaggerated and illegitimate praising: "To try to please or win the favour of (a person) by obsequious speech or conduct"; and "To praise or compliment unduly or insincerely."

As we trace the evolution of the word's meaning, it becomes a little less pejorative as we get closer to the twentieth century. In societies that were both hierarchical and Christian, flattery was dangerous. It was seen as both morally reprehensible and potentially destabilizing. During the Renaissance, as societies became more democratic and mobile, flattery began to lose some of its more derogatory connotations. It was seen less as a cosmic sin and more as a worldly foible. The *OED*'s later definitions give a sense of this. Number 4: "To gratify the vanity or self-esteem of; to make self-complacent; to make (one) feel honoured or distinguished." Flattery both indulges vanity and boosts self-esteem. Shakespeare shows both senses: the more traditional view of flattery as a sin and the more modern one of flattery as something, well, kind of nice. He does so in a single line from *Julius Caesar:*

When I tell him, he hates Flatterers,
He says, he does; being then most flattered.

Even today, we flatter people by telling them that they are immune to flattery. (And if they agree, they are not.)

When we say we are "flattered" by something, or that we find a remark "flattering," we mean we are pleased and a little honored, but too modest to really acknowledge it. We are cheered and charmed, made a little complacent, perhaps even beguiled. It is a little pat on the back. When we say "You flatter me," it is like saying "You indulge me," or 'You're pampering me, and I rather like it."

When we flatter ourselves, we are indulging our own fancy. We are puffing up our own self-image. The *OED*'s ninth definition makes the improving of image most explicit: "To represent too favourably. . . . Said esp. of painters or the like." This is the painter who makes his subject look handsomer, prettier, younger, wiser than the person looks in real life. The famous Hyacinthe Rigaud portrait of Louis XIV as an old man gives him the supple legs of a young Baryshnikov. From Horace Walpole's *Anecdotes of Painting in England:* "Oliver said to him, 'Mer Lely, I desire you would use all your skill to paint my picture truly like me, and not flatter me at all.' " But, of course, that is the ultimate flattery, to say that a flattering image is merely the most ordinary realism. Few of us can really bear reality, so it must be air-brushed a bit.

The *OED*'s last definition gives a sense of flattery as being a kind of moral laxness, a lazy indifference, even a kind of unfussy generosity. "In a weaker sense, to gloss over, palliate (faults)." This is flattery of omission, of not mentioning an obvious fault, of overlooking some mistake. The *OED* cites a sermon from the sixteenth century that gives this meaning: "Here learn not to flatter with anybody when they do wickedly, for Christ, perceiving his disciples to be unbelieuers, flattered them not, but rebuked them for their faultes." If Jesus had wanted to flatter them, he would have overlooked their faults. We see this in the kind of social omissions we use to flatter people, in pointedly ignoring some public failure as if to suggest it didn't matter or was beneath notice. We also flatter sometimes by saying nothing.

Chapter 1

Everyone
Has a Hierarchy

You Scratch My Back and I'll Scratch Yours

Watch people watching chimpanzees at the zoo. They smirk and point as though observing a troupe of loose-jointed slapstick comedians. We smile precisely because they appear . . . well, like us, only smaller, more hirsute, and, let us say, less mature. It has often been pointed out that apes hold up a mirror to humankind, but it's a kind of fun-house mirror in which we see a distorted version of ourselves, a kind of comic caricature of our great-great-grandparents, a home movie of humanity at an earlier stage of development. If we were gazing at a group of toddlers in a cage, we might not find the sight so amusing.

Chimpanzees are our closest relatives. We share 98 percent of our DNA with them. Like us, apes are social animals that live in groups. And like us, they form social hierarchies. But chimps and humans are by no means the only species that create hierarchies. The modern notion of animal hierarchies evolved in part from a Norwegian biologist by the name of Thorleif Schjelderup-Ebbe who spent an awful lot of time during the 1920s observing chickens. He noticed that when you stuck a bunch of hens together, they soon formed a linear system in which each bird knew its place, from the top hen down to the bottom. A pecks B, B pecks C, C pecks D, and so on. Schjelderup-Ebbe gave this process a name: pecking order.

Chimps, too, have a pecking order. At the top of the primate pecking order is the alpha male. It's not hard to spot him. Take a group of school-children to the chimp run at the zoo and ask them to pick out the "boss" (or better yet, the "principal") among the chimps. They will instantly point out the one chimp who is standing straighter, who seems to strut about in a haughty manner, whose chest is puffed out, and whom the other chimps seem to pet or stroke. The alpha male is king of the heap, leader of the pack, the chief, the top dog, the head honcho, and everyone in the group literally and figuratively bows down before him.

*   *   *

The alpha male is surrounded by a kind of court made up of other chimps who are less dominant than he but more dominant than others. (Call them corporate vice presidents.) Other males, when walking near the alpha male, keep their heads slightly lowered. They almost look like they're cowering. The alpha male can look pretty scary. His hair often stands on end as he parades around. This has the effect of making him look larger and more threatening. Subordinate males, by bowing and scraping, make themselves look smaller and less threatening. The alpha male lords it over the beta males, who lord it over the gamma males, and so on.

Scholars call this a "dominance-subordination hierarchy," which essentially means that each animal, in its quest for food, mates, and other resources, makes some kind of compromise to fit into its social system. Like the hens, chimps learn who is stronger and weaker and form alliances based on those assumptions. And there is some evidence that establishing a stable hierarchy is conducive to, well, if not happiness, at least fecundity and stability.

There are benefits to kowtowing to the alpha male and staying in his good graces. In fact, it's in the genetic self-interest of chimps to do so. The reason is that the alpha male, in addition to having first dibs on the best food, shelter, and shade, also controls access to females. Some alpha males monopolize virtually all the ovulating females. Studies have shown that alpha males alone are responsible for 80 percent of the copulations with fe-males in a given group. Rank has its privileges. *Le droit de seigneur.*

Being the extra male in chimp society, unlike at uptown Manhattan din-ner parties, is a very undesirable thing: surplus, subordinate males are usually social parasites and eminently expendable. They don't get a very good dinner partner at all. The surplus males generally get access to females only through the alpha male. That's like the fraternity president deciding which women, if any, each guy in the fraternity gets to date. And since chimps, like all creatures, are intent on getting their genes into the next generation, this is a pretty desirable goal. Chimps, like fraternity pledges, will go a long way toward pleasing the big guy to get a date for Saturday night.

The Prince, for Primates

The collective noun for certain primates—like a pride of lions, or a gaggle of geese—is a "shrewdness of apes." The term is apt because chimps are clever manipulators. They trick each other, they hide food from rivals, they flirt behind one another's back, they cry wolf, they stage coups, they play jokes on one another. They're connivers.

In fact, they are shrewd politicians. The title of Frans de Waal's absorbing work on life among the primates at a zoo in Arnheim, Holland, is *Chimpanzee Politics*. Politics, he decided, was the only word to describe the intricate relations among chimps in groups. Politics is concerned with power and status, he says, and chimps pursue both with the same avidity that we do. "The social organization of chimpanzees," De Waal writes, "is almost too human to be true."

Every primatologist, including de Waal, will tell you stories of the subtleties of chimp obfuscation, of the artful manipulation of one chimp by another, of smaller males currying favor with larger males, of shifting alliances and secretive takeovers. The theory goes that it was just such social interaction—the forming of a complex hierarchy—at a very early stage in human history, that drove the development of the brain's great leap forward.

The word that primatologists use over and over to describe chimpanzee behavior is "Machiavellian." Dominant male hominids, anthropologist Robin Fox writes, are "controlled, cunning, cooperative." Machiavelli could not have put it better. De Waal writes that they "never make an uncalculated move." Chimps are also highly opportunistic. They don't dillydally and postpone like Hamlet. If they see weakness in a competitor, they exploit it—immediately.

Chimps are strategic. They display traits that in humans we call guile or deceit. De Waal suggests that male chimps often form what he calls "triadic alliances." As though he were writing a political thriller, de Waal narrates the story of how one venerable alpha male is toppled from power by a young rival, only to have the outgoing alpha form an alliance with another powerful chimp to overthrow the pretender. King Lear had it easy by comparison.

Chimps use such alliances to form what he calls a "minimal winning coalition." Whereas male chimps, he suggests, are out to gain dominance and do so through forming coalitions, female chimps are more interested in forming coalitions with females that they like, not necessarily ones that will help them increase their status. Female chimps form a status quo and stay with it. At the same time, they want and need to eat, and females often barter sex for food.

Like all animals, chimps do whatever is best for their own genetic self-interest, and deception has proved to be an integral part of that self-interest. A male chimp, after a clandestine sexual encounter with a female who is part of the alpha male's harem, will prostrate himself with extra fervor before the alpha male, who is unaware of what has taken place. Chimps seeking to topple the existing order will act deferential to the alpha male, while secretly forming alliances with other chimps. Male chimps vying for group support in power struggles go out of their way to groom females and play with their infants—something they do not normally do—not unlike American presidential candidates wooing soccer moms and kissing babies.

The Chimps' Golden Rule

The most frequent social activity among chimpanzees is grooming. Grooming is both practical and social: It is a way of helping one chimp pluck ticks and other bits of matter from parts he cannot reach. But it is also a way of placating and petting another member of the group, of making nice. It has a calming effect. Soft spluttering and smacking sounds accompany the grooming, which is tedious, meticulous work.

Everyone at one time or another grooms the alpha male, but the alpha male grooms no one else. The less powerful male chimps groom the more powerful ones, and the female chimps groom the males—unless the female chimps are in estrus, in which case males groom them. Males tend to groom each other during periods of tension as a way of defusing any acrimony.

When the females are not in estrus, the males generally ignore them. When they are what primatologists call "attractive," the males can't seem to pay enough attention to them. A male will groom a female for hours, sometimes without getting lucky—that is, she will spurn his advances. He will also offer her gifts of meat and food, in the hope that this will make her more receptive to his overtures.

For females, sex is strategic. It is the most valuable currency that female chimps have to offer in the game of power and influence. Female bonobos, who are even closer genetically to humankind than chimps are, have at least twenty gestures and calls indicating a willingness to copulate. For female bonobos, sex isn't just sex: it is a way of getting food; it is a form of appeasement to reduce tension within a group, or when one group meets another—it is a way of keeping harmony.

*   *   *

The alpha male accepts his grooming as homage that is due him. But any chimp can't just walk up to him—or anyone else for that matter—and start grooming. Chimps must "greet" each other first. The greeting consists of various grunts and bows—all made while the subordinate chimp gazes up at the more dominant one. In some cases, a chimp performs a series of deep bows which are repeated so quickly that primatologists call this behavior "bobbing." Sometimes the greeter kisses the feet of the alpha male and brings along objects, like a leaf or stick, as a kind of offering. Another form of this "affinitive" behavior, as one primatologist calls it, is when a chimpanzee "pants in a friendly manner." Females, instead of greeting the alpha male, present their backsides to be inspected and sniffed. Sometimes the alpha male will permit subordinates to fondle his scrotum, which is considered a form of reassurance for both the dominant chimp and the subordinate one. It's a way for the alpha male to say, *I trust you,* and a way for the subordinate male to say, *I venerate you.* It's also frowned on in most corporate cultures.

Greetings function as a kind of ritualized confirmation of the social hierarchy, a kind of status head count of who's on top and who's not. It's also the equivalent of doffing your hat or saluting or bowing or opening the door for someone. One can tell who is up and who is down based on how chimps "greet" each other. Chimps are very much aware of their place in the group at all times, and can be quite put out if someone fails to greet them properly. In other words, If you diss me by not greeting me, that could lead to a fight.

For male chimps, part of the allure of power seems to be the status that comes with it. Jane Goodall wrote that chimps often "run serious risks of injury in pursuit of higher status." As we've already seen, high status often means high reproductive success. For male chimps as distinct from females, the pursuit of status seems to be the main reason for affiliating themselves with other chimps. A male chimp doesn't go off for a beer with a colleague just to shoot the breeze; there has to be something in it for him.

Chimps Are Us

It may seem curious to begin a book about flattery with a description of chimpanzee behavior, but I trust by now the reason should be obvious. Their behavior should seem disconcertingly familiar. Unlike us, however, chimps don't have the ability to weave the elaborate explanations that we use to justify our more craven conduct. They just act on their desires. "Chimpanzee group life," says de Waal, "is like a market in power, sex, affection, support, intolerance and hostility." Sounds like Washington and Hollywood. "The more scientists have studied primates," primatologist John Mitani writes, "the harder they have found it to identify the traits that distinguish us from our evolutionary cousins."

I've tried in most cases not to anthropomorphize my description of chimpanzee behavior, but it's not easy. I'm not even sure it's valid not to do so because, after all, we are their descendants and their behavior is so like ours. We're guilty of primatizing, or *animopomorphizing,* our behavior all the time—we wolf down a meal, the halfback was dogging it on the field, the fraternity boys behaved like animals, a young writer apes the literary styles of the masters. Evolutionary biologists believe that primates may hold the key to understanding the roots of love, aggression, friendship, and language—why not flattery, which is composed of all them?

Chimps don't tell each other "You look marvelous," but the bowing, the grooming, the coalitions formed by the less powerful with the more powerful, the favors performed, all mirror the same quid pro quo dynamic that forms the basis of one kind of human flattery, the strategic kind. From an anthropological perspective, the obeisance before the alpha male is no different than courtiers bowing before Louis XIV, nobles kissing the feet of the pharaoh. (De Waal writes of a "hollow" greeting between a deposed alpha male and his successor that could be a description of George Bush's frosty greeting of Bill Clinton at the latter's inauguration in 1993.)

De Waal describes this type of primate behavior—the bowing, the groveling—as "opportunistic, a way of currying favor with those who can help you." "This universal human system," de Waal writes, "the collection and redistribution of posssessions by the chief, or his modern equivalent, the government, is exactly the same as that used by chimpanzees." Their concern with power, de Waal says, is not greater than that of man, it's just more obvious.

The less powerful chimps who subordinate themselves to more powerful ones in the hopes of advancement are no different than innumerable nameless vice presidents sucking up to their bosses for promotions, or young associates at law firms kowtowing to senior partners. The chimp males who groom receptive females and offer gifts of raw meat are the less-suave precursors to young men with flowers and candy, whispering sweet nothings to their prom dates.

Because we empathize with chimpanzee behavior, it might have sounded a bit harsh when I wrote earlier that females barter sex for food. But we say this about ourselves all the time, though in a less crass manner. I quote now from one of our culture's most perceptive anthropologists, Miss Manners. "It is customary to begin a series of dates with a great deal of entertainment, a moderate amount of food, and the merest suggestion of affection," she writes to a young lady seeking advice about courtship. "As the amount of affection increases, the entertainment can be reduced proportionately. When the affection is the entertainment, we no longer call it dating. Under no circumstances can the food be omitted."

Everyone's a Social Climber

"Our social system," de Waal writes, "is an ape social system." What so many evolutionary biologists call the unversal human hunger for status and the equally universal presence of hierarchy seem to be traits we inherited from our primate ancestors. Child behaviorists have shown that groups of children as young as one year old form status hierarchies. After losing a fight, children everywhere lower their heads in self-abasement. Everywhere, Darwin writes, "a proud man exhibits his sense of superiority over others by holding his head and body erect." A portrait of the alpha male.

And where there is hierarchy and an asymmetry in power relationships, there will inevitably be techniques, behaviors, strategies—call them what you like—that help the individual advance up that hierarchy. One of those techniques is playing up to someone stronger in exchange for protection or some advantage. That's a description of strategic flattery.

"It's good to be the king," Mel Brooks once said in an otherwise forgettable film, but if you can't be the king (say, you're Prince Andrew), you have to elect a different strategy. In nature, as in life, a submissive strategy can be a winner. An animal may have to surrender some of its food and bow its head, but it avoids the bruising battles among powerful males as to who will be the alpha male. Some males make a quick calculation: It's better to find some place where it's safe and warm, and pick up the pieces afterward.

Let's say you are tramping around in the ancestral state and you're feeling cold and hungry and weak. You come across a six-foot-eight mound of alpha male muscle tucking into a succulent piece of filet that he has just killed and roasted. Yes, you can try to thump him over the head and steal his supper—or you can try to ingratiate yourself in some way in the hope that (a) he won't kill you and (b) he might even decide to share some of his repast with you. Which do you think is the better strategy? The genes that tell you not to punch the fellow in the nose but to sidle up to him and casually mention what a fine and noble nose he has are more likely to survive into the next generation. Becoming buddies with him, whether through flattery or some other means, will be in your genetic self-interest.

In fact, evolution seems to have ultimately favored sycophantic weenies over self-reliant bruisers, the Uriah Heeps and Eddie Haskells and Eve Harringtons over the Samsons and the Schwarzeneggers. Smooth talk trumps brute strength every day of the week. Survival of the fittest is not survival of the strongest but sometimes of the most unctuous. When the species made what anthropologists call the Great Leap Forward fifty thousand years ago, it was the smaller, smarter chaps who triumphed over the big bruisers. MIT professor Steven Pinker has dubbed this the revenge of the nerds. The men that survived—and we are their descendants—were not the guys on the gridiron but the ones keeping stats in the locker room. It was the triumph of Woody Allen over Hulk Hogan.

*   *   *

Status hierarchies are endemic in nature and in human societies of all kinds, and where there are status hierarchies, there is flattery, for flattery is a technique for raising your status. No society in human history has ever been purely egalitarian. Anywhere that there is what sociologists call asymmetrical relationships, there will be subordinates trying to ascend to dominant status. And where there is upward mobility, there will be flattery.

Let's be frank, befriending someone of high status is a wise survival strategy in any society. Let's say you've buttered up the king, now he can give you an exemption from having to go off and fight scary infidels in the Crusade. Where do you think you'll have a better chance of creating an heir? Shouldering a lance on a horse in Spain or pairing off in a galliard with a damsel at court?

Of course, low status is never as desirable as high status (as Sophie Tucker said, "I've been rich and I've been poor, and rich is better"), but sometimes there are benefits. "If one function of low self-esteem is to keep high-status people satisfied with your deference," the author Robert Wright has said, then you're going to do better in the long run than those who challenge the big boys and get sent to the bell tower. When in doubt, suck up. A faithful number two who never complains and never forgets to buff up the boss (think of Alpha Gore) often gets his shot to be number one.

Fame in our society confers high status. Some would say the highest status. In Manhattan, where I live, I come across many people who seem to measure their worth and self-esteem according to how friendly they are with famous people. The friendship or acquaintanceship with the famous allows them to name-drop with others or get their own names dropped in gossip columns as friends of the famous. People will do almost anything, it seems, to cultivate the acquaintanceship of the famous. Other folks are meant to be impressed by such "friendships," and often they are, because they share the same obsession.

As abject as this seems, few people are immune to it. As Robert Wright confesses with admirable candor, "If we have a friend who is, say, mildly famous, we cherish even his meager gifts, forgive his minor offenses, and make extra sure not to let him down." The flattery comes in not so much from saying, "How brilliant!" but from holding the famous friend to a less rigorous standard than we hold our regular, nonfamous friends. If you're meeting your sister for tea and she is forty-five minutes late, you will probably upbraid her for her selfish tardiness, but if it's Madonna, you're more likely to let it pass.

To describe someone as a social-climber or a self-promoter is generally not considered a compliment. But in fact, they are simply neutral terms for fundamental human behavior. It's just that some people are more annoyingly shameless about it. Based on the principles of evolutionary biology, social-climbing and self-promotion are as old as the hills and have proven to be evolutionarily successful strategies. Social climbing is in our genes.

Now, of course, in the ancestral state that didn't mean giving a lot of money to the Metropolitian Museum of Art in order to get invited to fancy-dress charity balls. Instead, we gave the alpha male some of our freshly killed woolly mammoth, or we picked ticks out of his beard. In any case, such behavior has always been genetically rewarded. It was rewarded in primate culture, in the courts of Tutankhamen and Elizabeth I, and it's rewarded on Wall Street, in Washington, and in Hollywood.

In the ancestral state, modesty didn't get you anywhere. Nowadays, the best way to social-climb and self-promote is not to be seen to be doing so. Those who are labeled social-climbers and self-promoters are either so successful as to cause envy or so graceless as to make their machinations obvious. In either case, it's a strategy that can backfire.

People who dine out on their relationships with celebrities always emphasize the "friendship." "We're really good friends, you know." It wouldn't do, I suppose, to say, "I just hang around with Madonna because it increases my status." But in fact, you could make the case that friendship in general—let's not even mention celebrity friendship—may simply be an outgrowth of the pursuit of status. Natural selection doesn't reckon with friendship. From natural selection's point of view, Robert Wright suggests, "status assistance is the main purpose of friendship."

In chimp society, most male affiliations are a result of the pursuit of status, and those affiliations, in terms of loyalty, trust, and helpfulness, at least reflect the outlines of what we would term friendship. That is, from the outside, two chimps with such an affiliation look to us like friends. The instinct for friendship may just be an adaptation that helped in the pursuit of status.

"Liking," writes Robert Trivers, "is the emotion that initiates and maintains an altruistic partnership. It is roughly a willingness to offer someone a favor." Liking is certainly a precursor to friendship, and flattery makes us more likable. The equation is, we like people who are nice to us, and we're nice to people whom we like. In exchange for receiving the flattery, the other person offers friendship. That's the favor. That's the exchange.

Nature's Golden Rule

In *The Descent of Man,* Darwin's late work that deals with the idea of how man himself evolved, the father of evolution writes of the "lowly motive" of aiding others in the hope of future return. As a Victorian, Darwin looked down on such a transaction. He believed that generosity should exist for its own sake, without any underlying motive of repayment. He noted that such base transactions occur almost universally among animals.

Evolutionary biologists have come up with a term for this "lowly motive": they call it "reciprocal altruism." They have discovered that even though natural selection suggests that every organism seeks to maximize its genetic self-interest, it appears that some amount of cooperation, rather than complete selfishness, actually helps just about everyone. As it turns out, it's in our self-interest to be a little disinterested.

Reciprocal altruism is not quite what we think of as charity or generosity. Reciprocal altruism is rather a kind of calculated favor, an action or gesture performed for an expected return. Whereas altrusim is defined as behavior that benefits someone else at some personal cost and without thought of private gain, nature practices a more selfish altruism. The idea is, *Sure, I'll help you, if I think you'll help me in return—otherwise, no deal.*

Evolutionary biologists, using game theory, have even come up with an equation that sums up the way reciprocal altruism works. It is basically "One good turn deserves another"—with the added proviso that "If you screw me, I'll screw you." It is the do-unto-others-as-you-would-have-them-do-unto-you formulation, but allowing for the repayment of injury as well as kindness.

In *Adaptation and Natural Selection,* George Williams describes reciprocal altruism with mathematical elegance: "Simply stated, an individual who maximizes his friendships and minimizes his antagonisms will have an evolutionary advantage, and selection should favor those characters that promote the optimization of personal relationships." Flattery is a strategy for optimizing those personal relationships and thus has an evolutionary advantage. There's little doubt that in the wild, or in the boardroom, flattery maximizes an individual's chances of surviving. It's a form of cooperation but a slightly devious form. While reciprocal altruism is indirectly selfish, flattery is explicitly so.

Flattery, at least in nature, doesn't have to be conscious. We carry out evolutionary logic, says Wright, not by conscious calculation but by following our feelings and intuitions, which he calls "evolution's executioners." Certainly, in primate culture, chimps are not thinking to themselves, *The alpha male just used some sticks and leaves to build himself some shelter; I'll tell him, "I love your work," and then maybe he'll let me get in out of the rain.*

Flattery can occur without design or premeditation. We know, even without thinking, that when we praise someone we are more likely to be liked by that person. Studies from the 1950s among college students suggest that we like people we influence, especially if they are of higher status. The study was done among fraternity brothers, and it showed that young men were more likely to like the people they helped if they perceived those people to be of higher status. But it was something that they were utterly unaware of. So, if you find yourself telling someone "That was a brilliant idea," especially someone of high social status, you may be fulfilling some deep evolutionary logic rather than simply being a common lickspittle.

*   *   *

Flattery among both primates and humans is an indirect form of competition. That is, it's a way of avoiding the direct competition that can be extremely dangerous to one's health. Direct competition in nature can result in a punch in the nose or a crushed skull. Direct competition in the workplace can mean that it becomes glaringly obvious that you're doing inferior work. Isn't it better to compete in a way that you're hedging your bets? Isn't it better to compete in an oblique way where you have a better chance of success?

Flattery is the choice of a competitor who knows that he is likely to fail in direct competition, either because he is weaker, or because he is excluded from the dominant hierarchy, or for any one of a thousand other reasons. Flattery, then, becomes a way of overcoming handicaps real or imagined, drawbacks natural or social. And if it turns out that your work is superior on its own merits, so much the better. Then you don't have to worry about achieving something you didn't deserve.

Plus, the price is right. Human flattery is a cheaper form of reciprocal exhange than anything that occurs in chimp culture for one simple reason. Most of our flattery is verbal; a chimpanzee generally has to really *do* something. A compliment, however extravagant, a fawning thank-you note, an unctuous introduction, all require very little investment. Grooming or providing a fresh drumstick takes a little more effort.

In nature, a creature is in effect saying, *Show me the advantage—before I help you out.* Because their own investment is labor-intensive, it requires a real commitment. With human flattery, the offer is insubstantial. It's just words. Perhaps the desire to put flattery into words was one of the forces behind the evolution of language. It was Darwin, after all, who noted that language evolved in part as a way of manipulating people to one's own advantage.

There's No Punishment for Lying

Reciprocal altruism isn't ladling out soup to homeless people or bathing lepers in Calcutta. It's not pure, or even very honest. Natural selection doesn't care what your motives are. It permits, even encourages, deception. In other words, you can get away with seeming nice without actually being nice, or you can take credit for a good deed without performing it. Reciprocal altruism kicks in anyway. In fact, selection will probably favor deception as long as one party doesn't realize he or she is being deceived. Evolutionary psychology also suggests that some of our own deceptive motives are hidden from us not by accident but by design.

In nature, imitation is more than just the sincerest form of flattery; it's also a survival technique. Nature isn't interested in truth. Natural selection doesn't favor honesty or candor. Organisms do whatever is in their own genetic self-interest, and if that involves deception, so be it. Because foul-tasting butterflies are typically brightly colored, and birds have learned to avoid them, some rather tasty butterflies have evolved their own pattern of bright colors in order to fool hungry birds. This phenomenon is known as mimicry. Noncolorful, nonpoisonous snakes have come to mimic the bright colors of highly poisonous snakes in order to deter enemies. Yellow-and-black-striped hover flies, which don't sting, look just like wasps. Beauty in nature is often deadly, or at least not very toothsome. "Genes for mimicry are favored by natural selection," the evolutionary biologist Richard Dawkins writes in *The Selfish Gene*. So why wouldn't genes for flattery be favored? And the flatterer, unlike the savory butterfly, has no natural enemy in nature. "Of all wild beasts preserve me from a tyrant," wrote Ben Jonson, "and of all tame, a flatterer."

Robert Trivers, who was one of the first to write about the idea of reciprocal altruism, suggested that deceit in nature may also engender its own detection. "If deceit is fundamental to animal communication," he writes, "then there must be strong selection to spot deception and this ought, in turn, to select for a degree of self-deception, rendering some facts and motives unconscious so as not to betray—by the subtle signs of self-knowledge—the deception being practiced." In other words, we deceive ourselves as a kind of protection. We often believe we're being honest even when we're not. That's what makes good liars so believable.

With so much deception out there in nature, selection must have favored some animals that are adept at spotting that deception, or else all nature would be made up of tricksters. At the same time, natural selection must have favored deceivers who do not know that they are dissembling. If we apply this to flattery, the idea would be that there must be some folks out there who are able to sniff out the Machiavellian manipulation of false praise, and by the same token, there must be flatterers who don't know that they are flattering someone.

"The tendency to tell lies," Jean Piaget wrote in 1932, "is a natural tendency . . . spontaneous and universal." With flattery, there is a positive reinforcement for undetected lies. Of course, flattery does not have to be a lie, and if it is not, so much the better. But there seems to be little difference in the benefit from the same praise spoken truthfully or untruthfully. You get the same reward for saying "I love your new haircut" whether you believe it or not. The point is whether the flatteree believes it, and she usually will, especially if she is not sure about the cut.

Trivers's point that selection must favor those who can detect deception doesn't seem to be very accurate in the case of flattery. The reason flattery works is that it is usually undetected. People tend not to overly question what they want to hear. We are more inclined to embrace the lovely falsehood that we want to hear than the unpleasant truth that we don't. Plus, in the case of most flattery, what is the genetic advantage in uncovering it? None, really, as long as the flatterer is not out to do us harm.

Of course, deceptive flattery can hurt. Natural selection may well favor males who are adept at deceiving females about their future devotion and commitment. *Sure, honey, I'll stick around and provide for the kids.* By the same token, it ought also to favor females who are good at spotting such deception. Men may be programmed to lie (and even believe in the truth of their own falsehoods), and women to try to spot those lies. In fact, studies show that men routinely depict themselves as more kind, sincere, and trustworthy than they actually are. "We evolved from apes whose males forcibly abduct females," says Robert Wright, "into a species whose males whisper sweet nothings." Consequently, he says, "the whispering will be governed by the same logic as the abductions—it is a means of manipulating females to male ends."

The result is female skepticism. In every species, Darwin suggested, the male is the wooer. The root of the word "woo" comes in part from the Latin *vovere,* to vow. Men make vows that they will be loving and faithful, and women must evaluate the sincerity and durability of those vows. Another definition of "woo" is "to solicit or entreat especially with ingratiating importunity." Ingratiation is the strategy that is meant to melt away female doubt.

Everyone seems to benefit moderately from reciprocal altruism, but you can make a far bigger score if you exploit the system and then get away with it. If a stranger trusts you to guard his dinner and promises that he will share some of it with you when he returns, you can actually steal it, stuff yourself, and not be bothered with having to take the less choice cuts when he returns. So is it worth the risk? Well, sure, you get more nutrition and energy in the short run, that is, as long as you're not caught with your hand in the cookie jar. Exploitation—provided you don't get nabbed—trumps cooperation anytime. But while this often works for an individual and in the short term, it ultimately becomes counterproductive if too many individuals do it for too long. Then reciprocal altruism turns to reciprocal mean-spiritedness, and we all lose.

"Organisms evolve only when their benefits outweigh their costs," Steven Pinker writes in *How the Mind Works*. Flattery has also evolved through a cost-benefit equation. In fact, in the cost-benefit calculus, flattery is a no-brainer. It has very little cost—even if someone thinks you are insincerely flattering them, it's not like you've done something illegal. People like it. The writer and editor Michael Kinsley has suggested that insincere flattery is the most flattering kind because it shows that people are so beholden to you that they even use subterfuge in order to ingratiate themselves. *I don't believe you, but I appreciate the effort.* There is no punishment for false flattery. There's no real cost, and as for the benefit, the sky's the limit. Flatter the king, and you could be right there next to him. Flatter the boss, and you can wind up the number two—or even the boss herself.

Chalk It Up to Chemistry

Of course, the reason flattery works may all come down to chemistry. To serotonin, anyway.

Flattery may well cause a biochemical reaction in the brain that's very pleasant, and chimps and humankind may share that same response. A recent study by UCLA professor Michael McGuire of male vervet monkeys showed that dominant males had twice as much serotonin in their blood as subordinate males. They discovered that if an alpha male was overthrown, his serotonin dropped, while the serotonin of his replacement shot up. Serotonin levels seem to be both a cause and an effect, but the most fascinating aspect of how the serotonin level of the monkeys varied was McGuire's finding that he could deplete the serotonin of a dominant male simply by keeping him behind a one-way mirror where his peers couldn't acknowledge his dominance displays. In other words, it was the sight of submissive behavior on the part of his minions that seemed to trigger the neurohormonal changes in the alpha male that led to increased serotonin. In short, what we might call flattery in the form of bowing and scraping and other submissive behavior was the very thing that caused the increase in serotonin. So when a courtier bows low and says to the king, "You are wise beyond the ken of prophets," the king's serotonin meter gets a little bump, and it makes him happy. It's good to be the king.

Serotonin is a neurotransmitter, a chemical used in sending information from cell to cell in the brain. In fact, serotonin is basic to life. Worms and sea slugs make it as well as monkeys and college professors. Recent studies have suggested that serotonin, among other things, quiets the sensory neurons that mediate pain and hunger and also pacifies neurons in the brain's limbic system. Low serotonin seems to play some role in depression (people who attempt suicide have extremely depleted levels of it) and violence (a study of career criminals in the Netherlands shows that they have extremely low levels of the stuff). By the same token, higher levels of serotonin seem to be conducive to greater happiness or contentment. Prozac works by boosting the supply of serotonin in the system, allowing it to remain longer, making you happier all around.

McGuire writes in his study that it's the perception of submissive behavior rather than the actual achievement of power itself that raises the monkeys' serotonin level. The idea is that the flattering behavior, rather than whatever action you took that makes someone want to flatter you, is what gives you the positive reinforcement in the form of serotonin flooding your brain. Negative feedback, McGuire writes, diminishes the levels of serotonin. We can assume that flattery—which is, by definition, positive feedback—boosts serotonin. Whether high serotonin is the result of high status, or the achievement of high status is the result of having high levels of serotonin, no one seems to know. But there is a clear correlation between high status and high serotonin, and we do know that high status makes folks feel better.

Many scientists who have studied power make the point that power itself makes you feel pretty darn frisky. (McGuire and a colleague did another study that showed that the officers of fraternities had 25 percent higher levels of serotonin than regular pledges.) "Every study indicates that mental health and self-satisfaction are connected with position," says professor David Kipnis of Temple University. "The more resources you control, the better you feel." By the same token, the fewer resources you control, the worse you feel. Power may corrupt (and make you happy), but powerlessness corrupts absolutely.

Any way you slice it, it seems that flattery, or something like it, is biological. Whether it's favored by evolution because it helps you get your genes into the next generation, or it triggers a happy chemical reaction because it helps you to survive, no one knows. But flattery seems to help you survive and thrive, and when you are on the receiving end of it, it makes you feel powerful. And that, as Henry Kissinger has kindly told us, is the ultimate aphrodisiac.

But natural selection doesn't know from morality. Traits are selected not because they are good or bad, but because they are useful in helping a creature to survive. Flattery, I believe, is one of those traits. In the eyes of natural selection, it is neither moral nor immoral, it is simply useful.

So don't feel guilty if you use flattery to get what you want. It's nature's way. Conscience, as H. L. Mencken said, is just "the inner voice which warns us that someone might be looking." And remember, if someone is looking, just tell her how good-looking she really is.

Chapter 2

You *Can*
Take It with You

Don't Change—You're Perfect Just the Way You Are

Egyptian civilization was ancient even to the ancients. The Greeks of the first century gazed on the pyramids with the same awe with which we regard the Parthenon. Egypt was a thriving culture a thousand years before the Minoans of Crete built their palace at Knossos. It was a religious nation nine hundred years before Moses led the Israelites into the desert. Egyptian civilization lasted for nearly three millennia, beginning about 3100 B.C., a span of time 50 percent longer than the period from the birth of Jesus till the creation of the 233-megahertz chip that I am using to type this sentence.

Imagine for a moment all the dazzling, life-transforming changes that took place between the birth of Jesus and today. Take that same interval, and you would have the period during which ancient Egyptian civilization altered hardly a smidgen. If change is the single constant of modern civilization, change was the constant enemy of ancient Egypt. To the Egyptians, change meant chaos; it was the enemy and was to be avoided. Ancient Egypt feared any kind of variation in its culture and over three millennia changed far less than did Europe and America in the two decades between World Wars I and II.

The Egyptians loathed change because in their cosmology the world was perfect the moment it had been created by the gods, and anything that altered that diminished its perfection. Their attitude was, *It ain't broke so don't fix it.* Everything was as it should be—fixed, complete, proper. Perfection meant eternal changelessness.

Egypt had a deeply conservative culture. Harmony was the status quo. We think of social change as a key to evolving cultures. But in fact, inertia was the foundation of Egyptian society, and they managed to cultivate it for thousands of years. Mark Twain once defined an Englishman as a man who did things as they had been done before. He didn't know any ancient Egyptians.

It was a hierarchical society in which there was a place for everyone, and everyone knew his place. At the top was the god-king, the pharaoh, and underneath him in descending order were viziers, provincial governors, senior officals—all of whom came from the nobility—followed by priests, scribes, low-level bureaucrats, workers, servants, peasants, and slaves. There wasn't much social mobility—and where there is strict hierarchy and little social mobility, flattery becomes as formalized and rigid as the hierarchy it mirrors.

The role of flattery in a conservative culture is as changeless as everything else. In a culture where there is social mobility, flattery has to adapt to change and varies as the hierarchy varies. Flattery can often be an instigator of change, an engine of social mobility, a way to climb up the ladder. But in a culture with no ladders, flattery is as static and stratified as the hierarchy.

Flattery in ancient Egypt was impersonal and monumental. It was more macro than micro. The pyramids are the grandest tombstones the world has ever known; tributes, as Samuel Johnson remarked, "to the insufficiency of human enjoyment." They were monumental exercises in vanity and were outsized advertisements for their occupants, great public works projects using hundreds of thousands of people. They were monuments meant to outface eternity, and each was designed to flatter a single man.

The kings of ancient Egypt were not servants of the gods but gods themselves. As both king and god, the pharaoh was all things to all people. The pharaoh was head of both church and state—not that there was much difference. From the beginning of Egyptian culture, the kings were generally depicted as prodigious in size, while everyone else—even their wives— were Lilliputian. In 1500 B.C., an Egyptian civil servant wrote of the king: "He is a god by whose dealings one lives, the father and mother of all men, alone by himself, without equal." Try topping that as a compliment.

In the Egyptian cosmology, the king was essential to maintaining the equilibrium of the divine order. On earth, he was the very center of a very centralized Egyptian life. Ultimately, all offices depended on the king, all favors and honors came from him, all wealth and power flowed from him. One pharaoh, Achtoes II, was said to have remarked: "Royalty is a good profession." But a hard one to crack.

Egyptian society was itself a pyramid. The pharaoh at the apex, the vizier underneath him, followed by nobles, and high bureaucrats. The vizier was the second-in-command to the king. But because he could not be the king, he found consolation in allocating to himself as many titles as possible. The vizier was not just a vizier; he was the Sealbearer to the King, Sole Companion to the King, Overseer of the Fields and the Royal Residence. In the case of governors, what began as delegated power to run civil administrations eventually was transformed into a hereditary right. The army was probably the best route of social advancement in Egyptian society. A brave warrior of humble origins might ascend to the civil service. Another path was to become a scribe. This was seen as a meritocratic occupation, but typically only the offspring of the well-to-do were educated enough to get a place. (Apart from making lists, scribes spent most of their time writing encomiums to the king.) At the bottom of the pyramid and by far the largest group were the peasants and workers.

For the Egyptian aristocracy, the greatest earthly ambition was to win the pharaoh's esteem and the greatest reward was to receive his royal favor. The upper class was a small hereditary caste of soldiers, priests, and bureaucrats who supervised public works, dispensed justice, and ran the elaborate Egyptian bureaucracy. The most important accolade for any member of the Egyptian aristocracy (and it was routinely carved on their tombs) was, "He was greatly favored and esteemed by the king." Their entire lives were often spent in pursuit of a single compliment from the pharaoh. And, of course, they pursued this by complimenting the king over and over again.

Just in case you didn't know how to flatter the pharaoh properly, there were what we would now call etiquette handbooks, precursors to what were known in the Renaissance as courtesy literature. (See Chapter 6.) One of the best-known was *The Instructions of the Vizier Ptahhotep,* written during the Old Kingdom and studied by untold generations of ancient Egyptian schoolboys. Like Machiavelli's *The Prince* and Castiglione's *The*

Courtier, it offers advice and instruction on how to behave at court. Like Lord Chesterfield's letters, the great courtly manual of the eighteenth century, it is written in the form of advice from an aging vizier to his unworldly son. It combines commonsense observations concerning everyday life with pointed and detailed recommendations regarding court etiquette. This is not the folksy wisdom of a wise old uncle but the hard-and-fast precepts of the head of a military academy. After all, Egyptian etiquette varied not a jot for centuries.

For example, the author is very specific as to how one should behave with one's superiors: be humble and obsequious. Always.

If you are one among guests
At the table of one greater than you,
Take what he gives as it is set before you;
Look at what is before you,
Don't shoot many glances at him,
Molesting him offends the ka.
Don't speak to him until he summons,
One does not know what may displease;
Speak when he has addressed you,
Then your words will please the heart . . .
He will give to him whom he favors.

First, ingratiation, then the reward. At the end of this section, Ptahhotep adds, "Laugh after he laughs, and it will be very pleasing to his heart." *Laugh after he laughs.* It is one of the perfect and most elegant rules of toadyism. Modern sociologists have an inelegant name for it: opinion conformity. It is a rule that has always been successful; it was part of the flatterer's credo.

Ptahhotep, unlike later guides to courtly life, is not interested in charm. Charm was not on his radar screen. In a system as rigid as that of ancient Egypt, there isn't room for charm, if it even existed. Ptahhotep's recommended use of flattery is purely strategic.

"He will give to him whom he favors," the Vizier writes. Both the humility he counsels and the favor that will be given are purely formulaic. The equation is, *be humble and he will favor you, and he whom he favors will be given much.* But there is no alternative to humility, for monkeying with the status quo will only get your head chopped off.

> *If you are in the antechamber, stand and sit as fits your rank,*
> *Which was assigned you the first day.*
> *Do not trespass—you will be turned back . . .*
> *Do not malign anyone,*
> *Great or small, the* ka *abhors it.*

Embrace the status quo. Don't say a discouraging word. Do not reach beyond your grasp. Stick to your station. Don't question your superiors. Don't ever rock the boat. In a conservative society, it is best not to criticize. The powers that be are running things as they want them to be, so any criticism, however oblique, will seem to be pointed at them. Advocating change in a society that hasn't changed for centuries is not likely to endear you to the powers that be. Criticism will always boomerang. Maligning someone is the opposite of flattery, and it is the thing that the *ka* loathes more than anything. He is saying something not unlike what your grandmother told you: If you don't have anything nice to say about someone, don't say anything at all. (But in our modern culture of flattery, beware, for silence is very often interpreted as criticism.)

But not all silences are equal. Ptahhotep writes about one form of silence that can be particularly flattering: listening. Listening intently is a potent form of ingratiation. It makes the speaker feel good, and raises his estimation of the listener. In the popular business handbooks that have been so successful over the last few decades, listening is always described as the secret weapon of subordinates and Fuller Brush men everywhere.

Listening, Ptahhotep suggests, is not only beneficial to the self (you don't learn while you are talking, as the Japanese proverb goes), it is ingratiating to the speaker. It will also make the speaker think you're clever.

> *He who hears is beloved of god,*
> *He whom god hates does not hear . . .*
> *Teach yourself to be a hearer,*
> *One who will be valued by the nobles . . .*
> *Failure follows him who hears not.*

God hates those who do not listen because they are not paying attention. Lack of attention is the opposite of flattery. It is a kind of enmity. No one likes to be ignored.

We think of great flatterers as eloquent speakers, but great listeners flatter by their intent attention. Listening can be a kind of action. There are aggressive listeners who flatter the speaker by seeming to soak up every phrase, every syllable, every nuance. Watch Bill Clinton at a town meeting. When someone is asking a question, he will wrap the microphone in his arms (it's a sign that he's not going to talk until the speaker finishes), and lean toward the speaker, often inclining one ear in his or her direction. His brow becomes furrowed in concentration, his eyes limpid pools of empathy. What voter is not flattered to have the leader of the free world paying such rapt attention?

But not all of Ptahhotep's advice revolves around currying favor with the leader. Some of it is strategy on how to become beloved as a leader yourself. The leader, he suggests, must win the people's trust. But, even in this, there is an ulterior motive: to pump up one's own reputation.

> *If you are among the people,*
> *Gain supporters through being trusted;*
> *The trusted man who does not vent his belly's speech,*
> *He will become a leader.*
> *A man of means—what is he like?*
> *Your name is good, you are not maligned . . .*
> *One praises you without your knowing . . .*

From Ptahhotep to Plato to Castiglione to Dale Carnegie (as we will see), the currency of greatness, the most desirable end of ambitious men, is to win the praise of others. A thousand years before Aristotle, Ptahhotep is suggesting, as the Greek philosopher later would, that reputation was the supreme quest of ambitious men. For Ptahhotep, the pursuit of trust is not so much an end in itself as a quest for reputation, a quest for being known as a trustworthy man. While it may seem a trifle shady, his advice is not at all hypocritical. There was no sense in ancient Egypt that reputation and behavior could be at variance.

A Little Slice of Heaven

For the ancient Egyptian, the real business of living was the proper preparation for death. This made perfect sense because when it came to death, the
Egyptian view was, you *can* take it with you. In fact, to reverse Jack
Benny's famous quip ("If I can't take it with me, I'm not going"), the
Egyptian attitude was, if you don't take it with you, you won't have a very
good time. Which is one reason they buried people with all manner of cushions: You wanted to be comfortable en route to the afterlife. And the Egyptian nobility never traveled coach.

They believed in an afterlife that was just like this life, only better. Life
after death was thought to be a kind of greatest hits album of earthly pleasures. Better food. More money. Ageless beauty. Perfect sex. All play and no
work. Death without tears; death but no taxes.

The walls of Egyptian tombs showed the expected afterlife: People are
boating on the Nile, fowling in the marshes, picknicking by the river, drink-
ing wine in cool gardens. Their idea of heaven was simply earth at its best.
Heaven wasn't so much a better world as a return to the Edenic paradise that
life was at the moment of Creation.

* * *

Because ancient Egyptian religion was besotted with death, the ultimate
form of achievement was your rank not in life but in death. There was a
pecking order in death that was even more rigid than that in life. Any man
who could afford a proper tomb spared no expense in outfitting it with
everything needed for the afterlife—which was basically everything you
needed for the present life: food, clothing, furniture, tools, and games to
while away eternity. The idea was to plan for a very long trip. To tell a man
that he was well prepared for the afterlife was a high compliment. Tutankhamen was buried with enough fresh fruit and vegetables to feed a di-
vision of the Egyptian army. Kings and nobles were buried with the things
they liked best in life. (Abiding by the same ancient principle, Frank
Sinatra's family buried the crooner with a flask of Jack Daniel's in his
pocket, a pack of Camels, and a Zippo lighter.)

We know the name Tutankhamen not because he was a great pharaoh—
on the contrary, he was a totally undistinguished one, a callow young king
who didn't achieve much of anything—but simply because his tomb was
discovered intact. He came to the throne at ten, in the fourteenth century
B.C., died at nineteen, and never saw a battlefield. Yet his tomb is teeming
with images of him as a great warrior. Tut driving a speeding chariot. Tut
leading his forces into battle. Tut returning triumphantly from the front
with a gaggle of prisoners. The magnificence of his tomb—and the record
of its inscriptions—would suggest a Napoleon, yet in the run of Egyptian
history, Tut was a nobody, a shadow, a cipher.

His court and entourage flattered him even after he died—*especially*
after he died. If reciprocal altruism helps creatures get their genes into the
next generation, the reciprocal burial policy of the Egyptians did what to
them was even more important: It got their souls into the next life. Anyone
could and did make it into this world; it was getting into the next world that
was the trick.

In the case of Tutankhamen, this form of after-death flattery was even
more exacting in death than it would have been in life. No expense was
spared. His actual tomb, the innermost coffin, was molded from 242
pounds of solid gold. His mummified body was wrapped in hundreds of
yards of fine linen and packed with 143 precious objects: golden sandals,
gold rings, necklaces, bracelets, pendants, amulets. There were countless
graceful fans to cool him in case he got too warm, statues of dozens of servants to wait on him, plus two full-size chariots and a folding camp bed. A
beautiful painted timber chest, the panels of which depicted him in battle,
contained his footwear of choice and is helpfully labeled SANDALS OF HIS
MAJESTY. LIFE, HEALTH, STRENGTH!

*   *   *

For a very long time in Egytian society, the afterlife wasn't available to
everyone. Heaven wasn't the least bit democratic. For more than fifteen centuries, the pharaoh was the only person in Egyptian society who had something to look forward to after death. Only he would sail on into eternity. The
great tombs with all their wealth, with all the thousands of man-hours taken
to create them, were all to usher this one man into eternity—which was not

at all like the No. 3 train at rush hour. The Egyptian heaven was populated only by pharaohs. It was the most exclusive club imaginable. In one religious text, a king asks the creator god, Atum, what is the duration of his life. Atum replies: "Thou art destined for millions of millions of years, a lifetime of millions." Flattery for the ages.

After their death, the pharaohs were usually embalmed for seventy days. The mummified body would be exhibited to the people on a barge. The walls of the pharaohs' tombs had murals showing thousands of mourners. In fact, Egyptians often hired professional mourners who would beef up a royal funeral and weep on cue. The birth of the funeral claque.

By about 1800 B.C., the afterlife had expanded to include the pharaoh's family, aristocrats and the royal court. The nobles achieved immortality through proximity to the king—and if that did not give them incentive for flattery, I don't know what would. The closer you were to the pharaoh, the more likely you were to get a shot at the afterlife. You very much wanted a tomb with a view of the pharaoh's, for it was the pharaoh who brought you along for the ride. When it came to funerary real estate, it was location, location, location. You wanted to be even closer to the king in death than in life. Here was the ultimate reward for a lifetime of sucking up: immortality.

Heaven was slowly becoming more democratic. Servants might be brought along, particularly if they had proven useful to their master during life. This doesn't sound like such a bad deal until you discover that faithful retainers were killed so that they could accompany the pharaoh on his journey. The good news: you're going to go to heaven; the bad news: you're leaving in twenty minutes. This is an extreme form of self-flattery, killing your servants so that they can serve you in death as well as in life.

By the end of the Middle Kingdom, the afterlife had been fully democratized. All men and women could expect life in another world after this one. Now there was something in it for them. They were vested in the system. But, of course, as the opportunities of the working class expanded, the gentry had to make sure they still had one-upmanship. Just as ordinary Egyptians got a shot at the afterlife and a tomb, the aristocracy started building second tombs for themselves, farther from the city and the tombs of the rabble, a kind of after-death country house.

Monuments to Eternity

The kings of Egypt were less interested in building metropolises for the people than necropolises for themselves. It's as though all the buildings Donald Trump ever developed were located in one place and were designed to house only one tenant: himself. And not until after death. (Actually, given his outsized vanity, that doesn't sound so farfetched.) In fact, it's more like the president of the United States, from the moment he took office, using the entire federal transportation and construction budget to build not just a presidential library for himself but an entire city, which would only be used as his final resting place. The moment a pharaoh ascended his throne was the moment he began planning his tomb.

Take Cheops's Great Pyramid at Giza. It was started when he mounted his throne; it took twenty years to build, required tens of thousands of laborers, and is composed of some 6 million tons of stone, much of which had to be brought from as far as five hundred miles away. And this before the discovery of the wheel. The main engine for moving each of these 750-foot-long pieces of granite was human muscle.

In fact, the pyramids themselves and the techniques used to produce them were pioneered by a courtier to please his king. About 4,700 years ago, Imhotep, vizier to King Djoser, constructed a step-sided pyramid as a funerary temple to his boss. The boss liked it. And from then on, every courtier tried to outdo the previous pyramid to please his pharaoh's edifice complex.

As a pharaoh, Ramses II was unmatched in terms of vanity construction. Ramses ruled for an estimated sixty-seven years and had a mania for construction. He built a series of temples for himself at Abu Simbel that one entered by passing through two sixty-seven-foot statues of himself carved out of the side of the mountain. This would be like Teddy Roosevelt's deciding to dedicate Mt. Rushmore all to himself. Just so no one could ever mistake who is buried there, the two statues of Ramses at Abu Simbel show him seated, while the figures of his immediate family come about halfway up to his knees.

For the pharaohs, the tombs were advertisements that signified the importance of their occupants. In the Valley of the Kings, where the mountainside is honeycombed with tombs, the pharaoh and his court inscribed their accomplishments on the sides of their tombs. These inscriptions on the outside of the temples were permanent billboards touting the greatness of those buried within. The builders and artisans were like a resident staff of press agents for the pharaoh, touting his image, polishing his record.

Ramses regarded himself as a king among kings, a warrior among warriors. But his military fame rests less on his own exploits than on his own words. His actual military record is modest, but accounts of his valor and courage were inscribed on the walls of every major temple of his era. Like every pharaoh, he never failed to claim success where failure had occurred, never hesitated to invent a victory where nothing at all may have happened. There were no newspapers or television reports to contradict him. For Ramses, the first draft of history was carved in stone. Ramses outdid the other pharaohs not so much in battles but in sheer wall space. Pictures depict him as a giant wiping out whole divisions of enemies. One temple says that the portrayal of the defeat of Egypt's enemies is meant to be "a lesson for a million generations." In ancient Egypt, the word was father to the deed. If it was said or written, it had happened. (Ramses did know how to flatter his wife, though. The inscription above the entrance of her temple reads, SHE FOR WHOM THE SUN DOTH SHINE.)

Egyptian names were forms of flattery and self-advertisement. Nefertiti, the name of the legendary Egyptian beauty, means "the Beautiful One is come." Egyptian kings had five names in their full titulary. Names, like words themselves, had a kind of totemic power in ancient Egypt. To undermine that power, the new pharaoh would often order the name of his predecessor to be erased from his tombs. It was as though the name itself would haunt him, and if it were effaced, it would lose its power. An Egyptian saying was, "To speak the name of the dead is to make him live again." That is what pharaohs sought to do for themselves and sought to undo for their predecessors. Not only must I succeed, my predecessors must be erased.

On the walls of the tombs of both kings and their circle were listed the tomb-owners, ranks, titles, and the offerings each had received. They were mini-autobiographies. They strike the modern reader, as the scholar Miriam Lichtheim notes, as "excessively self-laudatory." But they are not so much epitaphs as petitions for eternity. These inscriptions are each person making his or her case to the gods for eternal life. The idea isn't to be modest.

Hyperbole is the order of the day. They're like job application letters that begin, "I'm the best person for this job and here's why."

The style of these inscriptions eventually became formulaic, with the catalogue of virtues recited in symmetrically structured sentences. For those underneath the pharaoh, their autobiographies consist entirely of a recitation of the favors they did for the king and how much the king loved them in return. It is both self-flattery and an account of how they were flattered by the king.

Certain claims are repeated over and over. The inscriptions always assert that the deceased was kind, generous, honest, just, magnanimous, and tolerant. In *The Autobiography of Weni,* the inscription of the Sixth Dynasty governor of Upper Egypt and chamberlain to the king is typical of the kinds of puffery the nobles gave themselves. It reads in part: "His majesty made me senior warden of Nekhen, his heart being filled with me more than any other servant of his." He says the king asked him to quietly resolve a dispute in the royal harem. "Only I alone; because I was worthy, because I was rooted in his majesty's heart; because his majesty had filled his heart with me. . . . Never before had one like me heard a secret of the king's harem; but his majesty made me hear it because I was worthy in his majesty's heart beyond any official of his, beyond any noble of his, beyond any servant of his." Okay, we get the idea.

The smaller private tombs have their own mini-billboards crowing about how wonderful the occupant is. From the stela of the Bulter Merer of Edfu from the Middle Kingdom:

I was responsible for slaughtering and offering in two temples on behalf of the ruler. I offered for thirteen rulers without a mishap ever befalling me. . . . I was not spat in the eyes, owing to the worth of my speech, the competence of my counsel, and the bending of my arm. I did what the great ones liked, what my household praises; a person beloved of his companions. I have stood out in front; I have attained reveredness.

The nature of his work had entailed a lifetime of sycophancy, and he boasts about what a good job he did of it.

If Only Life *Did* Imitate Art

To the pharaohs, size mattered. They were generally depicted on a scale that dwarfed the natural world. They were giants who bestrode the earth; everyone else was a pygmy. When it came to depicting the pharaoh, there was no such thing as realism. Naturalism was perceived as insufficiently flattering. To flatter, one must improve upon nature. The pharaoh was always shown larger, handsomer, younger, and stronger than he was in real life.

In Egyptian art, all the devices that artists use to show perspective—foreshortening, overlapping figures, relative size—are almost totally absent. It's not that the Egyptians did not understand perspective; the point was that the pharaoh was never to be shown "in perspective." He was outside perspective. He was beyond perspective.

His portrayal was prescribed by convention. Austere and iconic, he was timeless, immutable, the still point of the turning world. Later, during the Fourth and Fifth Dynasties, known as the Old Kingdom, subsidiary characters, laborers, peasants, animals, were shown with some perspective and with more naturalism, but never the pharaoh. Others became more contemporary-looking, more rounded, but the pharaoh was outside of time.

Looking at one pharaoh's portrait after another, you could easily say, I see the family resemblance. For the expression on each pharaoh's face seems never to have varied over three millennia. Jaw-clenched, staring straight ahead, they were all detached, impassive, regal, impersonal. The pharaoh's body—even when old, wizened, and flabby—was always depicted as sleek, young, muscular, and perfectly proportioned. Later, by the end of the Middle Kingdom, the pharaohs became a little more human, a little less impersonal.

If you look at the schist statues of the Fourth Dynasty king Menkaure and his queen from the classic age of Egyptian sculpture, about 2500 B.C., the king has the torso of Jack LaLanne. Broad muscular shoulders, taut legs, and narrow waist. There's not an ounce of fat on him. The queen is a bit softer but still buff even by our rigorous health club standards. Their faces are completely without lines or wrinkles, staring off into the middle distance with a mixture of steely confidence and regal reserve. They are ageless, emotionless, eternal, as hard and everlasting as the stone from which they are carved. The idea was not to show their humanity but their ideality.

The Egyptians had a curious attitude toward art. First of all, they didn't have a word for it, and second, it was regarded more as prophecy or reportage than depiction. Art was literally akin to creation for the Egyptians, for they believed that the image of the thing had the same properties as the thing itself. Depicting an action in a relief or on a wall painting was the equivalent of making that action happen. It was a kind of *virtual* art, but without the computer graphics. For them, appearances did constitute reality in a very literal way.

The depiction of the pharaoh smiting his enemies was a way of guaranteeing that the event would occur. Traditionally, the pharaoh's enemies are shown hanging in rows like dead game birds, or kneeling in supplication to prevent their brains from being dashed out. Sometimes the pharaoh is shown holding dozens of captives by the hair. One classic image that is part of the royal iconography is known by art historians as the "smiting scene," and shows the king raining blows on a cringing foe. This picture appears in remarkably unvarying form for almost the entire span of Egyptian history. The collective name for Egypt's traditional enemies was the "Nine Bows," and this image was often drawn on the king's walking sticks, his footstool, and the soles of his sandals, so that he might trample his enemies all day long at his ease. Another example of wishful thinking is the celebration of what was known as the *sed,* a jubilee festival that commemorated the thirty years of a king's rule. Many kings had seds during their realm long before the three decades were up in the hopes that it might lead to such longevity.

* * *

There was one notable exception to the monotonous pictorial flattery of the pharaohs, and his name was Akhenaton; Akhenaton was the pharaoh of new ideas. He was a religious revolutionary. One thousand three hundred years before the birth of Jesus, he attempted to purge the Egyptian religion of its polytheism and replace it with the worship of a single god. This was a revolutionary notion, except for one problem: only Akhenaton was able to worship Him, and everyone else would have to worship Akhenaton. Yes,

Akhenaton came up with the idea of one God, but it was his private God only.

Akhenaton was a pear-shaped man with a long face, drooping shoulders, broad hips, and spindly legs. We know this because he commanded the court artist to show him the way he really was, not as some pharaonic superman. In his images, he looks like the "before" picture in a weight-loss ad. He even decided that his wife, Nefertiti, the legendary beauty, should be shown as she aged, with poor posture and a sagging belly. He took naturalism to an extreme. There were even paintings of the queen brushing her teeth. But Akhenaton's attempted revolution in both religion and art failed. His god existed only in his own lifetime, and his art proved to be a brief moment of naturalism amid the usual idolatrous flattery. His successor, who was depicted as tall, strong, and ageless, did his best to erase Akhenaton's name and image wherever it appeared. So, for the rest of Egyptian history, Akhenaton passed out of existence. It was the death of realism.

The Eloquent Peasant

The Egyptians' attitude toward language was not unlike their attitude toward art: It was something sacred. Not just a symbol of something but very near the thing itself. The word was the thing; the thing was the word.

The ancient Egyptians did not seem to have a word for "lying," and the idea of using speech to mislead or deceive was alien to them. What we would call false praise was to them not false but descriptive and prophetic. What seems to us like fulsome praise of the pharaoh was just someone trying to use language to capture something that seemed beyond language. Saying something that was not yet the case might have the effect of causing it to happen. It was not false speech but perhaps wishful-thinking speech. The Egyptians lived in a world of symbolism, but they were in fact very literal minded.

The Eloquent Peasant is one of the few pieces of literature that has come down to us from the Middle Kingdom, which spanned about three centuries, beginning about 2150 B.C. It is both a disquisition on the need for justice and a parable on the utility of fine speech. By our terms, the peasant of the title shamelessly flatters the judge from whom he is seeking justice.

But to the ancient Egyptians, fine rhetoric reflected fine morality. They did not yet realize, as the Greeks would, that a man may speak well but be a scoundrel, that fine rhetoric can be in the service of not-so-fine motives. Their attitude was, *If you say it, you must believe it and it must be true*. The word was father to the deed.

In the story, the eloquent peasant of the title appeals to the high steward Rensi after discovering that his donkey and supplies have been stolen by an unscrupulous master. He begins by saying, "O high steward, my lord, greatest of the great leaders of all!"

He continues:

> . . . *father to the orphan,*
> *Husband to the widow,*
> *Brother to the rejected woman,*
> *Apron to the motherless.*
> *Leader free of greed,*
> *Great man free of baseness,*
> *Destroyer of falsehood,*
> *Creator of rightness,*
> *Who comes at the voice of the caller!*
> *When I speak, may you hear!*
> *Do justice, O praised one,*
> *Who is praised by the praised;*
> *Remove my grief, I am burdened,*
> *Examine me, I am in need!*

Praised by the praised. Not only are you praiseworthy in and of yourself, you are venerated by those who are praiseworthy. This is the kind of thing that you hear at awards ceremonies like the Oscars, when winners routinely say how deeply meaningful the award is because it comes from one's peers.

This kind of ritual praise was absolutely necessary. Without it, the steward would be insulted. Even today in the Middle East, if you leave out what are considered ritual words of praise you are considered deeply insulting. The peasant's praise is also powerful because he is telling the steward what a good and decent man he is. What is clever about this is that he praises the steward for helping the powerless like himself—so in effect, he is praising the steward in advance for helping him. He is puffing him up to do the exact thing that he wants him to do.

After hearing the peasant's speech, the steward goes to the king and says, "My lord, I have found one among the peasants whose speech is truly beautiful." He then invites the king to come and listen.

On his second appearance before the judge, he tells him the following:

> *You are the whole land's rudder,*
> *The land sails by your bidding:*
> *You are the peer of Thoth,*
> *The judge who is not partial. . . .*
> *Speak justice, do justice,*
> *For it is might;*
> *It is great, it endures,*
> *Its worth is tried,*
> *It leads one to reveredness.*

To our ears, the peasant is trying to shame the justice into doing right. By telling him that he is fair, he will induce him to be fair. But to the king and the steward that is not what is going on. The king and the steward are transfixed by the peasant's speech. But they are listening to it earnestly, not ironically. Irony hadn't made it to ancient Egypt. Fine speech is rewarded because they perceive it as an example of fine thoughts and behavior. They don't see through it because there is nothing to see through.

In a sense, there was no such thing as flattery in ancient Egypt because there was no such thing as false or undeserved praise. Speech was considered either a true mirror of nature or a kind of literary prognostication. The idea of deception didn't really enter into either of those forms. Our modern sense of flattery is that there is some discrepancy between what the speaker is saying and the reality he is describing. The title *The Eloquent Peasant* was not meant to be ironic. Even if the eloquent peasant sounds disingenuous to us, his speech sounded earnest and sincere to Egyptians. The Egyptians didn't think they were telling untruths, even though by our standards, they certainly were. And if their flattery did come true, it wouldn't be flattery, would it?

Chapter 3

Flatter Me
or Else

God Is Insecure

In the beginning, God was lonely.

Yes, he had formed the heavens and the earth, he had made the light and the darkness, and put all manner of vegetation on the earth, but he had no one to share it with. And while a tree is certainly a lovely thing to look at, and nice to sit under on a summer afternoon, God wanted a little company, and who can blame him?

In fact, because he had no friends, no colleagues, no mother or father to speak of, he was more than lonely—he did not really know who or what he was. Everyone, even God, must figure out who he or she is in part by comparing themselves to others. Infants look everywhere but only begin to become self-aware when they recognize themselves in the mirror. God had created eagles and sea monsters and swarms of living things, but staring at a crow or a cow will not help a fellow figure out who he is.

Then, a lightbulb went off in God's head: I'll create a kind of clone, someone in my own image who will be a sort of mirror. "Let us make man in our image," he says in Genesis, "after our likeness." And in the mirror of his own self-image, God will finally be able to see himself, albeit in somewhat runtier form. God's plan had another fringe benefit. How better to find some congenial company, to meet someone with whom you have a lot in common, someone you can just really hang out with, than to create a version of yourself? And that's what God does. "So God created man in his own image, in the image of God he created him," says the narrator of the book of Genesis. As Jack Miles writes in his wonderful work, *God: A Biography,* God's quest for a self-image is the "sole and indispensable tool of his self-understanding." Even the Koran teaches that God created Adam in his own image so that he could contemplate himself as in a mirror. *So that's what I look like.* And, what's more, he got a buddy in the bargain.

When the first man becomes the first friend, God, of course, wants to play with him. But it's God's game and He makes the rules. First, he instructs Adam not to eat of the tree of the knowledge of good and evil, or else there will be dire consequences. In fact, that's really the only rule God makes. You'd think Adam could remember one pretty simple instruction.

But Adam was naive, and he is taken by surprise by the wily serpent who is playing an altogether different game. When the serpent persuades Eve to nibble the forbidden fruit, Adam also decides to have a quick bite. This episode is followed rather rapidly by another game: hide-and-seek. The Lord comes down to the garden, walks around a bit, and then says, "Where are you?" When a cowering Adam and Eve sheepishly come forth, Adam explains that he was afraid because he was naked. "Who told you that you were naked?" God says. Now, God is playing twenty questions. Like a prosecutor, God asks him directly if he's taken a bite of the forbidden fruit. Adam may be the first man, but he's no mensch. He blames it all on Eve. "She gave me the fruit of the tree," he says.

For this first crime, God decides a mere reprimand is not enough. The Lord tells Eve that from now on she will feel agony in childbirth, and then he casts them both out of Eden. He tells Adam that henceforth he will slave away for his daily bread "till you return to the ground, / for out of it you were taken: / you are dust, / and to dust you shall return."

The Lord seems excessively upset by this whole episode. After all, Adam is God's first prototype off the assembly line, he's a test model, an experiment. You can't really expect to mass-produce him right away. Surely, God must realize there are a lot of bugs in his software, and ADAM.2, ADAM.3 will iron out some of the kinks. But that doesn't seem to be on God's mind. God, the Lord of all creation, the fellow who created the heavens and the earth, seems to regard Adam as competition. What seems to concern God is not that Adam is imperfect, but that Adam might

be a threat to God's sovereignty. Why? Because Adam is no longer ignorant. Adam may have been created from the dust of the ground, but now,
the Lord says, he "has become like one of us, knowing good and evil."
"Don't get any ideas" is God's attitude. Don't get uppity on me. God is not
sure enough of himself to countenance a rival, however weak and puny and
inferior. Without even knowing it, Adam has kicked sand in God's face.

*   *   *

Did God create mankind, Jack Miles wonders, "because he wished to be
known, loved or served?" The answer, I think, is all three. Strange to say,
but Yahweh is a rather insecure fellow. He seems desperately in need of
positive reinforcement. A kind word goes far with him. But there aren't
many. Instead, he frequently resorts to boasting about himself to prop up
his confidence. He wants to feel powerful and he needs to feel revered. But
how is he going to raise the divine serotonin level? One way is through
praise or flattery. And the only way he has figured out how to get such
praise or flattery is by compelling it. Flatter me or else, he seems to be saying throughout the Old Testament.

The notion that God is a projection of human needs and mankind's own
anxiety is a theory advanced by many philosophers. Paul Tillich believed
that religion was necessary for mankind because of a deep-rooted anxiety
about the human condition. We're born, we get old, and die. Shit happens,
as the bumper sticker says. It makes sense to create a celestial mechanic, a
divine king, a Lord Most High who can provide meaning where there
might be none.

I am talking here about Yahweh, of course, the God of the Israelites—the
God whom the Israelites themselves invented. This is the God of the Old
Testament, not the New. He seems only a distant cousin to the Christian
God of the New Testament. Like Adam, he is also a prototype—the first
monotheistic God—and he has a lot of kinks that need to be ironed out.
Like a headstrong toddler, he's not quite sure of his own strength; he's testing things out and he doesn't like being told what to do. He is taking the
place of a passel of other gods, each of whom had specific tasks, so it
stands to reason that he's a little nervous. There's a lot of weight on his
shoulders.

If you look at the ancient Israelites, you'll find a rather ragtag people that needed some bucking up. They didn't have a homeland; they were blown from pillar to post; they were persecuted everywhere they went. There's a reason God is insecure; he's the projection of an insecure people. It makes a kind of counterintuitive sense: A God that needs flattery is created by a people who need security. If we create God in our own image, then a needy God reflects a needy people.

So when God tells Adam not to eat from the tree, this is the first of many tests that God gives to the people he himself has allegedly created. He not only tests Adam; he tests Abraham, Jacob, Moses, David, and, of course, Job. In the case of Adam, however, the test feels less like a game than a sting operation. Like a career FBI agent, God orchestrates the entire scene: He creates the garden, the serpent, the temptation. He sets the whole thing up, and of course, Adam falls into the trap. God records the whole thing on videotape. And because God is both prosecutor and judge, he sentences Adam without a trial, without even reading him his Miranda rights.

*   *   *

Until monotheism, most gods were local. If you walked from one town to another, you moved from the precinct of one god to that of another. It's like a variation on those road signs in the American Southwest: YOU ARE LEAVING THE REALM OF RA. YOU ARE ENTERING THE REALM OF BAAL. But the Jewish God was everywhere. You couldn't shake him or leave him behind, even if you wanted to. As Yahweh told Joseph, "I will keep you safe wherever you go." Like the Travelers Insurance slogan, he provided umbrella coverage.

In fact, his ubiquity proved more of a burden to his people than a boon. Yahweh is a God who demands your full attention. Don't even think about looking over his shoulder while he's talking to you. "It is part of the basic character of this God," the philosopher Martin Buber wrote, "that he claims the entirety of the one he has chosen; he takes complete possession of the one to whom he addresses himself." He is a meddlesome God who, at least in the early books of the Old Testament, can't ever seem to leave well enough alone. The God of Genesis isn't interested in being locked away in some primordial vacuum. He's an extrovert; he wants to be the life of the party. He doesn't sit around and mope; he takes action.

And don't get the idea that because he's universal he's also impartial. He's not. He's a god who plays favorites. But beware of becoming one of them. With mentors like Yahweh, you don't need enemies—but you get them anyway. Sometimes it looks enviable to be God's flavor-of-the-month, but don't get too cozy because he changes his mind without warning. He's flighty. He's mercurial. His smallest whim can upend your life in the blink of an eye. And don't even think about looking at another god. Yahweh even describes himself as jealous. "For you shall worship no other god," he says, "for the Lord, whose name is Jealous, is a jealous God." (It's one of his few moments of self-awareness.) If the Israelites so much as wink at another deity, God goes ballistic. He decries idolatry as a sin. But to him, idolatry is simply flattery directed away from him.

He's also very, very touchy. He's forever smiting people—his friends included; his friends especially—for what seem like the most trivial reasons. He treats misdemeanors as felonies. For example, after God leads David to victory over the Philistines, the Israelites are celebrating when a soldier named Uzzah stumbles and puts his hand on the ark of the covenant to steady himself. Watch out! "And the anger of the Lord was kindled against Uzzah; and God smote him there because he put forth his hand to the ark; and he died there beside the ark of God." And Uzzah was one of God's loyal soldiers.

God is no stoic. He complains incessantly. During the years in the desert, the Israelites grumble about the weather, the lack of water, the endless wandering. They're the original *kvetchers*. But they're outdone by God's moaning about their moaning. In Isaiah, he says, "For a long time I have held my peace, / I have kept still and restrained myself; / Now I will cry out like a woman in travail." He doesn't feel *our* pain—he wants us to feel *his* pain.

In the desert, he is obsessed with how the Israelites perceive him. He feels that they resent him no matter what he does. In his dialogue with Moses, God sounds positively Nixonian. His conversation could have come from the Watergate tapes. "How long will this people despise me? And how long will they not believe in me, in spite of all the signs which I have wrought among them. I will strike them with the pestilence and disinherit them." You don't want to be on *His* enemies list.

He's hypersensitive about anyone showing him disrespect—which of course is the flip side of flattery. Why does he destroy Sodom and Gomorrah, two entire cities populated by tens of thousands of people? Because they have shown "contempt" for him. God here is like the diminutive hot-tempered gangster who rubs out anyone who calls him Shorty. He's a God who is so insecure that he resents anyone who isn't. "Look on every one that is proud, and bring him low," he says. As Jack Miles writes, God has no cosmic opponent but himself. But he's a God who leads Israel down the path of destruction, killing tens of thousands, just to show who's boss. What's his catch-all explanation for all this? "That they might know that I am the Lord." That'll show them.

If at times God behaves like he is "rebelling against his Jewish mother," as Harold Bloom puts it, he also comes across as a Jewish patriarch who is not at all reticent about inflicting guilt on his ungrateful children. "Surely this instruction which I enjoin upon you this day is not too baffling for you, nor is it beyond reach," he says at one point. During the years in the desert, God routinely complains that the Israelites aren't grateful enough for what he has done for them. His attitude seems to be, *This is the thanks I get after all I've done for you?* While David is resting after a battle, the Lord tells the prophet Nathan: "Go and tell my servant David, 'Thus says the Lord: Would you build me a house to dwell in? I have not dwelt in a house since the day I brought up the people of Israel from Egypt to this day, but I have been moving about in a tent for my dwelling. In all places where I have moved with all the people of Israel, did I speak a word with any of the judges of Israel . . . saying, 'Why have you not built me a house of cedar?' " God sounds like a cranky father whose son is living in a big mansion in Scarsdale, but hasn't given a thought to his old man camping out in a little condo in Boca.

*   *   *

God, it must be said, was not above tooting his own horn. Modesty wasn't one of his virtues. Out of his own insecurity, he felt the need to boast about how unique he was. His attitude seems to be: *If I don't do it, no one else will!* It's also a way of telling the Israelites how he'd like to be flattered. He often gives them the template for exactly how he wants to be praised:

I am the first and I am the last;
besides me there is no god.
Who is like unto me?

And again:

I, the Lord, the first,
and with the last; I am He.

Like many self-flatterers, the Lord doesn't quite see himself as others see him. In fact, he has a rather inflated and inaccurate opinion of himself. In Exodus, he says of himself,

The Lord, the Lord God merciful and gracious, slow to anger, and
   abounding in steadfast love and faithfulness.

Talk about not knowing yourself.

In fact, God frequently demonstrates that he is quick to anger, anything but steadfast in his love, and generally pretty mean. A few pages after the above declaration about his mercifulness, the Lord orders the Israelites to put to death a man found to have committed the heinous crime of gathering sticks on the Sabbath. When the Israelites complain that he was unfair to some of the rebels, he sends a plague on them to show that they should not question him. When, after conquering Heshobon and Basham, some of the Israelites commence to worship Baal, the Lord sends another plague that kills 24,000 Israelites. Mercy and graciousness are not the first attributes that come to mind about this Lord.

But Yahweh's great and consistent lament seems to be, *No one understands me.* He sounds both wistful and bitter when he says in Isaiah:

Sons have I reared and brought up,
but they have rebelled against me.
The ox knows its master
and the ass its master's crib;
but Israel does not understand.

A Stiff-Necked People

For a universal God, the Lord is pretty parochial. In the Old Testament, God may claim to be Lord of all, but he is really just the god of the Israelites. Yes, he prefigures God of the New Testament, the Christian God of modern-day Christians—and that of Muslims, for that matter—but in the beginning, he seems to have time only for the Jews. After all, you might say that they chose him rather than the other way around. But regardless of who chose whom, I think it is fair to say that their relationship, in the parlance of pop psychology, is severely dysfunctional.

The character of the Israelites is in part responsible for God's insecurity. He needs reassurance and instead they give him grief. He wants to be loved and admired, and instead they ask, "So what have you done for me lately?" He wants to be flattered, and instead they ignore him and sometimes snub him. Throughout the Old Testament, the Israelites are pains in the butt. They're not exactly warm and fuzzy. They never suffer in silence. God refers to them on numerous occasions as a "stiff-necked" people. They're stubborn and refractory and they never make it easy for their cranky old Creator.

The Israelites may be self-absorbed but they're not stupid. They know on which side their bread is buttered. They seem to have no problem in flattering the earthly rulers who control their destiny. The advice in Ecclesiastes is often like the sort of worldly counsel that we will later see in Renaissance courtesy literature.

> *If the anger of the ruler rises against you, do not leave your place, for deference will make amends for great offenses.*

But when it comes to God, the Israelites are often reluctant to go down on bended knee. Instead of trying to mollify him, they always seem to be trying to dupe him instead. They treat him as though he's a slightly dotty uncle with a severe astigmatism whom they can fool with only a minimum of guile. Take Jacob, for instance. First, Jacob's mother Rebekah hoodwinks God by making Abraham think that Jacob is actually Esau. Then when God accepts Jacob, Jacob makes only a conditional agreement with

God. He puts God on probation, as Jack Miles puts it. "If God will be with me," Jacob says, "and will keep me in this way that I go, and will give me bread to eat and clothing to wear, so that I come again to my father's house in peace then the Lord shall be my God." Sure, I'll accept you, Jacob seems to be saying, just as long as you provide for me in the style to which I've become accustomed.

With Moses, on the long march through the desert, the Israelites are like a bunch of summer campers on an endless bus trip. They're hot. They're hungry. Are we there yet? Moses can't control them. "The people found fault with Moses, and said, 'Give us water to drink.' And Moses said to them, 'Why do you find fault with me? Why do you put the Lord to the proof?' But the people thirsted there for water, and the people murmured against Moses and said, 'Why did you bring us up out of Egypt, to kill us and our children and our cattle with thirst?' So Moses cried to the Lord, 'What shall I do with this people?'"

Enough already, he seems to be saying.

It is with this stiff-necked tribe that God decides to make a covenant.

·   ·   ·

The word "covenant" is really just a fancy term for a deal. And the deal between God and the Israelites was this: If you make me your one and only, I'll make you number one. If you flatter me with your worship, I'll make it worth your while. Stick with me, kid, and I'll do good by you. In exchange for the Israelites' making God their one and only, the Lord would make the Jews his special people, rid them of their outcast status, and deliver them to the promised land flowing with milk and honey. It would be, as they say in diplomacy, a special relationship. For the Jews, this seemed like a pretty good deal. So what's not to like?

The covenant is like the bargain of reciprocal altruism. The deal is meant to be mutually beneficial to both parties. God gets a people, and a people get God. God gets someone to worship him, and the Israelites get someone to worship. It's a win-win situation.

In fact, flattery itself is a kind of covenant. There is an implicit, unspoken agreement that is made when flattery is offered and accepted. If I flatter you and you embrace it, you implicitly agree to have a higher opinion of me. The covenant of God and the Israelites is that in exchange for the Israelites' worship, God awards them a higher place in the cosmic order.

This covenant between God and the Israelites was no casual handshake agreement. God drove a tough bargain. In fact, he made the Israelites an offer they couldn't refuse. God essentially said, *If you're there for me, I'll be there for you. But if you're not there for me, I'll kill you.* The Israelites really had no choice in the matter. If you don't worship God, Deuteronomy says, "You will be torn from the land which you are entering. . . . Yahweh will scatter you among the people, from one end of the earth to the other. . . . Your life from the outset will be a burden to you. . . . In the morning you will say, 'How I wish it were evening!' and in the evening, 'How I wish it were morning!' Such terror will grip your ears, such sights your eyes will see."

That doesn't leave much room for negotiation.

As part of the covenant, God selected Israel from all other nations and in return he demanded absolute fidelity. He enforced a loyalty oath and that oath is what Jews call the Shema, the central tenet of Jewish faith. "Hear, O, Israel: The Lord our God, the Lord is one. You shall love the Lord your God with all your heart, and with all your soul, and with all your might. And these words which I command you this day shall be upon your heart." In *A History of God,* Karen Armstrong writes that at the time the Shema was coined, which was the seventh century B.C., God was in competition with a lot of other gods, and he needed to corner the market on worship. This is a pretty stiff demand that the Lord makes in the Shema. He is God, after all, but it would be hard to come up with a more flattering oath. That's the point. No one or thing can or should be praised above God, so you want your name above the title.

Like the lawyers in the Paula Jones case, who tried but failed to find an airtight definition of sexual relations, God tried to impose an airtight definition of monotheism on the Israelites. *There shall be no other Gods before me.* But to the Israelites, there was a loophole. He did not say, "There shall be no other gods, period." He simply said, no other gods in front of him. So, the Israelites assumed, *Hey, there can be other gods, just as long as they're not our number-one God.*

With apologies to Henny Youngman, you could say the Israelites were religious, but they were not fanatics about it. They observed the covenant after their own fashion. They prayed to Yahweh in times of need, but when things were flush, they forgot about him. After the Israelites settled in Canaan and things were no longer so dicey, they turned to Baal, who was a fertility god. When God discovers that in Moses' absence the Israelites have started to treat the fertility god Baal as their top-dog god, the Lord doesn't just get mad, he gets even. "I will leave only seven thousand," he thunders, "every knee that has not knelt to Baal and every mouth that has not kissed him." In other words, everyone who has worshiped Baal will die, and the Lord proceeds to kill tens of thousands of Israelites, just like that.

As this story illustrates, fear is an unspoken component of the covenant. "The beginning of wisdom is the fear of the Lord" is an observation repeated three times in Proverbs. God's idea was, The Israelites are going to fear me if they know what's good for them. God was powerful—and capricious. He's like the Mafia don who gets respect in part because he's so unpredictable. He might hug you or he might plug you.

Fear, in fact, is a form of flattery, a type of deference. To show trepidation and nervousness before an opponent is a form of psychic groveling, an emotional prostration. Bowing and scraping, putting your head on the floor, prostrating yourself—as we saw with chimpanzees—is a ritualistic miming of fear. Some of the time, the Israelites only pretended to be afraid. But much of the time, the Israelites did not have to mime the fear; they were terrified. But they also realized that they could seduce God by showing that they feared him. This is exactly what the Lord seems to want from the Israelites—both real fear and the appearance of fear—but he only occasionally gets it.

*　　*　　*

Despite their disinclination to live up to their own part of the compact with God, the covenant went to the Israelites' heads. They began to flatter themselves that they were special. *We have been singled out by God. We're special. We are the Chosen People.* We may look like some ragtag bunch of good-for-nothings with no land or wealth, but we have a secret understanding with the Lord that puts us before every other people. We've got a secret. "A personal God like Yahweh," Karen Armstrong writes, "can be manipulated to shore up the beleaguered self in this way, as an impersonal deity like Brahman cannot." Which is exactly how they used him. God became the self-esteem guru of the Jews.

For the Jews, the sense of chosenness survived long after the time of the ancient Israelites. The twelfth-century Toledan physician and philosopher Judah Halevi wrote that the Jews had a special religious faculty and were therefore unique among the nations. Yes, the goyim could arrive at knowledge of God through the world, but only the Jews had a natural, subjective experience of the Lord.

Freud saw the Jews as almost comical in their sense of specialness. "Whence, then, did this tiny and impotent nation derive the audacity to pass themselves off as the favorite child of the Sovereign Lord?" he wrote. You could say Freud's view of Jewish self-flattery was an act of transference, evidence of his own mixture of insecurity and superiority concerning his Jewishness. "There is no doubt," he wrote, "that they [the Jews] have a very good opinion of themselves, think themselves nobler, on a higher level, superior to others." In the end, though, Freud offers a precursor to the modern self-help movement by suggesting that the Jews' belief in their own specialness—whether real or imagined—had the effect of making the Jews "proud and confident." Fake it till you make it, they tell you in the twelve-step programs. The Jews did.

Ultimately, the Israelites misinterpreted the covenant as a privilege rather than a responsibility. Israel was God's instrument, not God's favorite. The Jews seemed to think that the covenant was like winning the lottery, a prize with no strings attached. Sorry, there were *ropes* attached. Yes, the prophets said that God had selected Israel out of love, but it is the original definition of tough love. "Whom best I love I cross," says Jupiter in Shakespeare's *Cymbeline,* which was Shakespeare's summing up of the nature of God's covenant. Yahweh crossed the Israelites without ever seeming to really love them. Yahweh's ultimatum was, *Love me, or I will leave you.*

What God Wants, God Gets, Eventually

The covenant was a deal alright, but it was one in which one of the parties—that would be God—kept setting new conditions, rewriting clauses, revising the small print. The initial and fundamental requirement was pretty simple: "There shall be no other gods before me." But God kept raising the bar.

God went well beyond simply demanding that the Israelites tell him that he was their one-and-only. Over and over, he demands tribute, flattery, submission, adoration. And not just any adoration, but exactly on his own terms. He's a flattery autocrat.

Initially, he did not make moral demands; he made conditions. They were about power, not virtue: If you do *X,* I'll do *Y.* He constantly pushed the envelope of loyalty in ways that seem excessive. With Abraham and Job, he went beyond the boundaries of the covenant.

God not only demands offerings—which are a kind of flattery—he prescribes exactly the type and nature of offerings he desires. The Lord gives Moses a very specific shopping list of what he wants: "gold, silver, and bronze, blue and purple and scarlet stuff and fine twined lines, goats' hair, tanned rams' skins, goatskins, acacia wood, oil for the lamps, spices for the anointing oil and for fragrant incense, onyx stones, and stones for setting, for the ephod and for the breastpiece."

The Lord doesn't want just any sacrifice; he decrees that the sacrifices must have at minimum an R rating; they must be very, very bloody. In Exodus, he prescribes that the blood be drained from twelve oxen, collected in basins, half of it thrown at the altar and the other half sprinkled on the worshipers. "You shall kill the ram, and take part of its blood and put it upon the tip of the ear of Aaron, and upon the tips of the right ears of his sons, and upon the thumbs of their right hands, and upon the great toes of their feet. . . ." God commands the prophet Ezekiel not only to eat a scroll with God's words on it but to eat excrement as well. I don't recall that being part of the covenant.

Not only does he demand that Moses build him a temple, but he tells him how to furnish it, what patterns and colors to use on the walls, what fabrics the curtains should be made of. All of a sudden, God is a very finicky interior decorator who knows exactly how he wants the room to be for that fourteen-page layout in *Architectural Digest.* "They shall make an ark of acacia wood, and a cubit and a half its height. And you shall overlay it with pure gold . . . and you shall make upon it a molding of gold round about. And you shall cast four rings of gold for it and put them on its four feet, two rings on the one side of it, and two rings on the other side of it."

And he goes on and on, in numbing detail, about the lamps, about the tables, about how the cherubim should be carved, about the clasps on the ark, and even the fashion do's and don'ts for Aaron's garments. ("And you shall make the robe of the ephod of all blue. It shall have in it an opening for the head, with a woven binding around the chest. . . . On its skirts you shall make pomegranates of blue and purple and scarlet stuff. . . .")

The obsession with such minutiae makes him seem not omniscient but petty. The very specificity of his orders gives new meaning to the phrase *God is in the details*.

*   *   *

At first, God had seemed easy to please.

The moment Noah pitched up on dry land after the Lord had engineered a watery holocaust that killed every soul on the planet save Noah and his family, Noah builds a small fire to make a burnt offering to the Lord. "And when the Lord smelled the pleasing odor, the Lord said in his heart, 'I will never again curse the ground because of man.' " Wait a minute—is this the God we've come to know and fear? The Lord performs this extraordinary feat; he drenches the entire globe in water just to save this one fellow, and all Noah does to say thanks is throw a few sticks together and God is happy? This is one laid-back Lord, one easygoing deity.

At first, even with Abraham, the Lord seems pretty casual. When Abraham gets to Canaan, the Lord promises him all the land as far as the eye can see and that Abraham's descendants will build a great nation. Not too shabby. So what does Abraham do? He builds a small altar. That's all. And the Lord was satisfied. For Abe, not a bad deal, at first anyway.

Of course, there's one little hitch. Abraham has no heir. And he's ninety-nine years old. And his wife, Sarah, is ninety. No problem, says the Lord, "I will give you a son by her." For once, Abraham drops his mask of proud decorum: "Then Abraham fell on his face and laughed." Even Sarah has a giggle. "Shall I indeed bear a child, now that I am old?" she asks. Though God is a little miffed that Sarah laughed at him—when she denies it, the Lord says, "No, but you did laugh"—he insists that Abraham and Sarah will have a son, and that if they keep the covenant, that boy will be the father of a great nation.

There's a small catch, though. The Lord announces that Abraham must first be circumcised. Abraham doesn't say anything, but I think it would be fair to say that any man—and this surely goes double for a man of ninety-nine years—would find the prospect of adult circumcision (without the aid of even a local anesthetic) to be downright unappealing. For Abraham, this must seem like the unkindest cut of all. But the Lord absolutely demands it. "This is my covenant," the Lord says to Abraham, "which you shall keep, between me and you and your descendants after you: Every male among you shall be circumcised. You shall be circumcised in the flesh of your foreskins, and it shall be a sign of the covenant between me and you."

What is circumcision, really, but a kind of divinely enforced flattery? What could be more flattering than a ninety-nine-year-old man who is willing to take a knife to the most sensitive part of his anatomy and snip its skin off, all out of a sense of obedience? God does not tell Abraham what the purpose of circumcision is, or why he insists on it. Only that it must be done before he will make Sarah fertile. We've all heard explanations for biblical circumcision. The Israelites lived in the desert, there was not much water. It was more hygienic. But God doesn't tell Abraham any of that. He simply says, no cuts, no glory.

Abraham does the deed. It is a significant tribute to a God who has not been all that reliable. God had first promised Abraham a son twenty-three years before, when he was a relatively spry fellow of seventy-six. Ultimately, as Jack Miles puts it, "Abraham's penis is no longer his own possession." It is owned by the Lord, and a circumcised penis displays both Abraham's fidelity and the Lord's power. It is Miles's thesis that God is obsessed with controlling the Israelites' fertility. He notes that the Israelites' succumbing to circumcision is their surrender of reproductive autonomy.

Circumcision may be the world's oldest operation, but it also functions as a powerful metaphor. When Moses is speaking to the Israelites before they enter Canaan, he tells them that the Lord requires his people to both love and fear him, to serve him with all their heart and all their soul. And then Moses says, "Circumcise therefore the foreskin of your heart, and be no longer stubborn." It is the Lord saying, surrender unto me your body and soul, bare to me the most sensitive and private part of yourself, cut out your rebelliousness.

For Abraham, circumcision is just the tip of the sacrifices he must make.

If he thought circumcision was tough, wait till he gets a load of what else the Lord has in store for him. When Isaac—Abraham and Sarah's son—is a little boy, God calls on the prophet Abraham again. "After these things God tested Abraham, and said to him, 'Abraham!' And he said, 'Here am I.' He said, 'Take your only son Isaac, whom you love, and go to the land of Moriah, and offer him there as a burnt offering upon the mountains of which I shall tell you.'"

This is perhaps the most extreme loyalty test in human history. Only a deeply insecure deity would propose such a trial. Just how desperately needy must the Lord be to ask a hundred-plus-year-old man to sacrifice the son he has waited a lifetime for? How much loyalty can someone require? But Abraham is silent and early the next morning takes his son to the mountain. There, while gathering sticks for the fire, the boy cries out, "My father! . . . Where is the lamb for a burnt offering?" It is a heartbreaking question.

Another poet of biblical power tells the story this way:

Oh God said to Abraham, "Kill me a son."
Abe says, "Man, you must be puttin' me on."
God say, "No." Abe say, "What?"
God say, "You can do what you want Abe, but
The next time you see me comin', you better run."
Well, Abe says, "Where do you want this killin' done?"
God says, "Out on Highway 61."

Bob Dylan's God is the coldest of hit men.

Only when Abraham had carefully laid out the wood and snugly bound his son did an angel of the Lord appear and say, "Do not lay your hand on the lad or do anything to him; for now I know that you fear God." Some scholars have suggested that Abraham would never have actually murdered his son, but went through the motions because he knew at the last moment that God would stay his hand. I'm not so sure. But we're less concerned here with Abraham's motivation—which clearly was to placate what must have seemed to him an almost insane God—than with God's desperate neediness. "For now I know that you fear God," the Lord says. *Okay, I feel better now,* the Lord seems to be saying. Abraham's real or feigned fear was how he satisfied his God, by flattering the Lord that he was willing to kill his only son for him. So needy was the Lord that he pointed his finger to the one thing that Abraham loved more than any other, the one great gift that the Lord had given his faithful servant, and then asked him to sacrifice it.

The Gambler

What God demanded of Abraham was a cakewalk compared to what he required of Job. Einstein once said that God did not play dice with the universe.

Well, he played roulette with Job's life.

Job, more so than any of God's favorites, was the Unflatterer. Although you could interpret Job's astonishing loyalty as the greatest flattery of all, God did not. Instead, Job's mixture of mournful argumentativeness, followed by Stallone-ish taciturnity, seemed to irk God. Job did what was right because it was right (or seemed to him to be so), a principle that seemed rather foreign to the Lord.

God wants to be loved, respected, and flattered by Job for who he is, not for being the one and only superpower divinity. Like Willie Loman, God doesn't just want to be liked, he wants to be well-liked. It is precisely Yahweh's insecurity and, I would say, his immaturity, that makes him yearn to be loved in this way. It is Satan, a shrewd cigar-chewing appraiser of people, who knows that no one can love God for Himself alone. But God insists, which is why he makes the dreadful wager with Satan over Job's loyalty.

God guarantees Satan that he can do anything to Job short of killing the man and Job will remain faithful to the Lord. So, with God's approval, Satan slowly and methodically takes everything from the once-prosperous and content Job: his family, his fortune, his property, and his good name.

After Job has made his powerful plea to God for some explanation, a young fellow named Elihu who has been listening to Job's complaint attempts to answer Job's questions. Yahweh is angry, he says, because Job has sought to justify his own behavior rather than God's. But, in passing, Elihu says something interesting about the idea of flattery and what it suggests about God. He tells Job:

I will not show partiality to any person
or use flattery toward any man.
For I do not know how to flatter,
else would my Maker soon put an end to me.

Elihu suggests that God will not tolerate flattery of anyone but himself. And if God sees him or Job flattering anyone else, it's curtains. In fact, you could interpret the entire Book of Job as God's effort to wring some tiny compliment from his most faithful but ultimately most reticent servant.

Job finds God's fascination with man to be unfathomable. You made the heavens and the earth, you made lions and tigers, so why are you interested in a little worm like me? Job wonders:

What is man, that thou dost make so much of him,
and that thou dost set thy mind upon him,
doth visit him every morning, and test him every moment?

Despite all the pain and suffering God inflicts on Job, despite the fact that he loses everything that he values, Job never wavers in his allegiance to God—he simply wants to know *why?* But even this is too much to ask. Job is the model of the little guy with a conscience who stands up to a power much greater than he. Job displays the virtue that the ancient Greeks called *parhesia*—frankness. But that is precisely what the Lord does not want. He can't take the truth.

When the Lord famously answers Job from "out of the whirlwind," he begins by questioning Job's right to question him.

Who is this that darkens counsel by words without knowledge?

Then God, sounding like a bitter, querulous father, goes on to suggest why he thinks Job does not have the right to question him.

Where were you when I laid the foundations of the earth? . . .
Who determined its measurements—surely you know!
Or who stretched the line upon it?
On what were its bases sunk,

or who laid its cornerstone. . . ?
Have you commanded the morning since your days began,
and caused the dawn to know its placing. . . ?

And on and on. God recites his cosmic curriculum vitae—the creatures he has created, the mountain ranges he has raised, the land he has surveyed—as if Job were not aware of God's credentials. God does not think that Job lacks the moral authority to question him so much as the power. For Yahweh, might always makes right. How can such an insignificant little schlemiel contend with the Creator of all creation?

Finally, the Lord says,

Shall a faultfinder contend with the Almighty?
He who argues with God, let him answer it.
Then Job answered the Lord:

Job answers the unanswerable, and there is no rebuttal possible to what he says.

"Behold, I am of small account;
what shall I answer thee?
I lay my hand on my mouth.
I have spoken once, and I will not answer."

Job says, Who am I to question you? I who am nothing. But this is false modesty. Canny, shrewd Job is not really saying he is nothing, because Job knows the score. Job knows that morality is the great equalizer. That the most insignificant creature in all of God's green earth can question the Creator if the Creator is unfair and the questioner is just. On the scales of justice, power never outweighs mercy.

Initially, Job seems to offer the deference God seeks, but it is, in fact, mock deference. "I am of small account." (That is like a politician beginning his remarks with "Unaccustomed as I am to public speaking . . .") Mock deference shows his fear but also his indominability. He fears God enough to seem like he is praising him, but disdains what God is doing enough to make it ersatz praise. Mock praise is the opposite of the genuine article. He may flatter God by his fear of him, but he is insulting him by the disengenuousness of what he is saying. He is the ultimate ironist: he is mocking the very type of flattery that God craves.

"I will proceed no further," Job says, and then is silent.

God seems to regard Job's silence as submissive. But Job's silence is more defiant than deferential. It is not capitulation but a refusal to give in. But the Lord, in his craving for acknowledgment, does not see it that way. Job refuses to flatter, and God, so desperately needy, interprets it as the praise he so desires.

God Mellows

The Jews, of course, did not always treat God shabbily. Over the years, he got plenty of the praise and flattery that he longed for. The irony is that much of that praise came after God no longer seemed to need it.

As we've noted before, the names we call things are a prime avenue of flattery. In the case of the Israelites, reverence was expressed not by naming God but by not naming him. The accepted notion was that God was so awesome, so unknowable, so sacred, that it was considered insulting to pronounce his name at all. The divine name was written YHWH—only consonants, no vowels—and not pronounced in any reading of scripture. The idea was that human speech was simply inadequate to describe something as ineffable as God. As Maimonides suggested, it was better to talk of God in negative terms, what he was not, rather than what he was. God was the Unnameable.

Which brings us to the question: How do you flatter someone or something that is beyond comparison or comprehension, other than to say he, she, or it, is incomparable and incomprehensible? As many theologians have suggested, perhaps God is beyond flattery? It was Maimonides who said that God could not be flattered directly because one could only talk about him in allusive, symbolic ways. He cannot be compared to anything that exists. You cannot say he is good because he so far transcends anything that we earthbound mortals mean by good. In fact, Maimonides asserts that you cannot even assert that God exists. You can only deny his nonexistence.

Some thinkers mused that the Israelites eventually went over the top in the flattery department, praising the Lord too much. Rabbi Yohannan ben Zakkai wrote, "He who speaks or relates too much of God's praise will be uprooted from this world." Human praise, he suggested, was sublunary and God was transcendent, so how could words uttered by humans be anything but defective? But, of course, Rabbi Yohannan was simply trumping the others with his own praise by suggesting that theirs was too mundane. It's like the joke about the old and distinguished rabbi and the young rabbi who looks up to him. In the temple, the old rabbi drops to his knees, gazes up at the altar, and says, "Oh, Lord, you are everything, I am nothing." He then nods to the young rabbi, who does the same thing. After they rise, the janitor in the back of the temple, moved by the moment, falls to the ground and says, "Oh, Lord, you are everything, and I am nothing." The old rabbi turns to the young rabbi and says, "Look who thinks he's nothing."

Look who thinks he's flattering God. Your praise is merely insulting.

*   *   *

It is only at the tail-end of the Old Testament, when we get to the books of the Prophets, that the Israelites begin to give God the praise that he has always hankered for. This veneration, however, came at a time that the Lord himself was undergoing a change. For God has mellowed. He's no longer so demanding. He's not so easily riled. He's no longer so hard on the Israelites. He's matured.

Late in the Bible, he moves from being a God who rules through brute power to an ethical God, a God who prizes not just loyalty but virtue. In fact, he becomes disgusted with the kind of flattery he once accepted, the old practice of blood sacrifices. God calls them "vain offerings."

> *I have had enough of burnt offerings of rams*
> *and the fat of fed beasts;*
> *I do not delight in the blood of bulls.*

Now he tells us.

Once, God couldn't get enough of the fat of fed beasts. Suddenly, the old form of flattery, blood sacrifices, no longer pleases him. Instead, he says, he wants something very different. He wants the Israelites to change their hearts, to become new men themselves.

> *Cease to do evil,*
> *learn to do good;*
> *seek justice*
> *correct oppression;*
> *defend the fatherless;*
> *please the widow.*

God springs this out of nowhere on the Israelites. For hundreds of years, all they had to do was obey and build a fire and throw some meat on it. Now, God was asking for something that seemed easier but in reality was far more difficult. He's asking them to be good. He's asking them to be generous and kind. Obedience is no longer enough. As God says himself in Isaiah:

> *Behold, I am doing a new thing;*
> *now it springs forth, do you not perceive it?*

The old flattery is out; virtue is in.

The Lord had changed the nature of the covenant. Before, you could be a good Jew simply by obeying the commandments and worshiping the Lord. Now, that wasn't good enough—you had to be virtuous to boot. And in fact, it was more important to be virtuous—to do unto others as you would have them do unto you—than to be holy. It was the new way to flatter God.

In fact, the golden rule—as stated first in its negative form by Hillel in the first century B.C. ("Do not do unto others what you would not have them do to you") and later by Matthew in its more familiar form—is a summary of the covenant of flattery. Do unto others what you would have them do unto you. I flatter you so that you in turn flatter me. The golden rule is a form of reciprocal altruism, and mutual flattery is a subset of that.

The Israelites did not really understand the consequence of the Lord's "new thing." This new emphasis on virtue was a way of opening up Judaism; it was the door that led to Christianity. It made God truly universal. Christianity began as a form of Judaism open to non-Jews. And that's why it succeeded: it was open to all. The reason Christianity eclipsed Judaism is the same reason Microsoft came to dominate Apple: it licensed its operating system to anyone who wanted it. The Israelites, like Apple, had an elegant system, but they hoarded it. The Christians gave their operating system away to anyone who could use it, and it came to dominate the market.

*   *   *

By the end of the Old Testament, there is a kind of truce between the Lord and his Chosen People. As Jack Miles suggests, the Lord has become like a tired and weakened father, a forgetful old man who needs to be looked after by his children. The Israelites are now brimming over with praise for the Lord. The people and their leaders are elbowing each other out of the way to prostrate themselves before the Lord. But the Lord, distant, forgetful, weary, no longer seems to care. By the time the Israelites have come to praise the Lord, he seems ready to be buried.

When the Lord finally asks the Israelites to flatter him not by sacrificing sheep but by being good, he is showing how the desire to please, one of the motivations of flattery, can make people better. In order to please God, the Israelites had roasted zillions of cows and lambs, but now, in Isaiah, the Lord is asking them to help the oppressed. God begins to preach compassion and justice in the books of the prophets, and in order to flatter him, God's followers make those virtues the hallmark of the three great religions that have their origin in that era.

Job must wonder: Why the hell didn't He think of that earlier?

Chapter 4

Flattery
Is Undemocratic

The *Demos* Rules, Dude!

When you get right down to it, what is it that we really mean by democracy? I would say it's the idea that no one can lord it over you, that we're all equal, and that our voices are equal. In a democracy we hate the idea that some people are more equal than others (even if they are). That's undemocratic.

The ancient Greeks felt the same way, and they were the ones who invented democracy in the fourth and fifth centuries B.C. It was the great political innovation of classical antiquity, perhaps of all time. They didn't like the idea that some people considered themselves more equal than others, and they didn't like it when some people made themselves inferior to others.

That's why they loathed flattery. They saw it as a form of self-abasement. They saw it as deeply undemocratic. As Plutarch put it, the flatterer is born free but chooses to be a slave.

The word "democracy" derives from the Greek *demos,* meaning "people," and the verb *kratos,* "to rule." Thus, *the people rule.* The people shall govern. The people are sovereign. All power to the people. Government of the people, by the people, for the people. You get the idea.

Geography had something to do with the Greek invention of democracy. The remoteness of the Greek hill towns and fishing villages made these places ruggedly independent and self-sufficient. People formed deep attachments to their towns, much the way football fans today are fanatically loyal to their teams. We get the word "politics" from the Greek word for city, *polis*. The Greek word for citizen—*polites*—simply meant a person from the city. In a democracy, there is no higher title than citizen.

＊　　＊　　＊

In these small towns, or city-states, as they came to be known (Aristotle called them "the highest form of civilized life"), the entire body of citizens formed the legislature. Every citizen had to serve. Some jobs were filled by election, but many others were simply assigned by lot. There was no separation of powers: the legislature had executive and judicial as well as legislative functions. In that sense, it was about as pure as democracy can get. Ross Perot proposed the modern equivalent in 1992 when he said that Americans should be able to vote instantly over the Internet on whatever they wanted. The electronic forum.

The Greece of the archaic period from Homer all the way through the classical Greece of the fifth and fourth centuries B.C. was not a courtly society. Yes, there were kings and princes, but the assorted sycophants and hangers-on that surrounded them had not yet congealed into a court. It was the city-state of Athens in the fifth and fourth centuries that was experimenting with the idea of democracy. Citizens were permitted—encouraged—to speak their minds in the forum. To every free man his own soapbox.

But by our standards, Greek society wasn't very democratic. Women could not be citizens, nor could slaves (another decidedly undemocratic feature of ancient Greece) or anyone born outside of Greece or Athens. That meant about one in ten people actually qualified as citizens. (As Langston Hughes wrote in another context: "I still can't see/Why democracy means/Everybody but me.")

In short, citizens were born, not made, and no one could become one except by birth. But there was nevertheless a powerful egalitarian ethic, and the Greeks believed devoutly in their own fiction. By our standards, Athenian democracy was narrow and shallow, but it was still a democracy. And as Winston Churchill noted, democracy is the worst political system ever invented—except for all the others.

* * *

The Greeks were extremely wary about anything that might undermine their democracy or sense of equality. Of course, there were outside threats from rivals and enemies, but there were also threats from within. These latter threats were more insidious and harder to counter. For the Greeks, one of those internal threats was the idea and the practice of flattery.

They considered the very idea of flattery to be undemocratic. This was not personal flattery they were talking about. In fact, the Greeks were pretty much indifferent to personal flattery, and didn't really have much truck with it. They were much more concerned with public flattery—and by that they meant something very specific: the flattery of the public.

In inventing democracy, the Greeks also created the notion of public flattery, that is, the flattering of the *demos* (the people), a practice that they called—and we still do—demagoguery. To the Greeks, demagoguery was a way of playing on the vanity of the people as a whole. Individual, personalized flattery was not something they thought much about. What they did think about was the flattery of the public as a group—indeed, the flattery of the very idea of democracy itself.

It was only later, as Greek democracy itself came undone and as Rome replaced Greece as a military and cultural power, that flattery turned inward and became more private and personal. As democracy ebbed and imperial Rome came to power, there was no longer any *demos* to flatter; flattery was directed at the few rather than the many. As the egalitarian notions of democracy gave way to a politics centered on privilege and authority, frankness gave way to personal flattery. In Hellenistic Greece and in Roman society, thinkers concerned themselves with the triad of flattery, frankness, and friendship. The subject "How to Tell a Flatterer from a Friend" became a set piece among Greek and Roman thinkers. Flattery was a concern of these thinkers because they were increasingly interested in the disjunction between inner worth and outer position, between the private and the public, between virtue and hypocrisy. The use of flattery became a kind of hypocrisy litmus test.

Some Unflattering Words About Flattering the People

What was the flattery of the *demos*? In some ways, it mirrored the courtly
sycophancy that surrounded a king. If the people are sovereign, as they are
in a democracy, then aspiring leaders of the people might try to flatter them
as you would a sovereign. In Athens, demagoguery consisted of ambitious
politicians telling the people how fine and noble they were. The people,
demagogues claimed, were never wrong, their wisdom was infallible, they
were the sum of human goodness. Demosthenes wrote that Theocrines, a
corrupt young politician, always told crowds that he loved them as much as
his own family. The philosopher Isocrates contrasted himself with orators
who spoke only for their audience's gratification and not their moral benefit. Speakers who appealed to the audience's feeling of being left out or
marginalized were seen as populist toadies.

Sounds familiar, doesn't it? Every American president and virtually
every democratic leader around the world flatters the electorate. Ronald
Reagan made a career of telling the American people how aw-shucks won-
derful they are. "I have never failed when I trusted in the wisdom of the
American people," Reagan said time and again. On the day the House of
Representatives voted to open its impeachment inquiry, Bill Clinton said,
"I trust the wisdom of the American people. They almost always get it
right."

For the ancient Greeks, demagoguery was an acid that ate away at the
fabric of democracy. You could build walls around a city, you could train
every able-bodied man to defend freedom and democracy, but you were always vulnerable from within. As the historian Arnold Toynbee once wrote,
great empires do not die by murder but by suicide. In fact, it was a series of
irresponsible leaders drawn from the ranks of the public who in fourth-
century Athens literally gave demagoguery a bad name.

In his play *The Knights,* the great Greek comic playwright Aristophanes
draws a harsh caricature of demagoguery and an unflattering portrait of the
people who are suckers for it. No flattering of the *demos* for him. In the
play, his image of the demagogue is a humble sausage-seller at the gates of
the city whom Demosthenes schemes to make the leader of Athens. It is appropriate that the rising demagogue is a sausage-seller, as many Greek

philosophers likened flattery and demagoguery to feeding the people the less than wholesome foods they crave. As Demosthenes tells the sausage-seller, "To win the people, always cook them some savory dish that pleases them."

The sausage-seller is always offering treats to a character named Demos, providing him with a soft cushion, giving him his cloak when it is cold. He is unctuously helpful, and Demos is grateful. The Chorus takes Demos to task: "Demos, you are our all-powerful sovereign lord; all tremble before you, yet you are led by the nose. You love to be flattered and fooled; you listen to the orators with gaping mouth and your mind is led astray." After the sausage-seller has wormed his way into the heart of Demos, and become cynical himself about the process, he says at the end of the play, "Demos, I will care for you to the best of my power, and all shall admit that no citizen is more devoted than I to this city of simpletons."

* * *

Democracy was not universally revered in Athens. It replaced an aristocratic system, and the old aristocrats were not very happy about it. Nor were the philosophers. Plato, for example, was no small-*d* democrat. He thought democracy crude and unruly and inefficient. He regarded the rule of a philosopher-king or of an oligarchy to be much preferable to democracy. The people, he believed, were unfit to rule. Plato believed that the object of politics was virtue but that only the few, not the many, could ever aspire to this. You wouldn't catch Plato praising the essential goodness of the people.

One of his basic complaints was that the *demos* were too susceptible to demagogues and could not see through the flattery that was directed at them. One of the problems of democracy, Plato suggested, was that it "honored anyone who professes to be the people's friend." And every aspiring politician did so. But what really bothered Plato was something else. Democracy, he says, "dispenses a sort of equality to equals and unequals alike." Plato did not believe all people are equal, either in a literal or an abstract way. And he could not stomach the idea of the equal treatment of unequal people.

Plato had great enmity for those he regarded as demagogues. And for what he regarded as the principal tool of demagogues: rhetoric. In Athens, all citizens were encouraged to speak their mind at any political gathering. Freedom of speech engendered the desire not only to speak freely but to speak well. No ambitious Athenian of the fifth and fourth centuries could afford to be perceived as a dull and unpersuasive speaker. Lessons in oratory and rhetoric—the equivalent of verbal personal trainers—were all the rage for well-to-do Athenians. Handbooks on the art of speech were Athenian best-sellers.

Most Athenians regarded oratory as both a skill and an art. Plato was an exception. He derided rhetoric and fine oratory as a form of public flattery and the teachers of it as no more than instructors in how to pander. He thought such instructors corrupted the democratic ethos by teaching people how to be ingratiating, not how to be virtuous. The purpose of political oratory, he believed, was to improve men, not gratify them. We think of the word rhetoric today as a synonym for "empty speech," but rhetoric in Plato's day was a staple field of study, and criticizing it was a little like someone today denouncing algebra.

In Plato's dialogue *Gorgias,* the philosopher attempts to deconstruct the idea of demagoguery. Gorgias was a kind of fourth-century Tony Robbins, a wandering teacher of oratory and rhetoric who was fluent and charismatic and claimed he could turn anyone into a fine speaker. In the dialogue, it is the figure of Socrates who takes on Gorgias. From the start, Socrates uses his opponent's weapons against him by slyly flattering Gorgias. Socrates asks Gorgias to keep his answers brief, and after one or two, Socrates says to him, "My word, Gorgias, your answers are an absolute miracle of brevity, I must say." Gorgias is pleased.

Gorgias was well known for his flowery, poetic language. But his oratory, according to Socrates, existed mainly to call attention to itself. Socrates defines oratory as "a sort of knack gained by experience." Socrates goes on to say that the real name for oratory is pandering, and he places the art of flattery as a subset of oratory.

Plato objects to oratory for two reasons: It is morally neutral and does not make people more virtuous; it is a distortion of language for it is designed to make something unattractive appear beautiful. Cowardice is called prudence and stinginess frugality. It is ultimately a tool of tyranny, for it undermines democracy and allows would-be tyrants to fool the people into following them. Like flattery, oratory ministers to belief, not knowledge, to emotion, not reasoning, and often inculcates a false impression that has nothing to do with the truth.

Some Frank Words About Frank Speech

As insidious a problem as flattery was, there was a solution, and the Greeks called it "parhesia." We define parhesia as frankness or candor, or as frank criticism. The word has an interesting history that by itself traces the way ideas about flattery changed during Greek and then Roman history.

In the fifth century B.C., "parhesia" was the term the Greeks used for free speech. The idea was that a free man speaking before his fellow citizens was to speak frankly, truthfully, sincerely. Frank speech was transparent speech. Parhesia was regarded as a foundation of democracy. It was both a right and a necessity. Parhesia was the unpleasant truth, not the pleasing fiction. The Greeks believed a democracy could survive only if men were truthful and frank.

Later, parhesia came to mean frank speech in particular, not free speech in general. It eventually meant the words you used when you told someone something they probably did not want to know but needed to hear. "Frankly, Plato, your argument about rhetoric is full of holes." Parhesia was considered the antidote to flattery, which was regarded as the opposite of frankness. Those who used parhesia in public speaking were likened to physicians who cured their patients through inflicting some form of discomfort. Parhesia was the medicine, not the spoonful of sugar that helped it go down. Still later, parhesia migrated from the realm of the political to the personal. For Greek and then Roman writers, the answer to the question of "How to Tell a Flatterer from a Friend" was, of course, parhesia.

Parhesia was considered an essential virtue in counselors and advisors to leaders and princes. The philosopher Isocrates noted that princes must surround themselves not with flatterers but with those who would disagree with them. "Such frankness," Isocrates said, "is a virtue in a counselor, who must risk the ire of princes foolish enough to be offended when contradicted." Parhesia was speaking truth to power.

Flattery was seen as an abuse of free speech because it was a waste of free speech. Speech did not need to be free in order to flatter. You needed free speech in order to have frank speech. As Justice Louis Brandeis once said in a much different context, the necessity of protecting free speech is not to guard the speech that we love, but the speech that we hate. Parhesia needed protection; flattery did not. That is why there is more flattery in authoritarian states than in democracies. The right to free speech was necessary to protect frank speech, not to protect pleasing demagoguery.

Plato believed that a political leader needed to tell the people things that weren't palatable. He needed to tell them what we would call hard truths. Gorgias, by his own confession in the dialogue, confessed that he would never tell the people anything that might turn them against him. He might make it seem as though he were telling them some hard truths, but it would only be the illusion of real truth. Gorgias was the kind of leader that former Clinton advisor Dick Morris would understand, the sort of leader who polls and tests every line and phrase in a speech to make sure the voters would like it.

*   *   *

At the time, there were whole schools of philosophy that virtually revolved around the idea of parhesia. Just as frankness was considered critical to democracy, it was deemed absolutely essential in order to be both a good philosopher and a good friend. The Cynics were founded by Diogenes—he of the lamp and the search for an honest man—in the third century B.C. They advocated an ascetic self-sufficiency and the rejection of materialism. They were, in effect, the anti-Flatterers. Asked what the most beautiful thing in the world was, Diogenes replied, parhesia. The curmudgeonly philosopher was more than frank; he was often brutal. "Other dogs bite their enemies," he once said; "I bite my friends, so that I may save them." He advocated what he called "outspokenness," and said it was the duty of both the philosopher and the friend to speak the unvarnished truth all the time. This endeared him to neither friend nor foe.

Like the Cynics, the Epicureans believed that it was the duty of a friend to be frank. But the Epicurean philosopher Philodemus wrote that only the sage knows how to criticize in a balanced way. That's a pretty high bar. The Epicureans identified the good with pleasure and recommended a simple life in the company of friends. They were not romantic about friendship, seeing it as largely utilitarian and based on need. Which was all the more reason that friends needed to be frank.

Philodemus enumerated those whom he said were particularly resentful of frank speech. He cited politicians and the famous. Politicians, he said, are hungry for renown, and this makes them especially receptive to flattery and sensitive to criticism. Famous people, he says, regard all criticism as being an attack from impure motives. They see everyone as being jealous and resentful of their fame.

The Stoics, on the other hand, didn't give a damn about friendship or anything remotely sentimental. They seemed to regard friendship as something vulgar and for the masses. Secure in their self-regard, the Stoics barely noticed flattery; they did not approve of ingratiating themselves with anyone for any reason.

The End of Frankness

Aristotle did not share his mentor's animus toward rhetoric. Always more practical than Plato, Aristotle saw rhetoric as a tool. If you spoke well and persuasively in service of virtue, that only made you more virtuous; speaking well in service of selfishness and wickedness made you that much more despicable. You could praise virtue in order to make it more attractive, or you could praise the people in order to make yourself more attractive. Choose one.

Aristotle was more scientific about flattery than Plato. In Aristotle's famous doctrine of the mean, he placed flattery in the sphere of what he called the Pleasant. The mean is "friendliness," that is, a person "who is pleasant in the right way." The extreme is represented by the Obsequious person or the Flatterer. A person is obsequious "if he has no motive." If his motive is self-interest, says Aristotle, he is a Flatterer. (The extreme on the other side, by the way, is the Cantankerous or Ill-tempered person.) Flattery, according to Aristotle, is by definition always self-interested and intent on gain. Flattery is strategic, while obsequiousness is simply pathetic.

When it comes to flattery, Aristotle becomes a kind of ancient Mr. Manners. He finds flattery infra dig. He counsels people not to be overly friendly. He scorns the hail-fellow-well-met glad-handing-salesman type of personality, calling him obsequious. "To make themselves pleasant," he says, "they praise everything." Those who are especially susceptible to such praise, he says, are the Shameless, the Licentious, and the Powerful. Of this last category, he says, they are easy marks for flatterers because they are ever in search of honor. Neediness makes them susceptible.

His model of behavior is the individual he calls a man of Magnanimity, who possesses "greatness of soul." Aristotle's Mr. Magnanimity would not be the life of the party. He is cold, haughty, and humorless—all virtues in Aristotle's book. He is wholly without small talk. He does not care for personal conversation, says Aristotle, "because he does not care to be complimented himself . . . nor again is he inclined to pay compliments." He is as incapable of being flattered as he is of flattering. "Honor conferred by ordinary people for trivial reasons he will utterly despise, because that sort of thing is beneath his dignity."

Mr. Magnanimity is neither an ass-kisser to those above him nor an ogre to those below him. He is instead a kind of cocktail party Robin Hood, ignoring the socialites and giving comfort to the regular folks. "He is haughty towards those who are influential and successful," says Aristotle, "but moderate towards those who don't have an intermediate position in society." He is ultimately above human frailty and not a very realistic object of emulation. Butter wouldn't melt in his mouth.

Although Mr. Magnanimity is not very charming, the Greeks didn't seem to mind. They distrusted charm, and saw it as a kind of parlor room demagoguery. People who tried to make themselves liked were regarded with suspicion. Not all affable people were flatterers, but all flatterers were affable. They distrusted smiling. In the ancient Greek vocabulary of the face, a smile made you look foolish. It was a sign of lack of seriousness, of inanity. A leader would never consider smiling. Leaders were meant to look fierce. Only clowns and comedians smiled.

Friendship as the New Democracy

Unlike flattery, parhesia was dangerous. Just ask Socrates. He was put to death for what one might call too much frankness. Even though democracy continued after Socrates' death, his execution was evidence that all was not right with democratic values in Athens. Émile Durkheim has noted that a society that loses the ability to believe in its own myths is one that is slowly killing itself.

After the death of Alexander in 323 B.C., free speech was not so free anymore. In the Hellenistic Greece that followed, the notion of parhesia was gradually transformed from a political right to a private virtue. Candor went underground and became more personal than public. Parhesia, which had once stood for a political right, came to be seen as a private moral virtue. It became the frankness that was considered necessary between two friends, not the candor that was needed in the public forum. It was during this later Hellenistic period that Greek culture began to focus less on public issues than private ones, not so much on the public bond between all men but on the private friendship that existed between any two of them.

In Hellenistic Greece, friends of the king formed a council to advise him on policy, and by the second century this had eventually congealed into courtly institutions. Democracy subsided into bureaucracy. The world of friendship became a kind of private democracy. The political became the personal.

* * *

The Hellenistic Greeks idolized friendship. "Without friendship," Aristotle said, "nobody would want to live. It is absolutely indispensable for life." In Greek myth, friendship sometimes even rivals country as the wellspring of men's loyalty. Aristotle describes friends as having "one soul," from which we get the term "soulmate." But what the ancient Greeks meant by friendship is not always clear, and it's certainly different than our modern notion.

In ancient Greek society, you had kin, comrades in arms, citizens, servants, and slaves, but there was no such thing as buddies, pals, cronies, or boon companions. Homer does not contain a word or term for "friend" in anything like the sense we use it. "Dear comrade" comes closest, but it still sounds more like what one Member of Parliament calls another—"my honorable friend"— than a word for somebody with whom you might go to the movies. Women, of course, could not be your friends because they were not

considered capable of such a rarefied relationship. Nor could slaves or servants.

Ancient Greek society was a military culture, and they were interested in
the bonds that linked men in battle. For a Greek, there was no greater bond,
but it was not quite what we would call friendship. The story of the warriors Achilles and Patroclus has become a byword for friendship, but in fact
Achilles was more or less Patroclus's patron or mentor, and the two men
were probably lovers. "Friends" isn't quite the word for them.

Even though they revered the idea of friendship, the Greeks had a rather
utilitarian view of it. It was more about fulfilling reciprocal obligations than
it was about affection. The Greeks wrote paeans to the pragmatism, not the
pleasures, of friendship. Friendship was a kind of calculated cooperation.
The highest form of friendship, according to Aristotle, was a friendship
based on virtue. A sense of humor didn't rank very high in Aristotle's book.

We presume that friendship, like democracy, is egalitarian. The Greeks
did not. Aristotle said that in friendships between "persons of different
standing, the affection must be proportionate"—by which he meant the better or higher person must "be loved more than he loves." For the Greeks, it
is difference in standing that stokes the flames of flattery, which is the
enemy of true friendship. The ranks of flatterers, says Aristotle, come from
those he calls "friends of inferior status." That was the reason friends
needed to be from the same class.

The higher you went, the less you needed friendship. "When heaven
grants us luck," wrote Euripides, "what need of friends?" Basically, the
Greeks believed that friends could only be from the same class, and that
class must be the upper class. Anyone below was not fine enough to really
be friends. In keeping with this idea, the Greeks would have found the idea
of "opposites attract" to be incomprehensible. *Like attracts like* was the
principle they understood.

In Hellenistic Greece, the emphasis on equality yielded to concerns
about status. Philosophers were less concerned about the nature of friendship than about how that friendship could be perverted. The chief concern
was how a flatterer motivated by narrow self-interest would insinuate himself into the trust of a "superior" and achieve his own gain at the expense of
his "friend." As an egalitarian ideology gave way to one centered on privilege and authority, frankness gave way to sycophancy.

When in Rome, Flatter Like the Romans Do

Primus, maximus, optimus. First, greatest, best. These were the bywords of glory in Roman society. Like America in the twentieth century, everything in Augustan Rome had to be the first, greatest, and best. They did everything but talk about themselves as the lone superpower and yell "We're number one!"

Romans were a supremely status-conscious people. Much more so than Athens, Rome was a deeply stratified society. There was a place for everyone, and everyone was in his place. In an era of mistrustful and even paranoid rulers like Nero and Domitian, sycophancy masquerading as deference was the rule rather than the exception. Where leaders are paranoid, flattery is the only form of loyalty.

The first citizens of Rome spent a great deal of time, effort, and money establishing their place in aristocratic society and burnishing their reputations. Senators seemed to measure their status in how they stood each day among the chattering classes. While gossip columnists like Liz Smith and Suzy would have been unemployed in Athens, they would have been the toast of the town in Rome.

The grandees of Rome in effect employed personal publicists to puff their names and reputations. Every great man of Rome had a claque of toadies who surrounded him virtually every moment of the day, from the morning rounds of greeting, called the *salutatio,* to the evening dinners that lasted late into the night. Seeing these men walk through the square was like watching Sylvester Stallone enter a restaurant: Every eye turned because the great man was surrounded by an entourage of bodyguards and hangers-on, who exist mainly in order to call attention to Sly. For the members of these extended entourages, flattery was a way of life.

The Poet as Panderer

The romantic myth of writers is that they are ornery and independent, caring not for the opinion of others. Well, that myth was even more false in ancient Rome than it is today. Writers then as now had a symbiotic relationship with those they wrote about. Their subjects were dependent on the writer for glory and publicity, and the writer depended on his subjects for his livelihood. But the writers in ancient Rome were even more abject than writers today. There were no book contracts, no magazines, no newspapers, no writers-in-residence programs at universities. Writers counted on the largess of patrons, and that often had the effect of turning Roman writers into literary lapdogs.

Until the first century B.C., writing poetry wasn't considered the pursuit of a grown man. Sometime around the end of the first millennium, a fellow could more or less stake out a career as a poet. But it wasn't easy. Poets had a status that was perhaps only slightly elevated from astrologers. Poets, however, were generally from fairly well-to-do backgrounds. They had to be in order to afford the education necessary to give them the tools to write poetry. But most of them still needed patrons. Even philosophers, who were at the top of the pecking order in terms of prestige, still needed to take up residence in the homes of the wealthy.

Rome coined the idea of patronage. In classical Greece, there was no term for "patron" or "client." The original meaning of the word *patronus* was that of a master who manumitted his slaves but kept certain rights over them. The derivation is unfortunate; cultural patronage has retained some of the term's original sense. The protégé, like the freed slave, is never completely free.

In the early republic, Roman etiquette established rules in which a powerful benefactor lent protection and support to a dependent who was known as a client. The client, who might be a poet, a writer, a philosopher, or just a young man of good pedigree, in return provided loyalty and support. In effect, the client was a professional friend. It was a full-time occupation, with duties ranging from providing companionship, to instruction of the patron's children, to writing simpering odes to the patron himself. Juvenal complained that being a professional *amicus* was the only livelihood available to a man of modest means in Rome.

Young men offered themselves as apprentices to the great. Essentially, in exchange for support, they were pledging themselves to be professional flatterers. Juvenal quotes a note from a young man to his prospective benefactor telling him that even though his own power as a poet is frail, he promises that in return for help he will devote his entire career to celebrating his patron's name.

As a client, the poet could not be choosy. He was asked to produce verse for all manner of holidays, and domestic occasions such as birthdays and anniversaries, while suffering the further indignity of being called on to applaud his patron's often lame attempts to write his own poetry. He had to be ready to provide the words for gravestones, dedications, and the captions for paintings, statues, fountains, shrines—anything that needed an elegiac inscription. It was flattery on demand. Poems were "promised" to the patron, but they were not commissioned or paid for. That was considered unseemly. Nevertheless you find Martial writing in disappointment that after penning a poem that flattered a particular friend, he got no recompense whatsoever.

In his letters, Martial complains endlessly about the waste of time and energy having to truckle to his patron. He was expected at the morning *salutatio;* then he must escort him to the forum; later that evening he must appear for dinner, where he will figuratively and sometimes literally sing for his supper. In between, there are various household ceremonies, recitations, and the occasional appearance in court at his patron's side. What does Martial receive from his wealthy patron? He lists the following: a loan, a country house, a slave boy, some silver tableware, a toga, a cloak, mules, a chariot, and a boar. Outright gifts of money were rare.

Horace offers guidance to a poetic protégé on how to behave as a client. "If you are taken by the great man as a traveling companion on a trip to Brundisium or Surrentum, don't complain of your expenses and losses: that is like a kept woman constantly pleading that she has lost a bracelet or a dog." Don't accept everything that is offered, he says. Try to maintain a little distance. "If you set yourself up as a friend of the great," he writes, "you will be anxious not to be a mere sponger."

*   *   *

But poets did have a certain power, and it was the power of shaping posterity. Most flattery is momentary and fleeting; but not the flattery penned by Horace or a Martial or a Juvenal. That is praise that can be immortal, and that was why great men flattered poets. *Gloria et laus et aeternitas.* Fame, praise, and immortality. That is the promise the poet dangles so prettily before his patron. "Be valiant and win praise from men unborn," wrote Cicero. But it was men like Cicero who shaped that praise. History is written by the victors' poets. And the victors had to enlist their Ciceros. In the same way, American presidents give access to biographers while they're still in office to make sure that their reputations begin to get burnished even before they retire.

Sometimes an emperor is reduced to flattering a poet. The emperor Augustus, for example, sought to lure Horace to work as his secretary. Augustus wrote the following to Horace, who was the son of a freedman: "Your name came up in conversation when Septimius was present: you can ask him what I said about you. Even though you are so proud that you have rejected my friends, that does not make me haughty in return." Later, he chaffs Horace by saying he is cross with the poet because in a recent book of the poet's there had been no poems about himself. "Are you afraid that it will discredit you with posterity," he wrote, "if you look like a friend of mine?" Horace plays hard to get for a while, but he knows where his bread is buttered. When Horace is called to pen something for the emperor, he writes, "We hail you as superhuman in your own lifetime . . . we give you the preference to all other rulers, Roman and Greek." Panegyrics don't get much grander than that.

Many writers flattered themselves that they were true friends of their patrons. It's not unlike celebrity journalists who believe that they are pals of the people they cover. The greater the poet, the more likely he was to assume that he was a crony, not a client, of his patron. Other writers—often those without patrons—derided such poets as self-deceivers who were not friends but hangers-on of the famous.

Horace, for example, was sensitive to accusations that he was a sycophant to those with power. He notes in a letter to a colleague that genuine friendship is a mean between flattery and a boorishness that pretends to candor. But he is less concerned that he could be mistaken for a flatterer than fearful that any forthrightness might alienate his powerful friend. Horace gives himself away when he offers advice to his friend that could be a model to flatterers everywhere: "Sad types hate a cheerful fellow, jocular types hate a sad sack; fast people hate a sedentary fellow, relaxed types hate one quick and clever."

Sucking Up to Caesar

Whereas Greek thinkers were concerned with trying to protect the people from deceitful leaders, Roman thinkers were more concerned with protecting leaders from deceitful flatterers. While the Greek thinkers worried about preserving democracy, Roman thinkers worried about preserving power.

Counseling rulers to beware of flatterers was a literary growth industry in ancient Rome. Every writer, it seems, who had the ear of a powerful man advised his "friend" to beware of flatterers. Tacitus counsels a ruler to guard his values because "others will erode them through obsequiousness; adulation will break through, and flattery, and the worst poison to true affection, each man's own interest." Plutarch was concerned that silver-tongued flatterers would capture the ears of the powerful and exercise a pernicious effect. It is the flatterer "in great houses and great affairs," he says, that "often times overturns kingdoms and principalities."

Plutarch and the others never quite explained how flatterers overturn kingdoms and principalities. It was more the idea that flatterers had their own interests at heart rather than the state's or the people's. But the writers themselves were engaged in a subtle form of flattery and self-promotion: they flattered the ruler that he, above all others, might be immune to flattery, and they assigned themselves the role of guardian against pernicious flatterers.

Plutarch addresses his essay "How to Tell a Flatterer from a Friend" to Philopappus, a political leader and minor prince. He nowhere implies that Philopappus has a weakness for flattery; in fact, he suggests the contrary, telling the prince that a man of his virtue is immune to flattery. (Philopappus was apparently not immune to such a compliment, however.) The essay is meant to be a primer on how a ruler figures out who in his entourage is a flatterer with an ulterior motive and who is simply loyal.

Twenty centuries ago, Plutarch knew something that all the business ingratiation studies of the last twenty years have only recently demonstrated: that flattery works best on those who already have a high opinion of themselves. "For the man who is spoken of as a lover of flatterers," Plutarch wrote, "is in high degree a lover of self, and, because of his kindly feeling toward himself, he desires and conceives himself to be endowed with all manner of good qualities." Thus, when a minor young poet writes an ode to the many talents of a proud and self-confident prince, the prince says to himself, *Yes, what a clever young poet that fellow is to recognize how wondrous I am.*

Plutarch warns Philopappus against both "self-love" and "ignorance of self." He notes that each trait in its own way can make him an easy target for flatterers, and that the combination of the two is deadly. He suggests that love of self without knowledge of self makes one kindly but unthinking. "This fact affords the flatterer a very wide field within the realm of friendship, since in our love of self he has an excellent base of operations against us." Whereas knowledge of self without love of self makes us skeptical but insecure, a ripe target for flatterers as well.

Plutarch makes a number of distinctions between flatterers and friends. The friend is wedded to a moral system; the flatterer is not. The flatterer is a chameleon who changes color to suit the situation; the friend imitates only that which is good. While the friend appeals to that which is noble, the flatterer appeals to what is weak and vulnerable.

In answering his question of "how to tell a flatterer from a friend," Plutarch gives the standard reply of parhesia. Only a genuine friend will offer frank criticism; a flatterer never will. But Plutarch then makes a more subtle argument. He notes that truly clever flatterers, knowing that parhesia was the thing that separated true friends from flatterers, will imitate such criticism as a way of disarming the ruler. "The unscrupulous," he writes, "being well aware that frankness is a great remedy for flattery, flatter by means of frankness itself." Imitation may be the sincerest form of flattery, but imitation of sincerity is the most effective form of flattery.

Plutarch describes a flatterer's frankness as soft and weightless as a woman's undergarments. If a flatterer is frank, he says, it will be about something trifling, something that will only nick a person in the most superficial way. Something so small and picayune that it is a kind of flattery that they notice it at all.

Plutarch gives an example of criticism that is really veiled praise. He mentions a man who addressed Tiberius Caesar in the Senate with an air of making some somber criticism. "Caesar," the man declared, "you do not take proper care of yourself.... You are continually wearing out your strength in your anxieties and labor in our behalf." The technique is to tell the subject he has a flaw, but that the flaw is that he has too much of a given virtue—that is, he is too generous or too industrious or thinks too little of himself. With criticism like that you can't help but ingratiate yourself.

How to Spot a Flatterer

In order to help Philopappus avoid flatterers, Plutarch offers a kind of guide as to how to spot them.

Here are some ways, according to Plutarch, to discern and expose flatterers:

- Change one's views and opinions abruptly and see if the flatterer will follow.
- Remember, he says, flatterers "act the part of the friend with the gravity of a tragedian."
- Be aware of whether the individual in question praises your actions or yourself; if he does the latter, he's probably a flatterer.
- The flatterer will employ what might be called "third party" praise, and say things like, "Demetrius was saying just the other day how brilliant you are," or, "Have you noticed how people are staring at you?"
- If he is rough with his own servants and household, and soft with everyone above him, then he is likely to be a flatterer.
- Whereas true friends can convey affection and loyalty with a glance, a flatterer tends to rely on more formal means. Friends omit formalities, flatterers rely on them.
- Make a request of a friend and he will say, "Yes, if I can, it will be done." Make the same request of a flatterer and he will reply, "It is done."

· Watch how the flatterer behaves toward your other friends. While a real friend will befriend them, the flatterer will covertly try to steer you away from them.
· Flatterers are insecure and are only happy, he says, when they are abused. So if you abuse someone and that makes him happy, he's probably a flatterer.
· Flatterers pretend to an intimacy that is not the case and will take credit for actions that are not their own. Plutarch cites a wonderfully funny example. Melanthius, a flatterer, when asked how Alexander of Pherae was slain, replied, "By a stab through his ribs that hit me in the belly."

Plutarch's rules on how to spot a flatterer signal the final transition from flattery as a technique for persuading a whole class of people to flattery as a technique for influencing a single person. It is this latter idea that is closer to our modern sense of flattery, and will be given shape and form in the Middle Ages and the Renaissance.

Chapter 5

The Invention
of Romantic Flattery

All You Need Is Love—and a Rhyming Dictionary

Flattery has always been a seducer's art. It was Casanova who coined the seducer's credo: "Praise the beautiful for their intelligence, and the intelligent for their beauty." Flattery of any kind is useful to seduction of any kind. The sound of praise is almost always sweet.

As a technique of sexual seduction, flattery has generally been a male tool. As we saw with chimpanzees, the male seeks something from the female that she isn't necessarily willing to give him—or at least not without some token of his esteem. Sexual flattery has a very simple purpose: to persuade a woman to do something she might not otherwise do.

The seducer's strategy is pretty basic: I will make her like me (or trust me) by telling her something nice about herself, and she will reward me by sleeping with me. Male flattery is meant to pierce whatever counterstrategy the female has, which he assumes is to rebuff him. Romantic flattery is designed to be the key to the locked door, the combination of the safe, the gloss for breaking the code—choose your own metaphor.

Its modern forms are familiar. Everything from a man telling a woman she has the most exquisite eyes he has ever seen and then giving her a diamond bracelet, to a construction worker calling out "Nice ass!" to a passing female pedestrian. (My hunch is that the former has a better chance of success than the latter. Of course, the second strategy is designed to impress not the woman, but one's fellows.)

Sweet-talking is what we once called the gentle blandishments of a man courting a woman. In its definition, *Webster's Third International Dictionary* cites what is now a nostalgic-sounding line from John McCarten: ". . . manages somehow to *sweet-talk* the showgirl into a midnight supper at his apartment." Ah, the showgirl and the midnight supper. Its all so delightfully innocent.

To sweet-talk suggests romance as well as seduction. Nowadays, we generally don't make much of a distinction between the two, other than to suggest that a seducer is a cad. But that is because we live in a time when the language of love is the rhetoric of romance. We have elided sex and romance in a way that the ancients could not have conceived of. (Classical Greek had more than a dozen different terms for love, none of which meant what we mean by romantic love.)

Sexual flattery long preceded romantic flattery. Men flattered women in order to have their way with them. Love had little or nothing to do with it. Later, men seduced women by pretending to be in love with them, but that happened only after the conventions of romantic love became universal. Romantic love is a relatively modern invention.

In their 1958 song "Book of Love," the Monotones mused:

Tell me, tell me, tell me,
Oh, who wrote the Book of Love?
I've got to know the answer from someone from above
Oh, I wonder, wonder, wonder who, who,
Who wrote the Book of Love?

The answer to the Monotones' question is the Troubadours, and I don't mean another doo-wop group from the fifties. It was the troubadour poets of the twelfth century in the Provençal region of France who in many ways created the verbal and conceptual template for romantic love and romantic flattery. It is from them that we derive so many of our traditional assumptions about love—that love involves suffering; unhappy lovers are pale and thin; that love involves a pleasurable pain, an exquisite anguish; that ab-

sence makes the heart grow fonder; that a grand passion is life's great ambition; that, finally, *all you need is love*—all notions about love that we
think of as having always been around.

Clichés have to start somewhere, and many of our romantic clichés
began with the troubadours. It is hard to appreciate their originality because
they're so familiar. We hear lines from the twelfth-century troubadours
every day from movies, television, and romantic fiction. We live in an age
that mass-produces the sentiment first concocted by the troubadours. It was
the troubadours who wrote, wrote, wrote the Book of Love.

*   *   *

In many ways, we still abide by the laws of love they laid down eight
centuries ago. We have democratized them, we have secularized them, we
have turned them into greeting cards, but we have not changed the fundamental thrust of them all that much. "Real changes in human sentiment are
very rare," C. S. Lewis wrote about what the troubadours accomplished;
"there are perhaps three or four on record—but I believe that they occur,
and that this is one of them." We've just been refining what they started.

The troubadours were considered court poets, and they were a mixed lot:
Some were wandering minstrels or jongleurs; some were educated clerks;
some were poor, landless knights; a handful were women; and a few of
them were great feudal lords, like the duke of Aquitaine, Guillem de Pei-
teus, one of the original troubadour poets. Mostly, though, they were young
men on the make, amorous soldiers of fortune with a literary bent, knights-
errant who had traded armor for *amour*. Dante, who often quoted the troubadours in his work, called them "eloquent doctores," that is, masters of
doctrine and language. They were doctors of love.

*   *   *

The troubadours invented romantic flattery because they invented the
language of romantic love. They conceived its syntax and grammar. Virtually all the blandishments and endearments and sweet nothings that men
offer to women they learn from contemporary popular culture, and popular

culture began to learn them way back when from the troubadours. We kiss by the book, and we flatter by it as well.

You may think you're not familiar with the twelfth-century lyrics of the troubadours. And in fact the words, translated into English, don't quite have the familiarity of Beatles lyrics ("Love, love, love, / All you need is love"), but the romantic tropes are utterly familiar. We know them so well we don't realize we know them.

We'll start out with some simple garden-variety troubadour flattery. The poet is Marcabru, an orphan raised by a nobleman who wrote in the middle of the twelfth century. He's like the smooth-talking traveling salesman who sweeps the farmer's daughter off her feet.

> *Young girl of gentle birth,*
> *your father must have been a knight*
> *to engender in your mother*
> *such a courtly pleasant girl.*
> *The more I look at you, the lovelier*
> *you seem and the greater is my joy.*

Simple. Sweet. He is not only flattering her beauty but her sense of status by saying that she appears more noble than her birthright.

The troubadours were masters of romantic hyperbole. You know, there's no girl like my girl. Who's the fairest of them all? The answer was, whichever woman they were trying to seduce at the moment. The poet is Guillem IX, the duke of Aquitaine, one of the greatest of the troubadours.

> *For her I shiver and tremble, for*
> *Another like her*
> *has never been born.*

The idea is that to the lover his love is unique. One theme in troubadour poetry is that each troubadour's love is a nonpareil, and that God broke the mold after he created her. Until the troubadours, women were praised for their similarity to great beauties, not for their uniqueness. "Her beauty and her worth are unequaled" is another troubadour classic.

This time, the troubadour Peire Vidal:

For no one can despair when thinking
upon her, for in her joy is born.
And whoever praises
or speaks well of her
can never lie, for she
is the finest and gentlest lady
the world has ever seen.

The troubadours were the early PR gurus of another abiding romantic cliché: love at first sight. For them, love comes first through the eyes, and only then the heart. The whole idea of love at first sight is a tribute to another troubadourean notion: the irresistibility of passion. Guillem de Cabestanh:

The day I first saw you, my lady,
my heart abandoned all other thoughts,
and all my desires converged on you
for with your sweet smile and gentle look
you brought my heart such longing that I
forgot myself and all that was mine.

That I forgot myself. Love is so powerful that I was lost, that I was no longer myself. Love is so powerful it erases *I* and *me.*

Even though courtly love makes much of the lady's character, troubadour poetry suggests that beauty is only skin deep. They describe women from the outside in, not the inside out. Again, Guillem IX:

Her whiteness is
more than ivory's whiteness
Sun is pale where the whiteness glows.

Or, again. This time from the jongleur Cercamon:

The fairest woman who ever used a mirror never
saw anything as soft and white as ermine,
as she is, fresher than lily or rose—any flower!
And nothing makes me despair more!

In the last example, Cercamon also links her beauty with his own suffering. She is beyond reach. Oh, despair! And what is the result of such unhappy love? The lover becomes pale and thin. "But I can't go on, losing food and sleep like this," Cercamon sings. A robust lover, to the troubadours, was a contradiction in terms. Love makes you lose appetite for anything but love.

But being pale and thin is just the beginning. It's a mild nuisance compared to the lover's ultimate fate. In troubadour rhetoric, suffering is essential to romance, and the true lover is not just willing to miss a few meals for his love; he's prepared to die for her. In fact, he can't help it; he'll expire if he doesn't consummate his love. Give me love or give me death. Here again is Guillem IX, the duke of Aquitaine:

> If no hope comes to me shortly, some
> sign, some proof of her love,
> I shall die.

Bernart de Ventadorn, one of the classic troubadours, is also afflicted with the same ailment.

> Love, which way should I turn?
> Will I be cured through you?
> Or I'll surely die
> of longing and desire.

The conceit of dying for love is just that, a conceit that the troubadours helped create. And it is surely one of the most flattering things a man can say to a woman. In *As You Like It,* Shakespeare mocked the troubadours' convention of dying for love when he writes, "Men have died from time to time, and worms have eaten them. But not for love." The troubadours and Shakespeare know that hearts break but they do not stop beating.

For the troubadours, the ultimate verbal flattery is the inability to verbalize. Their flattery was in song, and so the greatest flattery was to be struck dumb with love. We saw this same idea in regard to speaking of Yahweh—the ultimate veneration is to be unable to speak at all. The troubadour Peire d'Alvernhe, writing toward the end of the twelfth century:

Oh, if only my desire had been
divined by her noble heart . . .
But I am ignorant of how to praise or flatter,
and thus my heart's feeling remain unspoken.

His poem suggests that his love is so pure that conventional praise and
flattery seem unworthy of his love. Other troubadours, like Bernart de Ventadorn, say that their love has left them "speechless." But, of course, they
do not then remain silent, they sing of their inability to sing. As Samuel
Becket said, when words fail us we must use them just the same.

In a fit of clever psychological displacement, the troubadours reserve
their wrath not for rivals or even husbands, but for flatterers. One of the
themes of their verse is that they, the troubadours, are not flatterers but true-
blue lovers, that their praise is both sincere and appropriate. These other
fellows (whoever they are) are false and shameless; they are panderers who
will stop at nothing. Again, Bernart de Ventadorn:

Oh, God! If only one could know
false from true lovers;
if only flatterers and traitors
had horns upon their heads.

The troubadours are trumpeting their sincerity by accusing other lovers
of being false. They know that there is no way of telling sincere praise from
false. And, indeed, the whole point about the effectiveness of flattery is that
the subject cannot tell the difference between true and false praise. So, always accuse your rival of falsity.

Love Will Find a Way to Her Pocketbook

Happy love has always been a literary oxymoron. The course of true
love never did run smooth—otherwise, you wouldn't have anything to
write about. Think of *Anna Karenina,* Abelard and Heloise, Tristan and
Isolde, Romeo and Juliet, *La Dame aux Camelias.* It wasn't until the ad-
vent of American movies early in the twentieth century that the image of

lovers walking off into the sunset was stamped on the popular imagination. Until then, love almost always meant a three-hankie ending.

The history of unhappy love may not have begun with the troubadours, but they certainly gave it their own spin. What they did was turn the pain of absence into pleasure. To them, suffering, not pleasure, was love's natural condition, and they took an exquisite pleasure in that suffering. "I have so much joy in my pain that I am sick with delight," wrote Christen de Troyes. Privation became an essential part of passion. With apologies to Shakespeare, the troubadours' motto could be, "The more unrequited, the more delighted."

The troubadours reveled in the paradox that love feeds on longing rather than fulfillment, that passion grows from scarcity, not plenty. Theirs is mostly the poetry of distance. The closer she got, to paraphrase the old hair color ad, the worse she looked. "My faraway love" is a staple form of address in troubadour poetry. Separation almost always made their poetry ecstatic. If they didn't have an absent lady to moan and moon about, they didn't have much of a poem. Absence made their art grow fonder.

Because they celebrated separation, they also created obstacles that would increase remoteness. We see this especially when medieval writers like Christen de Troyes used the tenets of courtly love as the themes of their stories. When romance became a narrative, impediments to love became essential. If the lovers have no obstacles to overcome, where's the drama? Boy meets girl, boy and girl fall in love and live happily ever after, is a story without much narrative drive. Boy meets girl, boy and girl fall in love, boy and girl must separate because their families are mortal enemies, or their class or background or religion or whatever keeps them from being together—now there's a story. The impediment *is* the plot. Because in our day race, class, or family are rarely considered obstacles to love, the story of modern romance is not of outer impediments but inner ones. Thus, the wrath of the Capulets descends into the rue of commitment-phobia.

The troubadours' glorification of passion was directly opposed to the classical tradition in which romantic passion was regarded not as one of life's great experiences but as a form of madness. (Love in ancient literature was mainly about sensuality or domestic comfort. Yes, Odysseus loved his wife, Penelope, and thought of her all those years of his wanderings, but it is not the romantic love of the movies, but more like the comfortable old-shoe love one has for a trusty Labrador.) The classical notion was that passion was the opposite of self-mastery. Passion was being out of control rather in control, and was only an illusion of freedom because real freedom comes from mastery and acceptance. In today's society, that's a description of a cold fish, or what the women's magazines would regard as a very bad bet for a relationship.

The troubadours' embrace of passion was also a revolt against the Church, where the idea of romantic passion was frowned upon. Yes, it was better to marry than to burn, Paul said, but not all that much better. The troubadours set up an alternative church, the church of love.

Today, we glorify passion and its synonym, instinct. "Trust your instincts." "Go with your gut." "If it feels right, do it." All of those clichés glorify passion and instinct, and seem to regard reason and contemplation as the consolation prizes in life's great adventure. Spontaneity trumps planning. "Just do it" is the reasoned counsel that Nike Inc. gives to millions of people around the world, as though impulse control was something to be avoided at all costs. The implication of "Just do it" is that people who choose not to bungee-jump from a bridge 150 feet off the ground are gray, timid souls who are not really living. It is almost fruitless to argue against passion and instinct these days; it is like being against motherhood and apple pie.

Passion has its privileges, though. The troubadours had a Cyrano de Bergerac complex—that is, they were for the most part men without a great deal of status seeking liaisons with women of a higher class. And this was at a time when class differences were seen as an insuperable obstacle to romance. But they had an ingenious solution: they promulgated the notion that passion obliterates class. That passion knows no boundaries. What they invented is the very modern and democratic notion that there is an aristocracy of passion. That true love o'erleaps boundaries of class and status and wealth. What they pioneered is the standard movie cliché of the mail-room boy, cop, football player, elevator operator, private investigator (choose one) who falls in love with and wins the heart of the heiress, wealthy widow, daughter of the town banker, niece of the rich boss (choose one). Their love is sanctioned by their passion.

Passionate love is thought to be both democratizing (it makes us all equal) and ennobling (it lifts us from our lives of quiet desperation). It is

nothing less than a privileged form of understanding. "Whoever loves passionately," Denis de Rougement writes in *Love in the Western World*, "is
supposed to be thereby made one of an exalted section of mankind among
whom social barriers cease to exist." This is an idea that the troubadours
wished to propagate—in part because they were young men on the make,
Sammy Glicks with mandolins, and were looking to raise their status. Their
strategy was to use their passion and their poetry to vault over their weak
résumés.

In the European literary tradition, barriers of class were traditionally the
cause of social upheaval, disaster, and tragedy. In the modern, more American tradition, barriers of class are either shown to be illusions or just a
jerry-built hurdle for the bride and groom to leap over. The troubadours
were like Americans in the sense that they sought to erase social boundaries, but in their case, it was mostly motivated by a desire to line their wal-
lets. Yes, they're intrigued by their noble patroness, but they were probably
more interested in procuring a horse than engaging in horseplay.

The irony is that while the troubadours helped invent the "Just Do It"
philosophy, it was a strategy designed to level the romantic playing field.
There was nothing the least bit spontaneous about their spontaneity—it was
strategic, calculated, studied. The model for their behavior was not the
modern thrill-seeker but the French poet Céline, who once said he wrote
and rewrote his poems for weeks to give the illusion that they were dashed
off in a quarter of an hour.

Someone once said that in the union of Fred Astaire and Ginger Rogers,
he gave her class and she gave him sex. This is the traditional bourgeois
marriage exchange between men and women. But in the case of the troubadours, who were often penniless, they played Ginger to the aristocratic
lady's Fred; they provided the illusion of sex while the gentle ladies gave
the poets entrée to high society.

*   *   *

The troubadours did help create the template for romantic flattery, but
they made a mistake that has characterized romantic flattery ever since. Another seducer's axiom: Good flattery is general; great flattery is specific.
They never seemed to have understood this lesson.

Perhaps because their ladies were often fantasies, most of troubadour flattery is abstract. There is nothing specific about the woman being flattered. The woman's skin was always as white as snow, her eyes were always clear and beautiful. There were no rhapsodies to the funny hazel-greenness of her eyes with their golden highlights. Their praise is generic. From their verse, you would never be able to pick one object of affection from another in a police lineup. As one critic said, it seems like a series of poems by a single author forever praising the same fair lady.

Shakespeare mocked the conventions of courtly flattery and in doing so created one of the greatest love poems ever written, Sonnet 130.

My mistress' eyes are nothing like the sun;
Coral is far more red than her lips' red;
If snow be white, why then her breasts are dun;
If hairs be wires, black wires grow on her head.
I have seen roses damasked, red and white,
But no such roses see I in her cheeks;
And in some perfumes is there more delight
Than in the breath that from my mistress reeks.
I love to hear her speak, yet well I know
That music hath a far more pleasing sound;
I grant I never saw a goddess go;
My mistress, when she walks, treads on the ground.
And yet, by heaven, I think my love as rare
As any she belied with false compare.

The flattery of the troubadours is false compare not because it is untrue—although it probably is—but because it is general. Eyes that are always like the sun, breasts that are always as white as snow, is bad flattery because it is one-size-fits-all flattery. But that, for the most part, has been the way of romantic flattery ever since. That's what makes it useful for suitors and greeting card writers. You can buy the cliché off the rack and it fits whomever you give it to.

But the troubadours have an excuse.

Like all great love poets, the troubadours are as in love with the form of their poems as with the form of their love. The poets are not looking for new

ways to praise her in order to win her love but in order to win laurels as a
poet. They are rhetoricians of love, and what they are in love with is their
own voices. They boast that they are adept at "luf talk," which sounds like it
could be a medieval call-in radio show. The troubadours are, in fact, in competition with each other not over women, but over their verse.

Bernhart de Ventadorn writes:

> *It is no wonder that I sing*
> *better than any other singer,*
> *for my heart impels me more toward love,*
> *and I am better made for its command.*

He boasts not that he's a better lover but a better singer.

Their love is so literary that they often claim to be in love with women
they've never actually seen, but only heard of. They are in love with the
idea of love. Guillaume de Machaut: "Even if a mistress I have none, / yet I
am a faithful lover." Yes, faithful to the religion of love. This may be their
most original heresy and the one that started eight hundred years of love
foolishness. Earthly love had always been a subset of divine love. When
one person loves another, the Church said, it is really the reflection of God
in that person that is the source of the love. (Only men could love God directly. Thus, Milton's "He for God only, she for God in him.") But the troubadours helped spur the notion that earthly love and human passion were
the be-all and the end-all, and weren't just a divine hand-me-down. This
was not so much an adulterous love as an idolatrous one. The troubadour
Peire d'Alvernhe: ". . . a man without love's service is no better than a
wretched ear of corn." The poets may have been generic when flattering
their love, but they excelled themselves in flattering Love. "For such was
the paradoxical secret of courtly love," writes de Rougement; "stilted and
inanimate when addressed to women, it became all ardent sincerity as soon
as it was directed to the Wisdom of Love."

Their philosophy is a precursor to our modern notion that romantic love
is the peak human experience, the *summum bonum* of life. This was a radical idea in the twelfth century. Again, Bernart de Ventadorn sums up this
notion:

He is dead who in his heart
hasn't some sweet taste of love.

Even though they sometimes show women as venal (these fellows could shift from amorousness to abhorrence in a line), what they really did was put women on a romantic pedestal for perhaps the first time in literature. In their poems, they created an idealized woman, a kind of Platonic notion of perfect femininity.

In the troubadours' poetry, women, through love, become the source of all virtues, the seedbed of honesty, generosity, courtesy, and courage. In short, women made men better, or men became better because of them. "Through her," wrote Cercamon, "I shall be false or faithful, loyal or full of deceit, totally villain or totally courtly." As Jack Nicholson said to Helen Hunt in *As Good as It Gets:* "You make me want to be a better man."

The idealization of women was in the air. In the twelfth century, for example, the game of chess changed from having four kings who dominated the game to a lady or queen who took precedence over all the other pieces save the king, who was relegated to having the least mobility. Another example of this idealization was the rise of the cult of the Virgin. Some have suggested that the Church, in response to what they saw as the idealization of women as a function of courtly love, promoted the cult of Mary in order to compete. Indeed, as strict courtly tradition began to fade, *la donna* became the Madonna, and the church fathers made Mariolatry into a form of sanctioned ecclesiastical flattery.

How to Cheat with Your Wife

The troubadours were the Beatles of the early Middle Ages. They embodied a sensibility that captured people's fancy and set the model for much that would come after them. And if the troubadours were the Beatles, then Andreas Capellanus was a sort of Brian Epstein, a manager-promoter who helped explain their music and create the myth around them. Andreas Capellanus was the author of *The Art of Courtly Love,* published in 1174, right in the middle of the Troubadour era. Capellanus was a chaplain of the royal court, and his treatise was probably written for Countess Marie, the daughter of Eleanor of Aquitaine who supposedly created her own court of love. The book consists mainly of a series of dialogues between knightly suitors and young women. The dialogues are divided according to class. For example, there is a dialogue between "a man of the middle class and a woman of the higher nobility," as well as a dialogue between "a man of the higher nobility and a woman of the middle class" and all the variations in between. It is a precursor to all those modern self-help books that give the reader sample dialogue to use when you want to ask your boss for a raise or your husband for a divorce.

The book, which had considerable popularity in the Middle Ages, may have been something of a parody. It's hard to believe that the dialogues are not somewhat ironic and that Capellanus actually intended knights to peruse his book as a study guide to seduction. *(Let's see, my lady is only of the lower nobility so I should avoid praising her family.)* But authorial intentions, particularly when it comes to writing about romance, often have little to do with how a work is read.

It was thought for a long time that Capellanus's *Art of Courtly Love* was a kind of underground guide to the secret life of a distant civilization. Many scholars believed Capellanus provided a realistic picture of medieval courts and the courtly love that animated them. I'm inclined to think the world it depicts mostly a fiction. Just as nowadays when movies are accompanied by the legend "Based on a True Story," people tend to think the whole thing is completely true; we are fooled by the simulacrum of reality. For our purposes, it doesn't matter that Capellanus was misinterpreted. In fact, it is his almost universal misreading that helped create the foundations of our modern sense of romantic love.

Capellanus's work reinforces the staples of troubadour romantic love. Three of Capellanus's inflexible rules are: "Every lover regularly turns pale in the presence of his beloved," "He whom the thought of love vexes eats and sleeps very little," and "He who is not jealous cannot love." He defines love as a "certain inborn suffering derived from the sight of and excessive meditation upon the beauty of the opposite sex." He says love may be blind but that the blind can't fall in love: "Blindness is a bar to love, because a blind man cannot see anything upon which his mind can reflect immoderately, and so love cannot arise in him." And of course, he is one of history's first PR spokesmen for being in love with love: "A true lover would rather be deprived of all his money and of everything that humankind can imagine as indispensable to life rather than be without love." Finally, in a line that could be a lyric in a Burt Bacharach song, he warbles, "Love can deny nothing to love."

One of the things that scholars and historians took very seriously was Capellanus's apparent endorsement of the idea that the only place for love was outside of marriage, that true love and passion could only be adulterous. The idea, as C. S. Lewis wrote, was that any idealization of sexual love in a society in which marriage was utilitarian must involve the romanticizing of adultery. Lewis listed the characteristics of courtly love as Humility, Courtesy, the Religion of Love, and Adultery. Romantic love, by definition, was extramarital, for marriage, by definition, was unromantic. In troubadour poetry and the realm of courtly love, God always seems to be on the side of the adulterous lover—look at Lancelot and Tristan—and never the cuckolded husband. This despite the fact that adultery was both a divine sin and an earthly crime, punished in the Middle Ages by death. Well, for the woman anyway.

The type of adultery that Capellanus disdains is one that we find hard to understand: what might be called adulterous love within a marriage. Capellanus makes an assertion that was a commonplace in medieval theology but which we, given our belief in romantic marriage, find rather bewildering. Capellanus first cites St. Jerome in saying "A too ardent lover, as we are taught by the apostolic law, is considered an adulterer with his own wife." Whew! I found that hard to type, so alien is it to our conception that romantic marriage is the ultimate good, and that ardent love of one's wife (we celebrate uxoriousness!) is the ultimate boon. Lewis quotes the Latin: *"Omnis ardentior amator propriae uxoris adulter est"* —*Passionate love of a man's own wife is adultery.* Whereas the troubadours and Capellanus find nothing shameful about adultery, they find a husband who is nuts about his wife to be a pervert.

Capellanus quotes from letters by the countess of Champagne, who seems to have been the Agony Aunt or Miss Lonelyhearts of the courtly love set. She writes, "We declare and we hold as firmly established that love cannot exert its powers between two people who are married to each other." Her rationale is that marriage, being a contract and an arrangement, makes people duty-bound to each other, whereas love can only be given and exchanged freely. Women, she says, can only be rewarded by the king of love for service "outside the bonds of wedlock."

*　　*　　*

Capellanus believes that women are absolute gluttons for flattery. To engineer a seduction, he says, flattery is absolutely essential. "You cannot find a woman in the world," he says, "who does not delight in the praise of men above everything else and who does not think that every word spoken about her has to do with her praise. This fault can be seen even in Eve, the first woman, who ate the forbidden food." Women have been susceptible to such reptilian blandishments ever since.

Although Capellanus believes that flattery is infallible, he says it must be carefully and thoughtfully applied. Like Ovid, he endorses its liberal use, but he goes much further in defining the nature and type of those uses. For example, in the first dialogue, between "a man of the middle class" and "a woman of the same class," he says, "praise her home, or her family, or herself. For women, particularly middle-class women from the country, commonly delight in being commended and readily believe every word that looks like praise." He argues that the lower a woman is on the socioeconomic scale, the higher her susceptibility to flattery. Here's an example of what he suggests saying to a middle-class woman: "When the Divine Being made you there was nothing that He left undone. I know that there is no defect in your beauty, none in your good sense, none in you at all except, it seems to me, that you have enriched no one by your love." How could a nice middle-class girl resist?

Beware of the sophisticated woman, Capellanus warns. In the next dialogue, which takes place between a man of the middle class and a woman of the nobility, Capellanus counsels the fellow not to lay it on too thick. "If the woman should be wise and shrewd, he ought to be careful not to overdo the praise of her beauty. For if he should praise a noble and prudent woman beyond all measure, she will think that he isn't very good at the art of conversation or that he is making up all this flattery and thinks her a fool." His logic is that the more sophisticated the woman, the more immune she will be to flattery—or, at least, the likelier she is to detect it and question it.

With noblewomen he counsels a more indirect form of flattery. In fact, he suggests a rather risky tactic of saying that the man should say he will not flatter her because (a) the world already does and (b) she'll see through it. It is a kind of simulated romantic *parhesia,* in which he covertly flatters her by not flattering her. Here is the sample dialogue: "It doesn't seem at all profitable to dwell very much on the praise of your person, for your character and your beauty echo through widely separated parts of the world, and, furthermore, praise uttered in the presence of the person praised seems to have the appearance of clever flattery." In other words, I'll only praise you behind your back—which of course, when it gets back to her, as it surely will, is the most effective kind of flattery of all.

Capellanus posits another type of romantic flattery—the flattery among equals, the it-takes-one-to-know-one school of flattery. This can only be done, he advises, between two people of the nobility. From a nobleman to a noblewoman: "So much nobility is apparent in you, and you are distinguished by so much courtesy, that I believe in the presence of Your Prudence I may without fear of censure say all that which is lying in my heart waiting to be said." Because they are of equal status, the woman knows that the man is not trying to enhance his own status by seducing her.

If all his recommendations don't work, Capellanus offers some emergency tactics:

Throw yourself on her mercy. His sample line: "You are the cause of my suffering and the cure for my moral pain, for you hold both my life and my death shut up in your hand."

You can never get rid of me. Tell her: I will never cease to serve you, no matter what you decide.

Accuse her of being a cold-blooded killer. Capellanus advocates telling her: If you send me away, I will die, and that will make you a murderer.

One of the flaws in Capellanus's logic is that he bases her susceptibility to flattery according to class, not personality. Class may indeed make some difference, but it is nothing compared to self-esteem. Thus, an insecure countess may be more susceptible than a self-confident milkmaid.

.   .   .

My wife and I have a long-running debate about whether or not the troubadours, or anyone else, for that matter, really did invent romantic love and romantic flattery. The argument goes like this: I always insist that most of what we think and believe about romantic love we learn from popular culture. She nods her head in exasperated familiarity when I pretentiously cite La Rochefoucauld on the subject: "Few people would fall in love if they had never heard of love." Her argument is that the popular depictions of love mirror innate romantic feelings. Clichés, she says, exist for a reason—that they have evolved out of the natural, inherent feelings that all human beings have. In our continuing debate as to which came first, the feeling or the depiction of it, she usually wins. (I well know that in a marriage one usually loses in the long run by insisting on winning an argument in the short run.)

I generally think most people's attitude toward the idea of romantic love is that it's been around in much the same form as it is now as long as men and women have been around. To me, this is not unlike the fundamentalist attitude toward the Bible. To wit, that everything in it is literally true, and that the nature of faith and belief has not altered by one whit since the words were written. I think many of us share the same notion about love— that it is the same now as it was a thousand or ten thousand years ago, that it is something basic, indivisible, unchanging.

When I was a little boy, I used to watch a Saturday morning cartoon show that was based on King Arthur's court. There were knights jousting while their fair ladies looked on. Every episode showed a knight winning victory on some battlefield and then winning his lady on the romantic battleground. In school, I can recall drawing knights on horses over and over, in part because I had a silhouette of them down pat that actually looked like a knight on horseback.

When I was a little older, I loved to watch Andy Hardy movies on television. In virtually every Andy Hardy movie, there is a scene somewhere about the middle of the movie where the Hardy family is sitting at their well-stocked dinner table. Andy is looking glum, staring down at his plate, and listlessly moving the mashed potatoes around with his fork. Then someone says something rather banal and he gives a choked cry and storms out of the dining room. Judge Hardy then turns to Mrs. Hardy and says, "What the dickens has gotten into that boy, Ma? He didn't touch his food. He's pale. He doesn't sleep. He just moons around like a sick cow." Mrs.

Hardy smiles sympathetically and says, "Judge, can't you see that boy's in love?"

Now, Mrs. Hardy's description of the way young Andy Hardy was behaving in the movie is a textbook definition of the unhappy lover in the troubadours' poems. My wife would probably say that there is some natural physiological reason that young men turn pale and don't eat when they are in love, but I'm not so sure. From watching those Andy Hardy movies and others from the fifties as well as the family television shows of the mid-sixties, I learned not only that young men turn pale when they're in love, but that crushes make one unhappy, that boys are bashful around girls they like, that a young man is supposed to give a girl flowers, and that he's supposed to tell her how pretty she is. I discovered the rudiments of courtship not from my classmates or my family or experience, but from television and the movies.

Technology has changed one aspect of this kind of romantic education. As a boy, I went to see *The Sound of Music* once in a movie theater. I absorbed the idea that freedom and love were joined and that the Nazis were bad. When it eventually came to television, and was treated as a kind of national event, I probably watched it three or four more times through my boyhood and adolescence. A pretty fair exposure. But today, in the age of video and VCRs, children watch the movies and fairy tales that they like twenty, thirty, or forty times. My nine-year-old niece has seen *Cinderella,* with its moral that all girls should and will marry a prince, thereby solving all life's problems, thirty-five times. She has seen the *Lion King,* with its moral that all girls should and will marry a prince, thereby solving all life's problems, twenty times. She has seen *Snow White,* with its moral that all girls should and will marry a prince, at least fifteen times.

My guess is that what teenagers are learning about romantic love is still based on the principles of courtly love and troubadour poetry. Here is a description of the courtly love affair by the historian Barbara Tuchman:

The love affair moved from worship through declaration of passionate devotion, virtuous rejection by the lady, renewed wooing with oaths of eternal fealty, heroic deeds of valor which won the lady's heart by prowess, consummation of the secret love, followed by endless adventures and subterfuges to a tragic denouement.

Except for the scholarly language, that could be the thumbnail summary that appears on the video for the movie *Titanic,* which is now the most popular movie ever made, seen by millions and millions of young people all around the world, viewed by millions of teenaged girls a dozen times or more, and, I would wager, the single most important influence on the conception of romantic love among young people in the last twenty-five years—and it is a perfect illustration of all the tenets of courtly love, troubadour poetry, and the romantic flattery they spawned.

The theme of the movie is that there is an aristocracy of passion, that operatic romantic love is the *ne plus ultra* of experience, and that anyone who doesn't have it leads a sorry half-life. De Rougement's summary of courtly love ("Whoever loves passionately is supposed to be thereby made one of an exalted section of mankind among whom social barriers cease to exist.") could be the tag line on the movie poster.

When we meet young Jack Dawson (Leonardo DiCaprio) in the early moments of the movie, he is the very model of the modern-day troubadour. He's described in the movie's script as a "drifter," a "Bohemian," and an "artist." And although he may be poor and landless like many of the young knights who were troubadours, he is obviously a noble soul, an aristocrat of the heart.

When Jack first lays eyes on Rose DeWitt Bukater (Kate Winslet), she is wearing a yellow dress and white gloves and staring off into the distance. In the grammar of movie logic, we know that the instant Jack sees her he is experiencing love at first sight. We know that Jack is smitten even before he does: this is his true love forever—or at least for the next two-and-a-half hours.

While Jack is staring at her from belowdecks (she is of course higher, which is how we picture the aristocratic ladies of the twelfth century on their balconies with their courtly lovers kneeling before them), he and his pals see her young, rich, and arrogant fiancé, Cal, come up behind her and take her arm. As Jack's mate Tommy says to him, "Forget it, boy-o. You'd as like have angels fly out o' yer arse as get next to the likes of her."

But as late-twentieth-century moviegoers, we know that just as the millionaire can fall for the flower girl—or the hooker—the heiress can fall for the busboy. We know that poverty and wealth are only temporary impediments to true love.

Jack and Rose's first interaction occurs when he sees her at the stern of the boat planning to leap into the freezing Atlantic. Without thinking, Jack is ready to dive in after her. His actions only confirm what we already know about him: that he would be willing to die for his true love.

Rose tells him that there can be nothing between them—but Jack won't take no for an answer. His two mates comment on the action.

TOMMY: He's not bein' logical, I tell ya.
FABRIZIO: *Amore* is-a not logical.

Ah, yes, Amore *is-a not logical.* Here the troubadour sensibility speaks practically in its native tongue. Love defies logic. The troubadours elevated passion above logic as the supreme good. That is certainly Jack's attitude. His passion cannot be bottled up.

When Jack finally does find Rose, she tells him, "Jack, this is impossible. I can't see you." Jack replies (the scanning is mine):

Rose, you're no picnic.
You're a spoiled little brat even,
But under that you're a strong, pure heart,
and you're the most amazingly astounding girl
I've ever known.

The troubadours could not have sung it better.

Jack's speech could be a contemporary version of one of Capellanus's dialogues, the one entitled "A man of the middle class speaks with a woman of the higher nobility." Jack has followed Capellanus's advice perfectly. "For if he should praise a noble and prudent woman beyond all measure, she will think that he isn't very good at the art of conversation or that he is making up all this flattery and thinks her a fool." Jack does not do this. He seasons his praise with a little bit of reality, prefacing his declaration that she is astounding by telling her that she's "no picnic" and that she's a "spoiled brat." He's established his bona fides with a little frankness.

She is flustered and he says (again, my scanning):

I know I have nothing to offer you, Rose,
I know that.

But I'm involved now.
You jump, I jump,
remember?
I can't turn away without knowing
that you're going to be alright.

Jack is again following Capellanus, who tells the middle-class lover to throw himself on the noblewoman's mercy. She will be flattered that she has so much control. "You are the cause of my suffering and the cure for my moral pain," Capellanus instructs the middle-class man to say; "You hold both my life and my death shut up in your hand."

Rose does finally give herself to Jack, and in the famous scene before he consummates the relationship, Jack sketches her with pastels just as the troubadours sketched their ladies in words. And Jack's portrait is just as impersonal and clichéd as one of the troubadour's poems. Her skin, as we can all see, is as fair as snow.

Finally, when the ship is going down and people are trying to save themselves, Cal sees that she is going to stick with Jack. Cal says to her, "Where are you going? To him? Is that it? To be a whore to that gutter rat?"

Rose replies: "I'd rather be his whore than your wife."

Bingo! Unfaithful love is the only truly passionate love. Of course, she'd rather be Jack's whore than Cal's wife—that's where the passion is.

Then, out on the water, Jack does indeed save her life by sacrificing his. That's something the troubadours only do in their poems, but of course, this is celluloid, and we have to see it. He dies giving her the greatest compliment of all: "Sailing on the *Titanic*," he says, "was the best thing that ever happened to me."

It's the ultimate romantic flattery.

Chapter 6

The Courtier's
Guide to How to Flatter

Social Climbing 101

Courts of one kind or another have always existed. You can find them in chimp culture, in the Old Testament, in ancient Egypt, at Microsoft—wherever there is a king, a chief, a sachem, a boss man, a big cheese who holds power, there is a court around him consisting of those who want to partake of that power and prestige.

But the height of Western courtly life was the Renaissance. We're talking roughly from about the fifteenth century to the eighteenth and primarily in France, Italy, Germany, and England. It was a time when kings and queens often enjoyed absolute power. If absolute power tends to corrupt absolutely, it does so in part through the court that surrounds the ruler. Are courtiers at such courts beholden to such a ruler? Absolutely.

The engine that drove men—and women—at court was the pursuit of power, privilege, and status. These were the goals of the great and the humble, the gentle and the not-so-gentle, of the oldest and grandest duke and the youngest son of the most unassuming country squire. Each was in a different and ever-shifting place on the ladder of hierarchy, with the king or queen at the very top.

Courts were great chains of ingratiation. Courtiers were suitors to those above them and patrons to those below. It was for the most part a vertical, up-and-down hierarchy of rank. In short, there was always an ass to kiss above you and someone below you to kiss your ass. Unless, of course, you were the king, who looked up only to God and down on everyone else.

Courts were opaque to the outsider. It was a precinct without a window, a place without a front door. It was a region of codes and rituals, of obscure forms, of rarefied manners, of abstruse language. They were seen as—and wanted to be seen as—impenetrable. Their complexity was studied, designed to rebuff the invader. (The lowest members of the court, Renaissance bureaucrats, delighted in being obscure and cryptic to outsiders. Those least secure in their place are always even more jealous in guarding it.) There was a kind of obscurantist Catch-22 about courts: You could only become a member of the court if you knew its elaborate rules, but you could only know the rules if you were a member.

To the insiders at court, the codes of etiquette were as well known as the rules of law are today. Each person knew the behavior that was expected of him. They operated according to conventions molded by tradition, mandated by custom, and enforced by their own internal pressure.

Courtiers succeeded, as the Renaissance scholar Daniel Javitch has put it, because they tailored their behavior to "the exigences of Renaissance despotism." The courtier knew that the prince's rule was absolute and that he, the courtier, was absolutely dependent on the king's favor. Castiglione, the great guide to courtly life in the early sixteenth century, suggested that the courtier's relation to the prince is not unlike like that of Abraham's to Yahweh—if the king asks you to sacrifice your firstborn, you reply, "When, Sire?"

Most of the dealings between king and courtier were less dramatic and less direct. "Transactions with a despotic ruler," writes Javitch, "require ingratiating deceit." Ingratiating deceit, or more to our point, deceitful ingratiation, was the lifeblood of the courtier. Undisguised truth was something to be shunned.

In *La Civile Conversazione,* published in 1574, Guazzo writes of court life, "Commonly the greater are flattered by the lesser, and the more they are in prosperitie, the more they are beset with flatterers; who alwaies make their repaire thither where profite is to be reaped." Guazzo's description is a useful definition of flattery in general—that it is ultimately strategic ("where profite is to be reaped")—and of flattery at court in particular. The goal of being at court was to advance one's place, and the way one advanced one's place was through ingratiation, deceitful or otherwise.

The courtier was the successor to the medieval knight. Whereas the theater of display for the knight was the battlefield, the battlefield of the courtier was the drawing room. Whereas the knight was primarily a warrior, the courtier needed to be many things: a gentleman, a poet, a flirt, a good dancer.

The job of the courtier was to elevate the general view of his own worthiness, to puff up his reputation. One way to do this was through flattery of those who judged his worth. George Puttenham in *The Arte of English Poesie* (1589) puts it most candidly: the "profession of a very Courtier, which is in plaine terms, cunningly to be able to dissemble." *Cunningly to be able to dissemble* was perhaps the courtier's most useful and essential skill. And one of the things about which he cunningly dissembles is the esteem in which he held those above him.

Inside Out at Court

During the Renaissance, some courtiers provided a glimpse of the secret life of courts through their writings. These books, which came to be known as courtesy literature, were a kind of memoir-cum-handbook, a summing up of all that the courtier had learned about how to behave in society.

These were texts written by the elite for the elite to help them navigate the mysteries of court. But they proved to be a tool not so much for the aristocracy but for those aspiring to become members of it. They were written as *epideictic* literature—literature, that is, for show. The authors were, in a sense, show-offs; they wanted to display how clever and successful they were. But, instead, the books became guides for how to climb the slippery slope, renaissance Horatio Alger stories for aspiring courtiers.

Renaissance courtesy literature flourished at a time when the court began to change from being the center of frozen hierarchies to one that was a locus of social mobility. It was at that time that courtesy literature changed from a form that reflected the status quo to a tool of social change. Montaigne, among others, argued that flattery flourishes at courts when times are precarious. The idea is that in times of uncertainty, one way that insecurity manifests itself is as sycophancy and toadying. Flattery, Montaigne said, is a weed that grows best in an untended garden.

Courtesy literature thrived during what historian Lawrence Stone has called "the century of mobility, 1540–1640." Stone is speaking primarily of England, where there was what he called a "seismic upheaval of unprecedented magnitude." But that upheaval was also happening throughout the Continent. In England, it was primarily fueled by changes that had occurred first in Italy and France. The pressure of the Reformation, the rise of European humanism, and the expulsion of the Catholic Church from England were creating room for aspiration. There was a restlessness abroad and at home. It was an age of upward mobility.

Henry VIII opened the doors of court to the landed gentry. Elizabeth, his successor, faced what Stone called a "horde of aspirants." She presided over an elite under pressure from a burgeoning upper middle class. In a modern state, there was a growing need for an educated governing class to serve queen and country. During Elizabeth's reign, the upper class trebled at a time that the population only doubled. The number of baronets and knights grew from 500 to 1,400. This was dubbed an "inflation of honors," and is itself a kind of social flattery.

The older aristocracy saw itself as threatened. Courts were besieged with suitors: The legions of younger brothers of the nobility, the platoons of the lesser gentry, all were looking to scale the battlements of court. These pressures and the numbers of aspiring courtiers changed the values of rank at court. As Frank Whigham put it: "Too many suitors competing for too few rewards inflated the cost while deflating the value." As the aristocracy saw it, quantity devalued quality.

The need for an educated governing class increased the value of education, and education was one way a fellow could change his status. For the nobility, academia had long been regarded more or less as a finishing school or a place for younger brothers to fritter away their time. But now it became a kind of trade school for the aspiring gentry. By the early seventeenth century, the numbers of young men leaving university became a jostling army of those seeking preferment.

The idea that, at court, merit as well as birth would be the new measure seems fair to us egalitarian moderns. But not to Renaissance aristocrats. To them, it was patently unfair. They were born into a system in which birth was the sum of all things, and suddenly, the rules were changing. To a person who grows up in a system based on birth, a meritocracy seems deeply unjust. They had lived according to one set of rules, and now those rules were being rewritten. The new standard was *Esse sequitur operare*—Identity derives from behavior.

Change was everywhere. It stirred anxiety among some, hope among a few, confusion among the many. Sir Thomas Wyatt condemned what he called "newfangleness." The English poet Gabriel Harvey complained to his friend Sir Edmund Spenser that everything had become cheapened. In no age," he wrote, "so little is so much made of, every one highly in his own favour, thinking no man's penny so good silver as his own." Everywhere, he says, he sees asses dressed in lion's skins, and everywhere he senses envy, "the scab of injured merit."

* * *

The change in the nature of social status at court—from an exclusively birth-determined hierarchy to one where identity was based in part on actions and achievements—reflected and advanced the rise of individualism during the Renaissance. Virtue and status were no longer simply defined by your station at birth, but by your behavior. But there was another option that soon presented itself: faking it.

Just because identity now derived from behavior didn't mean it had to be verifiable behavior. It was as important to appear to be a certain way as to actually be that way. *Esse quam videri* was the motto of the ancients—To be, rather than to seem. But during the Renaissance, the formulation reversed itself: to seem to be often became just as good as being. And the great guide in how to seem to be were courtesy books.

A gentleman was once a rather definable thing. Those who were gentlemen could immediately identify those who were not. Those who were not usually knew immediately who were. But how to be one was another story. It was a kind of secret society whose rules—what to say to a lady at tea, how to bow at court—were unknown to nonmembers. But courtesy books, particularly Castiglione's *Courtier,* helped explain and define exactly what a gentleman was. With Castiglione as your guide, you could turn yourself into a valuable commodity, a reasonable enough facsimile of a gentleman.

* * *

Between 1500 and 1800, thousands of courtesy manuals were written and were avidly read by tens of thousands of people. The genre was not a new one. It hearkens back to the apothegms and exemplars of Aristotle, Quintilian, and Marcus Aurelius.

Courtesy books were written in part to defend the barriers of entry at court, but offered instead a way around those barriers. They provided doors of entry and windows of insight. They were like *Martha Stewart Living* for the uninitiated. The rules were being revealed to nonmembers. These books offered a key at precisely the time that more and more people were seeking entry. They offered a kind of ladder for the new legions of social climbers. If the great creation of the Renaissance was the individual, courtesy books were a kind of how-to guide, for becoming a person.

The original courtesy literature was exclusive, not inclusive. It was the inside rules for insiders. It was meant as an ornament for those at court, not a map for those who weren't. It was meant to be concealed from common sight. It was a kind of code that must be kept secret. Some of Castiglione's contemporaries even thought that *The Courtier* would help those at court weed out impostors. In fact, it had the opposite effect. It became a manual of mobility. In the courtesy books, social climbers found what the critic Kenneth Burke called "a repertoire of strategies."

Courtesy literature stoked ambition. The books that we are going to look at, led by Castiglione's *Courtier,* but including Machiavelli's *Prince,* and, later, works by Chesterfield, Bacon, and Montaigne, were publishing sensations. They circulated widely because there was a great demand for them. The self-help section of the Renaissance Barnes & Noble was by far the most popular part of the store. Courtesy books reflected the Renaissance's concern with the distinction between praise and flattery. Praise, even self-praise, was fine, but no one wanted to be seen either as advocating flattery or as being a flatterer. Flattery was considered *the* courtly affliction. In *The Civile Conversation,* Stefano Guazzo wondered whether it would be better for man to be reincarnated as an animal because in society "it availeth not for man to be vertuous, noble, or valient, because the flatterer possesseth the first place, the second the calumniator, and the traytour and trecherous person the third." Everyone routinely condemned flattery, even as they advocated its use. Just as the most Machiavellian leader is one who publicly condemns Machiavelli while covertly using his strategies, the best use of flattery was to denounce it even while uttering it.

The Art That Conceals Flattery

When it comes to Renaissance courtier's manuals, Castiglione's *Il Cortegiano—The Courtier—*was the Bible of advice books, the indispensable text. The book, first printed in 1528, was one of the great publishing successes of the Renaissance. Within a few years of its publication in Italy, it was translated into Spanish, French, English, German, and Latin. It was reprinted more than any other secular work during the Renaissance.

For 150 years, it influenced courtly, diplomatic, and fashionable behavior throughout Europe. No one said, "According to Castiglione," but many surely thought it. In England, Cromwell read it, so did Richard Burton, Francis Bacon, and Sir Philip Sidney. Shakespeare certainly knew of it.

Il Cortegiano was essential reading for every Renaissance aristocrat. For them, though, it was preaching to the converted. But Castiglione's book had a second and more important audience. The book was published when lending libraries were being invented, and it was from these nascent institutions that the book was borrowed and devoured by merchants and lawyers, young men who were searching for a little extra polish. For these men, the book was not an ornament on a shelf, but the ultimate how-to guide. In the copies that still exist from those days, the sections on how to dance and how to ride are the ones most frequently underlined and annotated.

In a sense, though, Castiglione was writing a kind of autobiography, for he himself was the very model of the paragon he wrote about. The son of a noble family from Mantua, he was a diplomat, poet, scholar, and soldier, the archetype of *l'uomo universale,* the *Renaissance* man. Castiglione was a courtier all of his life. The princes he served were all absolute rulers. At an early age, he entered the service of the rulers of Mantua. He then served at Urbino for a dozen years, until he, along with his superiors, were driven from the city by the troops of Pope Leo X. The pope eventually awarded him the job of papal nuncio to Spain. It is said that the Emperor Charles I deemed Castiglione to be the perfect gentleman. Raphael's portrait of Castiglione, painted in 1516, shows a tall, elegant man who looks directly at the viewer. He is formal but not too stiff, self-conscious but not self-absorbed. He was, in fact, a dreadful snob.

Whereas Machiavelli was writing for the prince himself, or an aspiring one, Castiglione was speaking to those who served the prince. He did not presume to speak for the prince, or even to him. Castiglione is nowhere near as coldly pragmatic as his countrymen. He is a kind of idealistic pragmatist who often deceives himself. Even when he is being shrewdly pragmatic or opportunistic, he glazes it with a coating of idealism. The difficulty in reading Castiglione is that he is wise without being self-aware.

The book consists of a series of conversations over a number of nights by a group of aristocrats at a court. The talk is by turns entertaining and didactic, amusing and tiresome. For Castiglione, it is a kind of *how-to à clef,* in that each person was modeled after someone he knew. Each speaker provides a different aspect of Castiglione's worldview.

The courtier, he suggests, has one goal and one goal only: to please the prince. But Castiglione has a higher opinion of his perfect courtier than his imagined prince, and the job of the courtier is a subtle one. Yes, he must please the prince, but without debasing himself.

"I consider the dealings the courtier has with his prince are those which he should chiefly endeavor to make agreeable," Castiglione has his alter ego Federico say. The courtier, Federico continues, should "devote all his thought and strength to loving and almost adoring the prince he serves above all else, devoting all his ambitions, actions and behavior to pleasing him."

This description of the courtier's raison d'être provoked an acid response from Pietro da Napoli, one of the aristocrats at Castiglione's discussion. "We would find plenty of courtiers like this nowadays," he says, "for it seems to me that in a few words you have sketched for us a first-class flatterer."

Castiglione, in the voice of Federico, takes exception to this. "You are very much mistaken," he says. "For flatterers love neither their prince nor their friends, and I am saying that this is, above all, what I want our courtier to do; and he can obey and further the wishes of the one he serves without adulation, since I am referring to those wishes that are reasonable and right." Ah, well. For Castiglione, it is the courtier who must judge what is flattering versus what is simply reasonable and deserved praise. The prince can't be trusted to do so.

Federico/Castiglione goes on in his attempt to refute the charge that his courtier is a flatterer, but he unconsciously digs himself in deeper. The courtier, he says, should have "the discretion to discern what pleases his prince, and the wit and judgment to know how to act accordingly, and the considered resolve to make himself like what he may instinctively dislike. Prepared in this way, he will never appear before his prince in a bad humor, or in a melancholy mood. . . . Our courtier will avoid foolish arrogance; he will not be the bearer of bad news, he will not be careless in sometimes saying things that may give offense, instead of striving to please. . . . He will not be an idle or lying babbler, nor a stupid flatterer or boaster, but will be modest and reserved, observing always, and especially in public, the deference and respect which should mark the attitudes of a servant towards his master." Whew! Well, I'm glad we've got that straight. Castiglione seems to think that simply saying that his courtier is not a flatterer somehow makes it so.

The deference Castiglione is talking about is a kind of flattery, the flattery of the claque. If the courtier can never be in a bad mood around the prince, if he must humor the prince's every whim, if he must indulge the prince's every mood, that is a kind of strategic deference that is the moral equivalent of flattery. In fact, all Castiglione is really doing is making a distinction between classy courtiers and low-class toadies. "So it seems that these people are in error who condemn a ruler for keeping in his rooms persons of little worth except in the matter of knowing how to give good personal service, for I do not see why princes should not be free to relax just as we like to do." They can have toadies around them who reflexively praise everything, who assert that the prince's belches are more beautiful than the arias of opera singers. But the difference is really just style.

Renaissance Cool

When Castiglione condemns flattery, he does it in part on the grounds that it is a kind of affectation or ostentation. He recoils from anything of the kind. But in his advice to his ideal courtier, he is in effect saying, Flatter the prince, but do it with grace. Do it with a certain style, do it with *sprez-zatura*.

Sprezzatura is Castiglione's great invention. We often translate "sprez-zatura" as "nonchalance," but that is too circumscribed a definition. The courtier, Castiglione writes, must always display *sprezzatura,* which he describes as a kind of unstudied grace, a sophisticated naturalness, a mastery that seems unstudied. What we sometimes call "cool." "I have a universal rule which seems to apply more than any other in all human actions or words: namely, to steer away from affectation at all costs, as if it were a rough and dangerous reef, and (to use perhaps a novel word for it) to practice in all things a certain *sprezzatura* which conceals all artistry and makes whatever one says or does seem uncontrived and effortless. . . . So that we can truthfully say that true art is what does not seem to be art; and the most important thing is to conceal it."

Sprezzatura is making difficult things look easy. It is Astaire dancing with a broomstick. It is Joe Montana casually zipping a pass over the middle. It is Picasso dashing off a Minotaur sketch. All of these examples are of people, Castiglione writes, who "seem to be paying little, if any, attention to the way they speak or laugh or hold themselves, so that those who are watching them imagine that they couldn't and wouldn't ever know how to make a mistake." Yet, all of them, Castiglione would say, use art to conceal the hard work that makes it all look so easy. Noel Coward once said that Frank Sinatra never made an esthetic mistake, but that was due as much to incessant practice as a perfect ear. Fred Astaire wore down his partners with endless practice all in order to make it look like he did not practice at all. *Sprezzatura* was the master trope of the courtier.

Castiglione used another word for this idea as well, *disinvoltura,* which is a kind of Renaissance cool, a lordly and dispassionate indifference, a kind of paring one's fingernails as the world goes by. It's never letting them see you sweat. This is the *sprezzatura* of Humphrey Bogart's Mister Rick in *Casablanca.* But the modern celluloid model of these traits is James Bond, who seems to do everything better than everyone else, with barely a bead of perspiration.

Sprezzatura required a kind of subterfuge, for it is the masking of effort. The courtier must display *sprezzatura* about his own *sprezzatura.* It is a way of pretending that something which is hard and difficult is a breeze.

The courtier was the ultimate Renaissance man, the gentleman who can do many things beautifully but does not seem to practice any of them. He performs them all nonchalantly, saying afterwards, as modest old-time athletes used to do, "It was nothing." As Castiglione says, "Nor yet will I have him to be acknowne that he bestoweth much studie or time about it, although he doe it excellently well." Two Elizabethan courtiers, Leicester and Hatton, were vying for the queen's favor. Hatton was said to have pleased the queen by his artful dancing. Leicester then proposed to the queen to bring in a well-known professional dancer who was even better than Hatton. "Pish," said the queen. "I will not see your man—it is his *trade*."

Castiglione's notion is that the courtier must even display sprezzatura in his flattery of the prince. It must be flattery that conceals itself, that appears spontaneous rather than planned. It must never seem that flattery is the courtier's trade. When he tells the courtier to shun ostentation and avoid affectation, he is talking about language as well. Flattery is overembellished speech. It is affected. It is language that draws attention to itself. The opposite of sprezzatura is rhetorical foppery.

Only because Castiglione is so cool himself, does he underplay the fierce competition for favors which was the ever-present condition of courtiers. The courtiers knew they had to suck up to the prince, but the smart ones knew they had to cloak that sycophancy in a kind of artificial naturalness. The courtier is nothing other than a beautiful parasite. He is a man of beautiful stratagems. One of which is flattery accompanied by ironic reticence.

*   *   *

Flattery is always welcome in whatever form it takes. But certain forms are more flattering than others. "Everyone," Castiglione says, "no matter how evil, likes to be thought just, continent and good." It's a shrewd point, and the notion is similar to Casanova's credo: The idea is that the way to suck up to Stalin was to praise his mercifulness. A new corollary to the seducer's credo: Praise the despotic for their goodness, the ruthless for their kindness.

Castiglione makes an even subtler point about flattery: It doesn't matter if we know we are being flattered. He notes that the ancients wrote essays on how to tell a flatterer from a friend. But all for naught. "Even so," he says, "we may well ask what use is this, seeing that there are so many who realize perfectly well that they are listening to flattery, and yet love the flatterer and detest the one who tells them the truth.

Praise is so welcome, so pleasing, so gratifying that even if we suspect, even if we *know,* it is not genuine, we lap it up anyway, and feel darn-right chummy toward the person delivering it.

Castiglione's point is similar to George Bernard Shaw's point that "what really flatters a man is that you think him worth flattering." The idea is, flattery is very flattering. We see the machinery behind the stage, but that doesn't stop us from enjoying the play.

Castiglione says we are so greedy for praise that we do not care who gives it or what the nature of it is. It is all welcome. But at the same time, he is telling his courtier, neither a flatterer nor a flatteree be. At best, he says, the courtier should be as immune from flattery as it is humanly possible to be, yet at the same time he should be able to offer praise with so much grace that it does not seem like flattery. "Let us leave these blind fools to their errors and decide that our courtier should possess such good judgment that he will not be told that black is white or presume anything of himself unless he is certain that it is true."

He says the courtier must stop his ears to flattery, but the only detection device he proposes is good sense, even while he suggests that the power of flattery usually overwhelms good sense.

The only excuse for flattery that Castiglione makes is that the perfect courtier is flattering the prince to protect him from unscrupulous flatterers. Yes, he is doing something reprehensible but only to protect his prince from something even more reprehensible.

And from Castiglione's description, the prince truly needs such help. Castiglione says the problem with holding power is that no one ever speaks truth to it. "In this way," he says, speaking of those attending on power, "far from being friends, they become flatterers, and to benefit from their intimacy they always speak and act in order to gratify, and they mostly proceed by telling lies that foster ignorance in the prince's mind not only of the world around but of himself. And this can be said to be the greatest and most disastrous falsehood of all, for an ignorant mind deceives itself and lies to itself."

Castiglione's view of flattery, then, is not so different from Aristotle's view of rhetoric. Aristotle suggested that rhetoric was neither good nor bad in and of itself, but was a neutral tool that could be used for good or ill. Flattery, Castiglione suggests, is just such a tool. In fact, he uses it himself throughout *The Courtier* in his flattering depictions and references to contemporaries and in his fulsome dedication.

Castiglione's influence continued long after his time. After James Joyce finished reading it, his brother told him that he had become more polite but less sincere. But isn't that the point? Joyce replied.

Just How Machiavellian Was Machiavelli?

If the great sage of courtesy literature was Castiglione, his Italian precursor Niccolò Machiavelli was the hard-headed political consultant. Whereas Castiglione is writing for the courtier and teaching him how to deal with the prince, Machiavelli is writing for the prince and teaching him how to deal with the courtiers. He is the prototype of the modern political handler.

For Machiavelli, flattery is more a tactic than a strategy. The distinction is a military one: Strategy governs the large-scale plan of a campaign; tactics are the specific and individual techniques of battle. Flattery is just one weapon in the prince's arsenal, or, rather, one weapon in the enemy's arsenal. When it comes to manners, Machiavelli doesn't really give a hoot about which spoon you use and whether your love poetry is gallant or not. But all of these things are a means to an end, just as flattery is.

Machiavelli is more interested in guiding the prince in how to receive flattery than he is in counseling the courtier as to how to give it. He is not much concerned with how to deceive through flattery. The deception he is most concerned with is how to conceal one's weaknesses from those below.

When it comes to how the prince should use flattery, Machiavelli is kind of a softy. Machiavelli's advice for the prince as to how to win over those below him: Flatter them with your trust. Or as the Mafia dictum goes (perhaps they learned it from Machiavelli?), keep your friends close but your enemies closer. "Because men," Machiavelli writes, "when they receive good from him of whom they were expecting evil, are bound more closely to their benefactor." Enemies are suckers for flattery precisely because they don't expect it. "Men who at the commencement of a princedom have been hostile, if they are of a description to need assistance to support themselves, can always be gained over with the greatest of ease."

If the prince places his trust in a courtier, the courtier is honored and obligated to the prince. This is how the prince instills obligation. This has a wider application as well. Machiavelli says the prince should trust his subjects as a whole. For example, he counsels a new prince to arm his people "because by arming them, those arms become yours, those men who were distrusted become faithful, and those who were faithful are kept so."

So where is the malign Machiavelli of the popular imagination? In fact, Machiavelli is a closet moralist. All things being equal, he would prefer his prince to be moral, but if morality gets in the way of power, he must jettison it. He is a pragmatist above all, but a pragmatist who would rather achieve his ends through moral means. Wherever possible, he prefers virtue and self-interest to be congruent. It's just that when the two are in conflict, the prince must opt for power over virtue.

Machiavelli does not take flattery lightly as a threat to the prince, but his recommendations do not offer much of a practical defense against it. Machiavelli has an entire chapter in *The Prince* on resisting flattery, Number XXIII, "How Flatterers Should Be Avoided." Flattery, he says, is "a danger from which princes are with difficulty preserved, unless they are very careful and discriminating." The friend of flattery, he suggests, is self-complacency and its handmaiden self-delusion. If the prince is not vigilant against it, he will fall prey to it. The danger "is that of flatterers, of whom courts are full, because men are so self-complacent in their own affairs, and in a way so deceived in them, that they are preserved with difficulty from this pest."

What is Machiavelli's prescription? It is much the same as that of the ancient Greeks: candor. The prince, he says, must promote honesty. The astringence of the truth is the antidote to flattery. "Because there is no way of guarding oneself from flatterers except letting men understand that to tell you the truth does not offend you." How un-Machiavellian.

But Machiavelli's defense against flattery is easily penetrated. It is fine for a prince to say that he only wants to hear the truth. Many a prince has said that and many a prince has beheaded the messenger of an unwelcome truth. A more Machiavellian counselor will listen to the prince's demand for honesty and tell him frankly what a wise ruling he has just made. Let someone else tell the prince that he has made a mistake. Machiavelli does not really provide his prince with a defense against such a strategy. And if Machiavelli cannot think of a defense against flattery, it might well be history's greatest stealth weapon.

Machiavelli being a Machiavellian was himself adept at strategic flattery. His last chapter in *The Prince* offers a glimpse of his technique for ingratiating himself to Lorenzo the Magnificent. First, Machiavelli dedicates his book to him. But Machiavelli is too smart to flatter Lorenzo directly.

Machiavelli does not so much tell Lorenzo that he is the man of the hour (that's what a common flatterer would do), but that the hour demands a great man, and only Lorenzo can fill the vacuum. "Italy, left as without life, waits for him who shall yet heal her wounds," he writes. "It is seen how she entreats God to send someone who shall deliver her from these wrongs and barbarous insolencies. It is seen also that she is ready and willing to follow a banner if only someone will raise it."

In other words, Lorenzo, we are waiting for you. Even God himself, Machiavelli says (taking out the really big guns), is begging for a savior for Italy. Machiavelli then puts it on a platter for his patron. "Nor is there to be seen at present one in whom she can place more hope than in your illustrious house."

He is not so much flattering Lorenzo as tempting him to a course that Machiavelli would like him to take. He manipulates Lorenzo through flattering the young king's sense of himself. How Machiavellian.

Take off Your Face and Let Me See Your Mask

In his address to the reader at the opening of his *Essays,* Montaigne comes across like a tough gumshoe in a Raymond Chandler novel. "This, reader, is an honest book," he says tersely. Not only that, it is a book, he warns the reader, in which "I have had no thought of serving either you or my own glory." In other words, don't expect me to play up to you or to try to ingratiate myself with you. I'm not going to flatter you, so get used to it. Which, of course, is the most flattering promise of all.

Montaigne informs the reader not to expect much in the way of fancy prose, either. He tells the reader that he is coming before him naked and unadorned. And just to make sure the reader knows his place, Montaigne says, I'm not even writing this for you. I'm writing this for myself.

This of course is an elaborate pose. Montaigne says he disdains rhetoric, yet he has used a wonderful rhetorical device in order to condemn it. As part of Montaigne's case against rhetoric, he condemns flattery as the very opposite of plain speech. Flattery is adornment. Flattery is artifice. Flattery is unnatural because it exists not for itself but to achieve some desired end. It is a gilding of truth.

But Montaigne is very sly. He is in fact flattering the reader by telling him, I'm not flattering you. He is saying, I so trust your judgment, your decency, your perceptiveness, that I am not cloaking my prose in the usual adornments designed to trick the reader. Instead, I'm speaking to you straight. Just the facts, ma'am.

This strategy is Montaigne's version of parhesia, the candor of a friend speaking truth to a friend. And with that candor, he is attempting also to win the reader over. We like Montaigne in part because he tells us how much he trusts us and because he is so crankily self-revealing. Long before Holden Caulfield, he is the original hater of phonies.

In fact, Montaigne flatters himself for his honesty. Later, he even admits that he well knows that honesty is ingratiating. "I have an open way," he says, "that easily insinuates itself and gains credit on first acquaintance."

Montaigne is the apostle of moderation. Anything exaggerated offends him. So it makes sense that he would dislike flattery. For flattery was over the top, excessive, *im*moderate. It is language stretched too far. To him, the flatterer is the archer who overshoots his target.

Ultimately, Montaigne suggests that the reason flattery works is rather simple: All of us have an immense, gaping blind spot when it comes to our opinions about ourselves. We are self-interested and always err in favor of the self. He quotes Erasmus: "Every man likes the smell of his own dung." Or as Montaigne writes, "Praise is always pleasing from whoever and for whatever reason it may come."

For someone who implies that he is incapable of flattery, Montaigne is very shrewd about how to use it. The flatterer, he suggests, must know how far to go too far. He quotes Tacitus as saying, "Benefits are agreeable as long as they seem returnable; but if they go much beyond that, they are repaid with hatred instead of gratitude." The flatterer must carefully gauge the benefit he is conferring. Giving a man a painting is one thing; giving him an entire house to hang it in is another. Montaigne says: Be careful not to serve your master so well that he will not be able to find a fair reward for your service.

Even more important, he says, if you are seeking to ingratiate yourself, never, never, never remind the person of the good you have done for him. Instead, recall the good he has done for you. We like people for whom we do favors; we're a little uncomfortable with people who do *us* favors. No one likes to be reminded of the gifts he has received but rather of the gifts he has given.

Whereas the beauty of truth, Montaigne says, is that it has one face, flattery, like deceit, has a thousand masks. He cites the Pythagoreans, who he says determined that good was certain and finite while evil was uncertain and infinite. Flattery can take an infinite number of shapes. "The way of truth is one and simple; that of private profit and the advantage of one's personal business is double, uneven, and random." Ah, but that does not mean that untruth, or that flattery, does not work. Montaigne, after all, is a man of the world. "I do not want to deprive deceit of its proper place; that would be misunderstanding the world. I know that it has often served profitably and that it maintains and feeds most of men's occupations."

Montaigne can be more than a little sanctimonious, and when it comes to plain speech, he is also falsely modest. He says his own speech is "inept for public negotiations, as my language is in every way being too compact, disorderly, abrupt, individual." Here is self-praise masquerading as self-criticism. He then contrasts his own straightforwardness with the exaggerated speech of court.

At court, he says, there is "so abject and servile a prostitution of complimentary addresses: life, soul, devotion, adoration, serf, slave, all these works have such vulgar currency that when letter writers want to convey a more sincere and respectful feeling, they have no way left to express it." Even the currency of flattery has been corrupted by embellishment and rodomontade.

Montaigne pretends to chide himself for not being able or willing to indulge in a little ingratiation. "I mortally hate to seem a flatterer; and so I naturally drop into a dry, plain, blunt way of speaking, which, to anyone who does not know me otherwise, verges a little on the disdainful. I honor most those to whom I show the least honor." First and foremost in that category is the reader. He honors the reader by not pretending to honor him.

As much as he dislikes flattery, Montaigne makes an even greater show of his disdain for the hothouse world in which flattery flourishes. In part, he hates court because of its demanding rhetorical obligations. Courtly ritual is a kind of slavery, and one of its obligatory chores is to flatter the prince. Only at court, he suggests, can one meet men "uncivil by too much civility, and importunate in courtesy." At court, he suggests, there is a tyranny of courtesy, a slavish adherence to empty forms. At courts, everyone seeks the favor of the prince. And, Montaigne suggests, they do not care how they curry that favor. "There is nothing that poisons princes so much as flattery, and nothing by which the wicked more easily gain credit with them."

The difficulty of being a king or a prince, he suggests, is that one can never know if one is receiving true praise or real affection. "The honor we receive from those who fear us is not honor," he says. He quotes Seneca: "The greatest thing in rule is this, / That subjects are required not only to endure / But to applaud their master's deeds." Montaigne asks, What value is praise if your subjects are not allowed to dispraise you? A man may be genuinely praising the prince, but without the opportunity to do otherwise, the praise is meaningless.

Don't Flatter Yourself

It is fitting that Sir Francis Bacon, one of the towering intellects of the seventeenth century and the man who helped establish the inductive method in science, would take a more empirical approach to flattery. In this, he resembles Machiavelli more than Castiglione, and in fact, Machiavelli's own dispassionate view of things was a considerable influence on Bacon. Bacon considered Machiavelli's pragmatism to be rather scientific, and Bacon himself is a kind of seventeenth-century sociologist.

Bacon's essays, in their leisurely style and their down-home homilies, are an homage to Montaigne. But his advice and counsel is less self-reflective and more systematic than Montaigne's, which may explain why his essays, along with Castiglione's, were reprinted more than any other secular work of the Renaissance. Bacon's work is like one of those small point-of-purchase advice books at Barnes & Noble, the kind that offer useful tips without all the philosophizing. Bacon wasn't sweating the small stuff in the seventeenth century either.

Perhaps because of his own scientific instincts, Bacon lugs along none of the moral baggage about flattery that Montaigne or Castiglione carry. He is agnostic when it comes to the morality of flattery. He does not rail against it as either an insult to virtue or an affront to language. He just thinks you're plain dumb to be a victim of it. If a man allows a claque of followers to grow around him, Bacon says, he "maketh his train longer, but his wings shorter."

The problem, he says simply, is not the flatterer but our willingness to be flattered. We are all essentially defenseless when it comes to flattery. We are defenseless, he suggests, because we do not defend ourselves against it. "For there is no such flatterer as is a man's self," he writes.

Bacon has a gimlet eye when it comes to the efficacy of different types of flattery. He posits four categories of flatterer: the Ordinary Flatterer, the Cunning Flatterer, the Impudent Flatterer, and the Arch-Flatterer.

The Ordinary Flatterer is the one-size-fits-all flatterer. "He will have common attributes which may serve every man," says Bacon. He will use the same rather bland tributes to every person he meets. To every woman, he will say, "You are beautiful," and to every man, "You are wise." His flattery lacks specificity.

The Cunning Flatterer searches for what we like best about ourselves and then extols it. "Wherein a man thinketh best of himself," says Bacon, "therein the flatterer will uphold him most." If he divines that you pride yourself on being a particularly good judge of character, the cunning flatterer will say, "Ah, you are such an astute reader of personality."

The Impudent Flatterer reverses this. He finds the quality a man is most insecure about, and praises that to the skies. He will "look wherein a man is conscious to himself that he is most defective and is most out of countenance in himself," and then reassure him. This is liable to backfire, something Bacon does not reckon with.

The Arch-Flatterer is the Self which, as he already noted, makes all other flattery possible. Vanity is the root of all flattery.

Bacon also makes a distinction between benign flattery and malicious flattery. He writes that "some praises come of good wishes and respects, which is a form due in civility to kings and great persons." He quotes Pliny's phrase *"laudando praecipere"*—to teach by praising. This is benign praise and is positive, as long as it is not exaggerated and magnified. (Bacon says it is more seemly to praise a man's office or profession than to praise the man personally.) On the other hand, he notes, "some men are praised maliciously to their hurt, thereby to stir envy and jealously towards them." He cites Tacitus's observation *"pessimum genus inimicorum laudantium"*—that is, "the worst class of enemies are men who praise you."

Bacon ultimately uses a monetary metaphor for flattery. "But if a man mark it well, it is in praise and commendation of men as it is in gettings and gains: for the proverb is true, 'That light gains make heavy purses;' for light gains come thick, whereas great come but now and then. So it is true that small matters win great commendation, because they are continually in use and in note." Little bits of flattery work like compound interest.

*   *   *

Bacon is not egalitarian. He has very little faith in the wisdom of the common man. Praise from ordinary folk is usually false and worthless, he says, the lowest common denominator of flattery. "For the common people understand not many excellent virtues. The lowest virtues draw praise from them; the middle virtues work in them astonishment or admiration; but of highest virtues they have no sense or perceiving at all. 'Species virtutibus similes' [appearances resembling virtues], serve best with them." Because fame, he says, is adulation by the hoi polloi, he has no use for it. Fame, he says, is like a river that bears light and swollen things and drowns things that are weighty and solid.

Bacon is also psychologically shrewd about the form of flattery that we have come to see as indirect self-praise, or oblique flattery, that is, praising the good qualities in others as a way of catching some reflected glory. The idea, he says, is to praise those good qualities in others that are conspicuous in one's self. He is not the first to talk about this—the Romans were there before him—but he explains it in an empirical way that others don't. He says it reflects well on you when you praise both a superior and an inferior for qualities which you have. The superior sees you as a kindred spirit and the inferior looks up to you as a model.

He seems to have realized this rather belatedly and awkwardly when he first published the *Essays*. While his final edition in 1614 was dedicated to George, duke of Buckingham, the second-most powerful man in England after the king, his 1612 edition was dedicated to his brother Anthony. He had originally intended to dedicate the first edition to Henry, Prince of Wales, but abandoned the idea when the prince died shortly before he finished the book. Nine days after the book was published, Anthony, Bacon's brother, wrote to Robert, the earl of Essex, an important figure at court. The letter had Bacon's approval.

> I am bold and yet out of a most entire and dutiful love wherein my german brother [Francis] and myself stand infinitely bound unto your Lordship, to present unto you the first sight and taste of such fruit as my brother was constrained to gather, as he professeth himself, before they were ripe, to prevent staling; and withal most humbly to beseech your Lordship, that as my brother in token of a mutual firm brotherly affection hath bestowed by dedication the property of them upon myself, so your Lordship, to whose disposition and commandment I have entirely and inviolably vowed my poor self, and whatever appertained unto me, either in possession or right,—that your Lordship, I say, in your noble and singular kindness towards us both, will vouchsafe first to give me leave to transfer my interest unto your Lordship, then humbly to crave your honourable acceptance and most worthy protection.

Either Anthony told his brother, "Hey, you're crazy to dedicate the book to me. I love you already, you're wasting a very big chit." Or Bacon realized it himself, but in either case, Bacon must have come to the conclusion that he was better trying to flatter someone who could help him. And the earl allowed himself to be flattered with the dedication.

Dear Boy

Lord Chesterfield—Philip Dormer Stanhope, the fourth earl of Chesterfield, the grandson of the Marquis of Halifax, the lord-lieutenant of Ireland

and secretary of state of England—is a writer who is remembered these days, when he is remembered at all, for something he forgot to do.

In 1747, Samuel Johnson had an audience with Chesterfield in order to enlist him as a patron for his dictionary. It was natural for Johnson to seek him out, since Chesterfield was known as a benefactor of writers. Johnson handed Chesterfield his plan for the dictionary; Chesterfield handed Johnson £10 and promptly forgot about the entire endeavor. When Johnson finally published his great work seven years later, after herculean labors and years of poverty, Chesterfield belatedly offered assistance, wrote two articles praising the dictionary, and requested a meeting with Johnson. Johnson rebuffed Chesterfield, disdained the praise as hollow, and wrote an acid letter to Chesterfield in which he famously defined the word "patron" as someone who "looks with unconcern on a man struggling in the water for life and, when he has reached ground, encumbers him with help."

Chesterfield's role as a footnote in literary history is unfortunate, for he is one of the great masters of English prose and a sage observer of human folly. His own sense of humor and self-confidence were robust enough that he conspicuously displayed Johnson's letter on a table for the admiration of his visitors, much the way journalists today post particularly nasty letters from readers on their office doors for general delectation.

Lord Chesterfield's *Letters to His Son,* first published in 1774, is one of the great works of Renaissance courtesy literature. The *Letters* consist of nearly three decades of fatherly advice to his only son, who was the product of a liaison with a French governess when Chesterfield was ambassador to The Hague. Philip Stanhope was, as George II put it when Chesterfield petitioned the king for a place for his son, a "bastard." For Chesterfield, however, Stanhope was his legitimate and loved offspring, and he never thought his son's irregular birth should be a liability to the boy's success. In this, and in this only, Chesterfield seems a trifle naive.

Chesterfield started writing letters to his son—"Dear Boy" is the way they are addressed—when Philip was seven. The letters began after a visit from his father, when young Philip expressed an interest in Chesterfield's writing to him. "If that be the case," Chesterfield promptly wrote, "you shall hear from me often enough; and my letters may be of use, if you give attention to them." So began nearly thirty years of epistolary advice, scolding, storytelling, and affection that did not stop until his Dear Boy died unexpectedly at the age of thirty-six.

In the letters, Chesterfield emerges as a charming drawing room Machiavelli who is enormously entertaining and impossible not to like. Whereas the Italian philosopher was a large-scale strategist, Chesterfield is more of a small-bore tactician. If you are going for a job interview, read Chesterfield. If you are negotiating with the Russians, read Machiavelli.

There were those, however, in the eighteenth century who found Chesterfield less than endearing. Some disparaged him as a foppish Francophile who had the impertinence to praise Voltaire over Shakespeare at a time when England and France had been at war for two decades. In some quarters, Chesterfield was regarded as a Continental subversive, a cultural apostate who recommended the sorts of values—self-interest before morality, adultery over marriage, and breeding above all else—that would undermine merrie olde Englande.

Although he was entitled by birth to be at the very center of English life, Chesterfield was something of a rebel by disposition. He spent two-thirds of his political life in opposition, and when he was secretary of state, it was said he stayed in the job for only a year because he couldn't put up with duplicity and wouldn't flatter the king enough.

After the *Letters* were first published in 1774, eleven editions appeared by 1800. By the turn of the century, they had also been translated into French, German, and Dutch. This was also the era of library societies, as they were known, and Chesterfield's *Letters* regularly crops up among the ten most popular books during the 1770s. As with Castiglione, ordinary folk read Chesterfield as a guide both to manners and the hidden world of aristocratic life.

*   *   *

One of the very first things that Chesterfield tells young Stanhope is that "decency" is all-important. But not, Dear Boy, in quite the way one might imagine. Decency is all well and good, Chesterfield says, but one of the reasons that you embrace it is "to gain the approbation of mankind." So begins one of the great themes of Chesterfield's worldly advice: that it is good to do good, not only because it is the right thing to do, but because it will win you esteem in the world's eyes. Yes, do the right thing for the right reasons, he counsels, but also because it will make people like you.

Being admired by society is one of the great objects of life, Chesterfield says, and he does his best to tutor his son as to how to achieve such regard. Conquer through kindness, he says, but also through what the French call being *aimable,* that *je ne sais quoi* quality that people like. This is what Chesterfield calls, over and over again, "the Art of Pleasing." The Art of Pleasing, he tells his son, "is a very necessary one to possess; but a very difficult one to acquire."

The Art of Pleasing, he says, consists in part of "a genteel easy manner" which "prepossesses people in your favour, bends them towards you, and makes them wish to be like you." Reserve, he says, is an absolutely essential component, but it must be a *pleasing reserve,* an amiable outward reserve that camouflages a real inner reserve. "Have a real reserve with almost everybody," he writes, "and have a seeming reserve with almost nobody; for it is very disagreeable to seem reserved and very dangerous not to be so."

But most of all, the single most reliable means of personal ingratiation is summarized by Chesterfield's golden rule: "Do as you would be done by is the surest method that I know of pleasing." This is the reciprocal altruism of pleasing: Praise others in the way that you surely would like to be praised. And you probably will be.

But how, exactly, do you *do as you would be done by?*

First, he says, *pay attention.* And by that he means focus intently on the person you are trying to please. Nothing is more ingratiating, he says, than benign attention. In other words, listen and look at the person you are trying to please the way Nancy Reagan looked at and listened to Ronnie. People like it when you hang on every word they say as if each one was a great pearl of wisdom that has astonishingly dropped into your lap.

Sometimes it sounds as though Chesterfield is describing the job of a concierge at a Four Seasons Hotel rather than that of a Renaissance courtier. "Observe the little habits, the likings, the antipathies, and the tastes of those whom you would like to gain; and then take care to provide them with the one, and to secure for them the other. . . . Such attention to such trifles flatters self-love much more than greater things, as it makes people think themselves almost the only objects of your thoughts and care."

Chesterfield's most explicit strategy of flattery is not unlike Francis Bacon's. It is to focus on a person's particular strength—or his particular weakness. "If you want to gain the affection and friendship of particular people, whether men or women, endeavor to find their predominant excellency, if they have one, and their prevailing weakness, which everybody has; and do justice to the one and something more than justice to the other. . . . Men have various objects in which they may excel, or at least would be thought to excel; and, though they love to hear justice done to them, where they know they excel, yet they are most and best flattered upon those points where they wish to excel, and yet are doubtful whether they do or not."

Chesterfield provides an excellent example of this. "Cardinal Richelieu, who was undoubtedly the ablest statesman of his time, or perhaps of any other, had the idle vanity of being thought the best poet too: he envied the great Corneille his reputation. . . . Those, therefore, who flattered skilfully, said little to him of abilities in state affairs, or at least but *en passant,* and as it might naturally occur. But the incense which they gave him, the smoke of which they knew would turn his head in their favour, was as a *bel esprit,* and a poet. Why? Because he was sure of one excellency, and distrustful as to the other." Thus, here is the rule: To flatter Tony Bennett, don't tell him what a great crooner he is but what a fine painter. To ingratiate yourself with Michael Jordan, don't tell him what a great jump shot he had, but that he was greatly underrated as a baseball player.

All of this advice, Chesterfield hastens to point out, applies to men only. For women, there is but one rule: Flatter them as much as possible whenever possible in any way possible. Chesterfield does not have a very exalted opinion of what he would most definitely call the weaker sex. "No flattery is either too high or too low for them. They will greedily swallow the highest, and gratefully accept the lowest; and you may safely flatter any woman, from her understanding down to the exquisite taste of her fan." You can't miss, he says.

Flattering a woman's appearance is pretty surefire. "Women have, in general, but one object, which is their beauty; upon which scarce any flattery is too gross for them to swallow. Nature has hardly formed a woman ugly enough to be insensible to flattery upon her person." But don't let lack of a pretty face throw you. "If her face is so shocking, then she must in some degree be conscious of it, her figure and air, she trusts, make ample amends for it. If her figure is deformed, her face, she thinks, counterbalances it. If they are both bad, she comforts hereself that she has graces; a certain manner; a je ne sais quoi, still more engaging than beauty."

He then offers his variation on the seducer's credo. A truly beautiful woman, he says, must be flattered upon her *understanding*. "Women who are either indisputably beautiful, or indisputably ugly, are best flattered upon the score of their understanding; but those who are in a state of medi-ocrity, are best flattered upon their beauty, or at least their graces; for every woman, who is not absolutely ugly, thinks herself handsome . . . whereas a decided and conscious beauty looks upon every tribute paid to her beauty as only her due; but wants to shine, and to be considered on the side of her understanding."

Women's opinions are of great value, Chesterfield tells his son, but not for the reason you might think. At court, Chesterfield says, it is women who are often the arbiters of men's characters. This is a job, he says, for which they have no aptitude, but no matter. "They have, from the weakness of men, more or less influence in all courts; they absolutely stamp every man's character in the beau monde."

*   *   *

When it comes to courts, Chesterfield is a contrarian. "It is a trite, com-monplace observation," he writes his son, "that courts are the seats of falsehood and dissimulation. But that, like many, I might say most com-monplace observations, is false. Falsehood and dissumulation are cer-tainly to be found at courts; but where are they not to be found? Cottages have them, as well as courts; only with worse manners." Courts, he main-tains, do not have a corner on the market of perfidy; it is simply that the court is the cynosure of society. If there is a real myth, he says, it is of rural innocence. At least court toadies have some style and charm.

Courts, for better or for worse, he says, are the finishing schools of society. Courts, he writes, "will gradually smooth you up to the highest polish. In courts, a versatility of genius and a softness of manner, are absolutely necessary; which some people mistake for abject flattery." Courts are the crucible of charm.

Flattery at court must never be indiscriminate. The players are too subtle. At courts, you find the Dream Team of flatterers. Here, for example, is Chesterfield's advice on how to talk to the king. "Were you to converse with a King, you ought to be as easy and unembarrassed as with your valet-de-chambre; but yet every look, word, and action, should imply the utmost respect." Never appear nervous. "Whatever one ought to do, is to be done with ease and unconcern." You must display sprezzatura even when, and especially when, you are flattering someone above you. The perfect courtier will always "join perfect inward ease with perfect outward respect."

Chesterfield cautions his son against what he essentially defines as the antiflattery: contempt. Even if you do not flatter people, he suggests, never ever treat them with contempt. Contempt disposes people against you forever. "There is nothing that people bear more impatiently, or forgive less, than contempt; an injury is much sooner forgotten than insult."

An insult is the polar opposite of a compliment. But even more than a compliment, an insult is an electronic bug that lodges forever in your hard drive. We sometimes forget the nice things people say about us; we rarely forget the negative things. Contempt constitutes the opposite of how he defines flattery. It is exactly how you would not want to be done by.

But for Chesterfield the reason to shun contempt is practical, just like the reason to flatter. The reason you never treat anyone with contempt is because you never know when such behavior will come back to haunt you. "Be convinced, that there are no persons so insignificant and inconsiderable, but may, some time or other, have it in their power to be of use to you, which they certainly will not, if you have once shown them contempt."

Just as anyone may help you, anyone may hurt you. The servant who handed you your coat whom you did not bother to thank may be the same man who could tell you that your enemy's cloak contains a dagger. The courtier offends no one, for anyone can help him rise and anyone can assure his fall. Do not—especially do not—show contempt to fools. You may be inclined to do so—who isn't?—but the reason they are fools is in part that you never know what a fool might do. "Abhor a knave, and pity a fool in your heart; but let neither of them unnecessarily see that you do so. Some complaisance and attention to fools is prudent." Yes, suffer some fools, if not gladly, at least with stoicism, because a fool can wound you as well as help you. Flatter fools by not abjuring them. "Their enmity," Chesterfield says, "is the next dangerous thing to their friendship."

*   *   *

The reason flattery works, according to Chesterfield, is simple: bottomless human vanity. "This principle of vanity and pride is so strong in human nature, that it descends even to the lowest objects; and one often sees people angling for praise."

Chesterfield offers the chicken soup defense of flattery: in other words, it can't hurt. To Chesterfield, flattery is a victimless crime. In fact, it is a form of generosity.

"Do not mistake me," he writes his son, "and think that I mean to recommend to you abject and criminal flattery: no; flatter nobody's vices or crimes: on the contrary, abhor and discourage them. But there is no living in the world without a complaisant indulgence for people's weaknesses, and innocent, though ridiculous vanities. If a man has mind to be thought wiser, and a woman handsomer, than they really are, their error is a comfortable one to themselves, and an innocent one with regard to other people; and I would rather make them my friends, by indulging them in it, than my enemies by endeavouring (and that to no purpose) to undeceive them."

A complaisant indulgence for people's weaknesses. Is there a better recipe for a civil society than that? It is a definition of a form of flattery that is a kind of worldly generosity. He is not saying we should indulge a madman's dangerous delusions or a tyrant's cruel hypocrisies, he is simply saying that we should not disabuse people of their small vanities. Does a woman think she sings rather well but is in fact tone deaf? Don't bother undeceiving her. Does a man think that we don't notice his toupé? Why tell him?

*   *   *

Stanhope was not his father's son, except in one ironic respect. Whereas Chesterfield was tall, graceful, and articulate, Stanhope was stocky, clumsy, and tongue-tied. When Stanhope, with his father's help, managed to make it into Parliament, he froze during his maiden speech, and then never rose to speak again.

Ever since Stanhope had reached his teens, his father had been writing to him that it was wiser to marry for wealth rather than for love. A man who marries for money, his father told him, has few happy days but no uneasy ones. A man who marries for love has some happy days and many uneasy ones.

But Stanhope followed his father's example, not his advice. It was only when Stanhope died after a brief illness at the age of thirty-six that Chesterfield discovered that his son had secretly married a French governess nine years before and fathered two sons. At the age of seventy-four, shortly after Stanhope's death, Chesterfield visited his daughter-in-law and his two grandsons on the Continent. The boys were eight and six and he immediately informed their mother that he would pay for their education. When he returned to England, he wrote them an affectionate letter ("Dear Boys") full of advice on how to please, a habit he continued until his own death five years later. Courtier to the end, pleasing even in the face of death, with his last words Chesterfield offered a chair to an old friend at his bedside.

*   *   *

Because Renaissance courts were a clear hierarchy, the purpose of flattery was also clear: to raise the perception of one's worthiness. This is what we find so annoying about flattery. It is a technique that helps people get what they don't deserve. Why is that witless, talentless courtier advising the king? How did this mediocre lickspittle get to be my boss? It just doesn't seem fair.

The nature of flattery itself began to change during the Renaissance. Flattery had always been rather generic. But as the idea of individualism flowered, flattery itself became more individual. Castiglione, Machiavelli,

Bacon, and Chesterfield all urged that praise be tailored to the person. They understood that we like our flattery to be monogrammed.

This lesson was not lost on the readers of these courtesy books. After reading Castiglione, ambitious young men took dancing lessons, but they also learned how to be ingratiating. These books taught the common man how to praise uncommonly.

Chapter 7

American
Transparency

No Room for Flattery

The American Adam was a divided fellow.

He had a heart that yearned for piety, but a head that was made for business. He had escaped the Old World but was not yet reconciled to the New. He was filled with the doctrine of original sin, but he was hell-bent on making something of himself. He embraced the plain style but liked to put on a fancy coat every once in a while. He stood up for the straight truth but often spoke out of both sides of his mouth. He knew that grace came from God and God only but that he could not be a slacker about it. He believed in free will but knew that God had divinely ordained everything. He was modern and medieval at the same time.

He was a mass of opposites.

He was composed of contradictions.

He was an American.

When European settlers came to America, they pushed the Indians into oblivion and Europe into the past. The world they had come from was now at the margin of modernity. For them, history was just beginning. America was not the end product of a long historical process, it was something new. The American Adam sought to liberate himself from the dead hand of the past, and to establish what Emerson called "an original relation to the universe." Westward the course of empire makes its way, said Bishop Berkeley famously, swiveling the compass of the contemporary 180 degrees. These settlers were the thin end of the wedge of modernism.

In Europe, one's identity had been inherited; in the New World, one's identity had to be invented. Henry James's name for his American Everyman was Christopher Newman. The early settlers were new men, but they carried a lot of Old World baggage like racism and a sense of entitlement. They identified with the ancient Hebrews and saw themselves as the new Chosen People in a New Canaan. They knew themselves as chosen in another way as well; they felt economically blessed. As Henry Adams said of the early settler, every stroke of the ax made him a capitalist and turned his children into gentlemen. In the Old World, every man was someone's son. In the New World, every man would be someone's father.

*   *   *

In America, Emerson said, "the only sin is limitation." Old World flattery thrived on limits; it was born of constraint and would die of freedom. "Let those flatter, who fear," Jefferson wrote, "it is not an American art." But in America, freedom and equality of opportunity gave birth to a new type of flattery: flattery of the self. This was not the hierarchical flattery of the Old World—it was lateral; it was each to each. In America, success was the empirical evidence of merit; nothing flattered like success.

Flattery in America was seen as unmanly. Truth was straight and hard and masculine, and anything that departed from it, like flattery, was regarded as effeminate. The act of flattering someone put you in an inferior position. There was a kind of masculine aversion to flattery in America. You can't flatter the Marlboro Man, and he won't flatter you. D. H. Lawrence's summary of the Hemingway protagonist conveys this same idea: "He doesn't love anybody, and it nauseates him to pretend he does."

Americans had what the writer Margaret Fuller called a "love of utility." In America, flattery was not about charm or romance, it was a tool. Not that it didn't have a similar function in the Old World, it's just that Americans were explicit about it. It was the apparatus of ingratiation. It wasn't something mysterious as it had been in the Old World; it was a way to get ahead, to make a deal, to get the corner office.

In a modern democracy, flattery had to become both more general and more specific at the same time. General in the sense that everyone was presumed equal; specific in the sense that everyone was now an individual. The American coat of flattery was made-to-measure *and* off-the-rack.

*   *   *

The Puritans who came to New England were of two minds. Here is what they knew: that man had been born in terrible sin, and only grace, which they could not earn and which God dispensed with no evident pattern or logic, could redeem them from eternal damnation. They knew they had to create a civilization out of what they saw as a primitive, untamed Eden. They soon learned they were good at it, and could turn a profit to boot. They may have believed in predestination, but they also believed they held their destiny in their own hands.

Their religion was unsparing. The old Church of England had promised salvation to everyone who received the sacraments. But that was far too easy for the Puritans. Only what they called "conversion," a transformation of the soul wrought by God, could save your sinful self. But grace was neither inherited nor earned. It was not a reward for human righteousness or achievement. There was not a whole lot you could do, but that didn't stop them from doing a whole lot. They were industrious and prized industry for its own sake. At the very least, work was good for the soul, even if it didn't save it.

Their ideology was absolutist. Thomas Hooker argued that you should not praise something merely because it was better than the ordinary. What is the point of praising some particular cloth, he said, just because it was less coarse than a rug? "Will not comparison make those things that are naughty in themselves seeme goode?" wrote Hooker. "Let that alone be held for goode, that is goode in it selfe, whose goodness is to be found in the nature of the thing." All comparisons, and therefore all praise, were odious.

In a predetermined world, there was not much room for anything that might alter your destiny, much less something as trivial as flattery. If you believe in a wintry and unpredictable God who has decreed everyone's divine destiny from the beginning of time, what is left for poor human flattery then? What good could a few smarmy compliments do you? Flattery is in part about manipulating your deserts, but if your cosmic destiny was already settled eons ago, what was the point? If you were saved, who needed flattery, and if you were damned, what did it matter?

The idea was, God could not be flattered.

What was the Reformation all about but a revolt against a kind of flattery? To Luther's way of thinking, papal indulgences were a sort of cosmic flattery. They were an attempted manipulation of one's divine destiny, in short, a bribe, and Luther said, the buck stops here. Flattery was a way of "earning" a kind of grace, and the Puritans knew that grace could not be earned.

Like the good, plain Protestants they were, the Puritans distrusted the fancy embellishments of the Old World Anglican Church, the red-robed bishops and the snowy surplices. What was flattery, really, but a fancy red robe, a shiny surplice over God's honest truth? The Puritans distrusted the flowing rhetoric of the Anglican ministers, their musical voices and fine phrases. Wasn't flattery fine phrases and insincere speech? The Puritans believed that the rich ceremonies and ornaments of the Anglican Church might cause men to mistake esthetic pleasure for divine grace. Beauty, like flattery, can charm men's souls. The Anglicans even put cushions on their seats.

The Puritan style was straight, severe, and unadorned. Its only ornament was plainness, the clean-swept floor, the empty whitewashed walls. Decoration was decadent. They worshiped in simple, spare foursquare timbered churches, with hard, uncomfortable pews. Their translations of religious works from Latin and Hebrew were deliberately flat-footed and clunky. They disdained "fancy, fawning words, and vainly-garnish'd expressions," as one preacher put it. They revolted against the confectionery style of Anglican preachers who sugar-coated unpleasant doctrine. Obscure phrases and exotic words seemed immoral, like painted marble. "God's altar needs not our pollishings," read *The Bay Psalm Book*. Flattery was the polish.

From the beginning, there was a kind of transparency to American life. Nothing was hidden. Plain speech was transparent speech. New England was a region of windows without curtains. The young American girl in Henry James's novel *The Europeans* is amazed when her visiting French aunt uses a shawl to put up makeshift curtains in her room. "What is life after all without curtains?" the young girl says to herself.

But the American Adam wasn't interested in curtains. He was a natural man who spoke the naked truth. Flattery curtained off the truth.

Work Is Good for the Soul and the Pocketbook

The Puritans were prototypical Americans in another way: They evolved into devout capitalists. They were, as Andrew Delbanco notes, both "ambitious and deeply suspicious of ambition." They were taught to strive for a certain "deadness of heart" toward the things of the world, but the world made them feel alive. Their religion was nonmaterialistic and otherworldly, but they took a deep satisfaction in worldly things. In fact, possessing worldly things suggested to them that they were destined for higher things. Accumulating capital, as Max Weber said, was regarded as a sign of God's grace. Prosperity equaled predestination.

Yes, there were the cold, hectoring ministers, but there were also lawyers, merchants, tradesmen, farmers, shopkeepers. Yes, the Puritans wanted their newfound land to be a city on a hill, in John Winthrop's famous image (which he poached from Matthew), but in that same speech Winthrop talked more about the New World being a place for successful plantations than about it being a moral beacon. He could have been talking about building condominiums on the hill where the views would be better.

Cotton Mather, the New England divine, suggested that every Christian had two callings, to serve the Lord and to be useful. The Puritans had it both ways. "How can you ordinarily enjoy any rest at night if you have not been well at work in the day?" Mather preached. "Let your business engross most of your time." Mather combs the Bible for anything smacking of get-rich-through-spirituality. He cites Deuteronomy, "Thou shalt remember the Lord thy God for 'tis he that gives the power to get wealth." The Lord as venture capitalist.

Historians note the bubbling up of a new sense of self in the New World that did not exist in the Old. There was an expanding sense of privacy, a loosening of class boundaries and a lessening of social deference. This all coincided with the rise of a market-oriented culture that saw a shift from a more closed religious society to a more open and diffuse capitalist one. By the end of the eighteenth century, the apex of society was populated not by aristocrats of inherited wealth but rich merchants and planters who acquired their money the *new*-fashioned way; they earned it. In America, if it wasn't for the *nouveaux riches,* there'd be no *riches* at all.

A staple of Puritan discourse was that men were to love the world with "weaned affection." The preachers told them that they were to be in the world but not of it. But the world beckoned. They became the original models of the American success story, and they soon learned, as generations of industrialists would after them, that nothing succeeds like success. They had an exaggerated sense of their centrality to history, and you can almost imagine them waving their fingers after a successful skirmish with the Indians and chanting, "We're number one!"

For all the mythology around the holiday of Thanksgiving, the Puritans weren't the most sharing of folks. As one English writer said, "A Puritan is such a one as loves God with all his soul, but hates his neighbor with all his heart." The historian Perry Miller deemed them "ambidextrous theologians." They did what was convenient and then rationalized it afterward.

For all the talk of predestination, most Puritan preachers believed salvation required a lot of work. Whereas the Calvinist tradition was to be rather passive in the reception of grace, the Puritan tradition was to work like a demon for it, all the while saying that good works and industriousness didn't count for much. Grace wasn't a free lunch. You couldn't ingratiate your way into heaven. God helps those who help themselves, said *Poor Richard's Almanack*. You had to put in the overtime.

They were strivers. They were upwardly mobile spritually and economically. John Winthrop was the distant precursor to the 1960s figure of the Reverend Ike, who wore sequins and preached that God liked those who helped themselves to the world's riches. In the Old World, being busy was a pain; in the New World, being busy was a virtue. There wasn't time for flattery.

As the Puritan gave way to the calculating Yankee, old-fashioned Protestantism gave way to the hard-work-and-success mode of the Protestant ethic. Puritanism went from a religion of acceptance before a distant and aloof God to a theology of ambitious individuals striving under the gaze of a proud father. They shifted from a religion of grace, as Delbanco writes, to a culture of discipline. And their ethics switched from the absolute to the situational.

Founding Flattery

Even today, two centuries after the Revolutionary War separated America from England, there are those who think of America as a cultural stepchild of England and Europe. These are the Anglophiles and Europhiles who, like so many eighteenth- and nineteenth-century visitors to America, consider the United States a rude, gauche place, a land, as Matthew Arnold wrote, that lacked "interest," a country that has achieved much but somehow managed to elude civilization. In 1791, Chateaubriand visited America and pronounced it a place with no activities but the practical, no values but the utilitarian, and no dreams but the mercenary.

Americans, for a very long time, were insecure about not only their achievements but their social graces. Emerson said that he felt like an "invalid" when he first visited Europe. That insecurity went much further back than Emerson, however. While the Founding Fathers were confident about the necessity of revolution, they were unsure of the etiquette of it. One of the first matters taken up by the new Congress was how the new president, George Washington, should be addressed. The Senate wanted to call him "His Highness, the President of the United States and Protector of the Rights of the Same." Others preferred "His Excellency." But Washington eschewed flattery and elected to be called plain old Mr. President, a republican title if there ever was one.

Washington knew that a revolutionary should throw off all the embellishments of Old World monarchy. Except one, manners. Throughout his life, Washington was known for his punctilious manners. And like the good American that he was, it was something he taught himself. American manners were learned from books, not courts. As a teenaged boy in Virginia, young George Washington painstakingly copied out 110 rules of etiquette from a translation of a book entitled *The Rules of Civility and Decent Behavior in Company and Conversation*. It was a primer that had been compiled by French Jesuits in the seventeenth century. Washington kept his handwritten copy of the *Rules of Civility* his whole life.

Americans of the eighteenth century were gluttons for advice and etiquette books. Washington was one of nature's aristocrats, but he wanted to learn how to be perceived as a man of the world. (As an acquaintance wrote in 1775, "There is not a king in Europe that would not look like a *valet de chambre* by his side.") But the young Washington wasn't interested in Machiavelli or Castiglione or even Lord Chesterfield. He was looking for something more practical, more useful, more utilitarian, more *American*. He didn't need or want a lot of philosophizing with his rules. He just wanted to know which was the dessert fork and whether to first turn to his left or his right for polite conversation during dinner.

Of the 110 rules he copied down, number 2 was, "When in company, put not your hands to any part of the body not usually discovered." So far so good. Number 7 is also of the what-I-should-have-learned-in-kindergarten variety: "Put not off your clothes in the presence of others." Number 12 is good advice for a future politician: "Bedew no man's face with your spittle by approaching too near him when you speak." And for those rubber chicken dinners on the election circuit, there is number 85: "Cleanse not your teeth with the table cloth, fork, or knife."

Washington never wanted anyone to outdo him in courtesy. Not for him Ben Franklin's radical informality. A Virginia colonel complained that at his morning levees the general's bows were more stiff and distant than George III's. As the French aristocrat, Barbé-Marbois, wrote of Washington, "I have never seen anyone who was more naturally and spontaneously polite." There is a story about a European visitor upbraiding General Washington for bowing to a slave. "Would you have him outdo me in courtesy?" Washington is said to have replied.

Not all the precepts in *The Rules of Civility* are rudimentary; some of them speak to Washington's more sophisticated and calculated civility. Rule number 1, for example, is a principle that Washington followed his whole life: "Every action done in company ought to be done with some sign of respect to those that are present." Washington unfailingly observed this, from the regard with which he treated common soldiers to his insisting to then vice president Thomas Jefferson that Jefferson leave the podium before Washington at the inauguration of John Adams. I'm just a semiretired gentleman farmer, he pointed out; you are the vice president of the United States.

When it came to flattery, the rules of civility were admirably direct. Number 17: *"Be no flatterer."* Fine, but take number 25: "Superfluous compliments and all affectation of ceremony are to be avoided, yet where due they are not to be neglected." That is Washington down to the waistcoat. He is the perfect republican aristocrat, a man who abjures ceremony when he can but follows it when he must. It was affectation that Americans disliked. Whatever you do, don't put on airs. Ceremony purely for ceremony's sake rubbed the democratic skin the wrong way. But the book's rule, as well as Washington's—and this is appropriate for a man who became the eighteenth century's Cincinnatus—was: When in Rome, do as the Romans do. Rule 42: "In a manner of saluting and resaluting, in a word, keep to the most usual custom."

Like the eminently practical man he was, Washington was not one to renounce flattery where it could help him. In 1757, when he was a colonel in the Viriginia militia and was eager to make his way up the military ladder, he wrote to the British commander-in-chief in North America: "Do not think, My Lord, that I am going to flatter; notwithstanding I have exalted sentiments of your Lordship's character and respect your rank, it is not my intention to adulate. My nature is open and honest and free from guile!" George got the promotion.

It is hard to know Washington's own response to being flattered. He seemed to take it with glacial modesty. He rarely revealed whether or not he was pleased. (He was never "visibly" pleased, as modern newspapers always put it.) He was premodern in the sense that he did not smile either in public or for his portraits. (And it was not just because George didn't want to show his dentures.) A smile meant you were not serious. When neurologist Oliver Sacks played a videotape of Ronald Reagan with the sound off for a group of autistic patients who had never seen him before, they thought he was a comedian.

But Washington took his mask very seriously. His face was as stony as his statues. When the wife of the British ambassador told Washington that she could read in his face how much he looked forward to retirement, he replied, "You are wrong, Madam. My countenance never yet betrayed my feeling." This was an exaggeration; many a lieutenant was chilled by seeing anger flash across his face. But if you flattered him successfully, you would not see his pleasure in his countenance. "He possessed the gift of silence," John Adams once said. Rage was fine, smiling was uncivilized.

The Rules of Civility counseled humility, even a feigned humility that would be a kind of social lubricant. False modesty is a type of flattery. It is a way of saying, No, I am unworthy, it is you who are more deserving. Washington was not a modest man, but he well knew that a public figure must seem so. In 1775, when Washington was chosen as commander-in-chief by the Continental Congress, he wrote to them, "I do not think myself equal to the command I am honored with." When he was elected to preside over the Constitutional Convention, he wrote that he "lamented his want of better qualification." And in his first inaugural address of 1789, he confessed that he was himself "peculiarly conscious of my own deficiencies." But there was never a time when Washington did not know that he was his country's indispensable man. He simply knew that he must not seem like he knew it.

Fur Cap Flattery

The real model for the new American, in both style and substance, or "meat and sauce," as he himself liked to put it, was Benjamin Franklin. (The idea, of course, was to be more meat than sauce.) In terms of manner and style, Washington was mid-Atlantic, somewhere between the Old World and the New. But Benjamin Franklin became the world's prototype of the American new man—self-made, self-invented, and self-propelling. Franklin became the international poster child for the new American. In France, during the American Revolution, Franklin ostentatiously vaunted his own simplicity, discarding flowing wigs for a fluffy fur cap that barely covered his unpowdered gray hair. In the evenings, he affected a wooden staff instead of a sword. He wore the plain dress of the democratic philosopher rather than the courtly finery of a diplomat. Revolutionaries don't wear black tie, as Nelson Mandela once said.

Franklin's *Autobiography* fits into the category of the instructional fairy tale. He presents his life as a series of do's and don'ts. Successful printer that he was, he refers to his mistakes as "errata." And new man that he was, he knew that errata could always be corrected in a new printing. For Franklin, his mistakes were not indelible mortal sins. Franklin didn't seem to regard any mistake as permanent, at least while there was still time for another printing.

Franklin always preached not to waste time, and he himself had little time for musing on mannners. But that does not mean that Franklin was oblivious to appearances, or rather, Appearances, as he called them. In fact, the good doctor was the original American spin doctor. He was the first American political handler and he was his own best client.

In his *Autobiography,* Franklin made reference to the differences, as he put it, between Appearances and Reality. Not for him the Puritan congruence between what a thing seemed to be and what it was. Whereas the Puritans were concerned about reconciling the two, Franklin understood that if you could not achieve the Reality, the Appearance was often quite as good. He was a master of what sociologists would later call "impression management." As he wrote in his *Autobiography* regarding the virtue of humility, "I cannot boast of much Success in acquiring the *Reality* of this Virtue; but I had a good deal with regard to the *Appearance* of it." As Oscar Wilde said, only superficial people do not judge by appearances.

Franklin's discussion of Appearance and Reality is not so different from Castiglione or Chesterfield. He is both more straightforward and more naïve—a very American combination. He tells stories on himself with a remarkable lack of self-consciousness. He writes of his early days in Philadelphia: "In order to secure my Credit and Character as a Tradesman, I took care not only to be in *Reality* Industrious & frugal, but to avoid all *Appearances* of the Contrary. I drest plainly; I was seen at no Places of idle Diversion . . . and to show that I was not above my Business, I sometimes brought home the Paper I purchas'd at the Stores, thro' the Streets on a Wheelbarrow." Franklin is simply saying, If you can't be the thing, at least look the part, for one way to judge a book is by its cover.

One of the Appearances he carefully cultivated was that of a republican indifference to appearances. Franklin was a master of this, particularly when abroad. It was the deliberate cultivation of a kind of republican insouciance that made Franklin the talk of the town in Paris. His informality was a *scandale*—but the people adored him for it. Like Princess Diana's, his portrait was affixed to everything from snuffboxes to teapots. John Adams wrote that his reputation was greater than Newton's, Leibniz's, or even Voltaire's. He was the first international American celebrity.

Although Franklin assiduously advocated modesty, he was actually an industrious public relations man in his own behalf. He was shameless in promoting and selling his own paper—as well as selling himself. He often inserted blind items about himself—to promote something that he was doing. If he lived in contemporary New York, he would be calling *Page Six* all the time to leak little flattering anecdotes about himself. He was a stickler for privacy during the Constitutional Convention, but when it was over he quickly made arrangements to have his own remarks published.

He was also the first Dear Ben–style advice columnist. He was the progenitor of what would become a peculiar American industry, the industry of self-help and self-esteem. Machiavelli, Castiglione, and Chesterfield all offered counsel on how to rise in the world; Franklin provided a blueprint. It was *Poor Richard's Almanack* that would become the model for Dale Carnegie's *How to Win Friends and Influence People.*

Franklin started printing the *Almanack* in 1732, and then printed annual editions between 1733 and 1757. The *Almanack*s were a collection of maxims, stories, advice, poetry, most of it hortatory. Each was a commonplace book with a purpose. It was also easy reading, simple, clear, colloquial—a tabloid, not a broadsheet. Max Weber cited *Poor Richard's Almanack* as the quintessential self-help manual of the Protestant ethic. "All Franklin's moral attutudes are colored with utilitarianism," wrote Weber," and they are virtues "only in so far as they are actually useful to the individual."

One of the first compilations of Poor Richard's maxims was published in a volume appropriately entitled, *The Way to Wealth,* a title that wouldn't be out of place on today's *Times* bestseller list. Franklin understood, as T. S. Eliot once said, that good writers borrow, but great writers steal. Many of his maxims were freely pinched from others. Franklin always preached the importance of sharing credit, but he always hinted that he was the one who deserved the lion's share of it.

Franklin differs from Chesterfield and Castiglione primaily in his directness. *Poor Richard's Almanack* is all meat and very little sauce. In that way, it would prove an influence on Dale Carnegie. For Franklin's test for every form of behavior is not its morality but its efficacy. It is the *realpolitik* of social relations; what works is always best.

Franklin, like Chesterfield and later Carnegie, basically encouraged a mild and ingratiating manner. Don't alienate anyone, he said, because they can come back to spite you. "Speak with contempt of one, from slave to king, / The meanest Bee hath, and will use, a sting." Better to soothe than to ruffle.

Franklin confesses in the *Autobiography* that he's rather curmudgeonly by nature, but he learned that alienating people with argument did not get him where he wanted to go. As a young man, he was prone to get in arguments, and adamant about his own opinions; he was, as the British call it, bloody-minded. But he learned his lesson, and he advises the reader to curb whatever argumentativness he may have. He decides he will never again contradict people, not because he doesn't disagree with them, but because it was a no-win strategy for getting what you wanted. "I made it a Rule," he writes, "to forbear all direct Contradiction to the Sentiments of others, and all positive Assertion of my own." This in itself is a kind of flattery, the flattery of not contradicting, the flattery of not disabusing someone of their error. It is echoed, almost two centuries later, by Dale Carnegie, who cites Franklin when giving his readers the advice that, as he says, "the only way to get the best of an argument is to avoid it."

Despite Franklin's career as a printer, writer, and publisher, he is skeptical about language. Words, he suggests, are very often the things that get in the way of truth. Much of *Poor Richard's Almanack* is an oblique condemnation of rhetoric and fancy speech. "There are no ugly loves, nor handsome prisons." You can't embellish reality; something is what it is. Franklin is very much the rationalist, the concrete philosopher. Another maxim: "What you seem to be, be really." Of course, to Franklin, that is merely advice to play yourself.

At the outset of the *Autobiography,* he tells the tale of John Collins, his best friend when he was a boy. Franklin envies young Collins for he was "naturally more eloquent, had a ready Plenty of Words," and his fluency helps him win many arguments. Franklin always portrays himself as halting of speech. But Collins gets his comeuppance: As an adult he proves to be a drunk and a deadbeat who betrays Franklin. Like Dante, Franklin relegates the smooth-talking Collins to a central ring of hell. That is what happens to men who are all sauce and no meat.

Franklin is always prejudiced in favor of action over reflection. "Well done is better than well said," says *Poor Richard's Almanack*. Such advice also betrays his distrust of rhetoric. "Here comes Glib-tongue: who can outflatter a Dedication and lie, like ten Epitaphs," says *Poor Richard's*. He distrusts glibness for the same reason Aristotle did: It can polish over ill intentions. For Franklin, flattery equals glibness.

"Hold your tongue" is probably Franklin's most oft-given advice. "He that would live in peace and at ease, must not speak all he knows, nor judge all he sees," says the *Almanack*. "The closed mouth catches no flies." Half-wits talk much but say little, he says. "Great talkers should be cropp'd, for they have no need of ears." Everywhere, he distrusts speech, and suggests one would almost always be better off being silent. Those who can, do; those who can't, speak.

But Franklin well knew the effect of flattery, whether delivered subtly or bluntly. "A flatterer never seems absurd: The flatter'd always takes his word," says the *Almanack*. He knew that self-interest took precedence over any other kind, and that everyone likes a compliment. It's an example of his pragmatism that he doesn't really bother criticizing flatterers. How could he? They were working the same side of the street he was. If the flatterer is industrious and achieves his end, so be it. It didn't bother Ben. He was well aware of the Reality that flattery worked. He just knew that for Appearance' sake, he couldn't be seen to recommend it.

Franklin praised candor, and knew the value of parhesia, but he knew better than to be candid himself. He knew that candor alienated. But he also knew that it is better to be seen to recommend it. Franklin may not have been much of a flatterer, but he wasn't particularly frank either.

Franklin's stories are always instructive, but sometimes they instruct in a way that he probably did not intend. Franklin tells an anecdote that is meant to convey how one defuses a conflict and is meant, I think, to illustrate how modesty and practicality can help you avoid a fight. In fact, the story is a beautiful illustration of the uses of flattery. Franklin writes of how he handled competition for the job of clerk of the Pennsylvania Assembly in 1736. In his first year, he had been elected unanimously; the next go-round, he had an opponent.

"My opposition," he writes, "was a Gentleman of Fortune, & Education, with Talents that were likely to give him in time great Influence in the House, which indeed afterwards happened. I did not however aim at gaining his Favour by paying any servile Respect to him, but after some time took this other Method. Having heard that he had in his Library a certain very scarce & curious Book, I wrote a Note to him expressing my Desire of perusing that Book, and requesting he would do me the Favour of lending it to me for a few Days. He sent it immediately; and I return'd it in about a

Week, with another Note expressing strongly my Sense of the Favour. When we next met in the House, he spoke to me, (which he had never done before) and with great Civility. And he ever afterwards manifested a Readiness to serve me on all Occasions, so that we became great Friends, & our Friendship continu'd to his Death. This is another Instance of the Truth of an old Maxim I had learnt, which says, 'He that has once done you a Kindness will be more ready to do you another, than he whom you yourself have obliged.' "

The maxim that best summarizes this idea is La Rochefoucauld's, that we ingratiate ourselves with people by asking them a favor rather than by doing them one. We like the people who ask us favors—it makes us feel magnanimous. Franklin is shrewd but disingenuous. He says he would not pay "servile respect" to his antagonist. I will suck up to no man! But, in fact, Franklin comes across as a servile schemer who is grateful for the man's attention and generosity. The weasel didn't even bother reading the book; he just borrowed it so that he could be seen to return it.

Flattery Is the First Refuge of the Political Scoundrel

Both Washington and Franklin attended the Constitutional Convention in Philadelphia in the summer of 1787. They were the odd couple among the Framers. Washington, the taciturn aristocrat who towered over the delegates, and Franklin, the still-puckish éminence grise of democracy who was carried everywhere in his sedan chair in order to alleviate the pain of gout and kidney stones. Washington presided over the convention, but sat silent for four months, rising only to speak on the last day to throw his support to the new constitution. Franklin was chattier, getting involved in the nitty-gritty of the arguments, proposing solutions to roadblocks, offering counsel and advice.

Neither was considered a small *d* democrat. Both were celebrated men of the age. Washington already behaved as though his visage was carved on Mount Rushmore, and Franklin, whom some considered a Tory at heart, was a little too aware that he had been fêted by the crowned heads of Europe.

But to be deemed a democrat was not an unalloyed compliment. It was in fact closer to an insult. Most of the Founding Fathers would have shuddered to be called a democrat. It was perhaps worse, even, than being called a monarchist. To most of the delegates, the word had a pejorative meaning. Democracy usually meant the rule of the mob rather than the reasoned rule of the people. The adjective "democratic" regularly preceded the noun "licentiousness." Pure democracy, most of them thought, was the recipe for pure anarchy. It meant license more than liberty. The *demos,* to them, was not so much an enlightened citizenry as a passionate mob. The whole purpose of the convention, said Edmund Randolph of Viriginia, was to "restrain the fury of democracy."

There were many at the convention who distrusted "the people" altogether. Elbridge Gerry, the Boston merchant who had been one of the signers of the Declaration of Independence, declared that "the evils we experience flow from the excess of democracy. The people do not want virtue, but are the dupes of pretended patriots." He spoke ominously of the "danger of the levelling spirit."

Today, the phrase an "excess of democracy" seems almost impossible to contemplate. We like to think democracy is an unmitigated good. The Framers sought to restrain democracy, and to that end, there was a property qualification for voting, and senators were elected not by the people but by the legislatures. The president was elected not by property-qualified white males, but by electors chosen by the legislatures. The people may rule, but the idea was to keep them as far away from governing as possible.

The source of the property qualification was the idea that men without property were men without character. To the Founders, poverty spelled idleness and sloth, rather than lack of opportunity. (Not so different from today's more conservative Republicans who equate poverty with a kind of moral laxness.) The Founders assumed that there was no lack of opportunity to work, ergo, if you were poor, you were lazy.

But the general feeling about the citizenry among the Framers was not that they were base and conniving; in fact, the opposite was the case. The people were considered naive and uneducated, too credulous rather than too shrewd. The reason they could not be trusted is because they might be too easily swayed by demagogic flattery. As Hamilton, Madison, and John Jay suggested a number of times in *The Federalist Papers,* the people are "corrupted by flattery." "A dangerous ambition," Hamilton wrote in *The*

Federalist No. 1, "more often lurks behind the specious mask of zeal for the rights of the people than under the forbidding appearance of zeal for the firmness and efficiency of government." He notes darkly that of "those men who have overturned the liberties of republics, the greatest number have begun their career by paying an obsequious court to the people."

This is an almost perfect mirror of the Greek idea that flattery undermines democracy and that a phony patriotism is the first refuge of a political scoundrel. The reason demagogues succeed, Hamilton suggests, is because the people are easy marks for such confidence men. Leaders must not take advantage of the people's credulity. The republican principle, he says in *The Federalist* No. 71, "does not require an unqualified complaisance to every sudden breeze of passion, or to every transient impulse which the people may receive from the arts of men, who flatter their prejudices to betray their interests." And there are too many politicians willing to play to those prejudices.

Hamilton, the brilliant, mercurial immigrant from the West Indies, was not above doing a little flattering of the *demos* himself. Beginning with the ancient Greeks, the ritual praising of the wisdom of the people has become one of the stations of the cross of democracy. The people, Hamilton writes, generally intend the public good. "Their good sense," he says, "would despise the adulators who would pretend that they always reason right about the means of promoting it. They know from experience, that they sometimes err; and the wonder is, that they so seldom err as they do; beset as they continually are by the wiles of parasites and sycophants."

Hamilton took the Greek idea and cleverly reversed it. The problem of demagogues who flatter the people is that it poisons the water for true patriots. How can anyone discern the honest words of praise of a true democrat from the false encomiums of the demagogue? "An overscrupulous jealousy of danger to the rights of people . . . will be represented as mere presence and artifice, the stale bait for popularity at the expense of the public good." Any concern for the people, then, will come to be seen as a ploy for popularity, as a stratagem to get elected. The result will be that "the noble spirit of liberty is apt to be infected with a spirit of narrow and illiberal distrust."

There is no real solution to this, and he proposes the same remedy that the Greeks did: frankness, candor, and not poring over the poll results every morning. "When occasions present themselves in which the interests of the people are at variance with their inclinations," Hamilton says, "it is the duty of the person whom they have appointed to be the guardian of those interests, to withstand the temporary delusions, in order to give them time and opportunity for more cool and sedate reflections." Politicians, he says, must have the courage to serve the people at their displeasure. Politicians must resist flattering the people to get elected, and then resist the popular but sometimes shallow wishes of the public once they are in office. Good luck. It is not much of a bulwark against the excesses of democracy, but it is pretty much the only one there is.

Packaging Praise

Ralph Waldo Emerson, the Sage of Concord, the apostle of self-reliance, the most beautifully American of American writers, was also the copywriter of much modern advertising: Be all you can be, Just do it, Go it alone.

In fact, the last of these three slogans was not a sneaker jingle but his advice to students in his famous address to the Harvard Divinity School in 1838. Emerson followed his own counsel, and just did it: His blunt critique of organized Christianity was so objectionable to the Harvard authorites that he was not invited back for thirty years.

Emerson's philosophy of self-reliance, of looking inward and having the courage to be yourself (there's another advertising slogan for you), is what modern sociologists call inner-directedness. It is also a strategy to make yourself immune to flattery. If you care not for the world's opinion, compliments or criticism just won't matter very much. One must be as indifferent to applause as one is to jeers.

"Society's praise can be cheaply secured," he told the divinity-school students, "and almost all men are content with those easy merits." But don't be content with them, Emerson says. Just as you would naturally question criticism, question praise. Merit often has nothing to do with society's opinion of you. And it's all relative anyway. "You would compliment a coxcomb doing a good act," he says, "but you would not praise an angel."

Emerson's oversoul, that part of every person which he says plumbs deep inside to find the truth of one's divinity, scoffs at flattery. "The soul that ascends to worship the great God is plain and true; has no rose-color, no fine friends, no chivalry, no adventures; does not want admirations; dwells in the hour that now is, in the earnest experience of the common day." Just as for Emerson evil is the privation of the good, falsehood and its handmaiden flattery are privations of the truth. Truth needs no fancy robe.

Emerson's rejection of flattery was both cultural and psychological. For him, flattery smacked too much of Old World courtesy and superficial manners. "We have listened for too long to the courtly muses of Europe," he wrote famously in "The American Scholar," and those courtly muses whispered blandishments. Flattery also meant a dissipation of self-reliance. If one listened to flattery, one could become addicted to it. "Great is the soul, and plain. It is no flatterer, it is no follower." Listening to flattery, he suggests, is becoming a follower, which to Emerson—and to Nike advertising—is the worst thing you can be.

Emerson's devotion to transcendental nature made him opposed to anything that he saw as unnatural. For Emerson, true speech is natural; flattery is unnatural. "Words are signs of natural facts," he writes in *Nature*. Flattery is a distortion of natural facts. "Every natural process is a version of a moral sentence." The lily itself is the natural fact; gilding it is a distortion. "The corruption of man is followed by the corruption of language," he says. It is "the desire for riches, of pleasure, of power, and of praise," he says, that makes "duplicity and falsehood take the place of simplicity and truth."

Emerson has a dreamy, idealized view of truth as an absolute. "The least admixture of a lie—for example, the taint of vanity, any attempt to make a good impression, a favorable appearance—will instantly vitiate the effect. But speak the truth, and all nature and all spirit help you with unexpected furtherance." In fact, it was Emerson's own lack of vanity, his soft rectitude, that made a good impression on people. He did not have to fake his sincerity; it was transparent.

Emerson idealizes friendship almost as much as he does truth. Like the Greeks, Emerson says the key to friendship is not flattery but frankness. "A friend is a person with whom I may be sincere," he says, and "drop even those undergarments of dissimulation." In fact, friends owe each other what he calls "rude truth"—which must be even more rough-hewn than plain

truth. "They resent your honesty for an instant, they will thank you for it always." Sometimes Emerson sounds like a modern mother disciplining her
children and saying, "Someday you'll thank me for this."

Although Emerson pens tributes to friendship, it is obvious that he
doesn't really care for it all that much. Friendship for him is always a
mixed blessing. Friendship is a distraction from the real work of self-
examination. He also sees friendship as camouflaged rivalry. His view resembles the United States and the Soviet Union's Cold War policy known
as Mutually Assured Destruction, or MAD. "Let [friendship] be an alliance
of two large, formidable natures, mutually beheld, mutually feared, before
yet they recognize the deep identity which, beneath these disparities, unites
them. . . . Let him be to thee for ever a sort of beautiful enemy." With
friends like that, who needs rivals? We love our enemy because he defines
us for ourselves.

Finally, for Emerson, the truth is not only natural, it is *masculine*. We
crave, he says, "this manlike love of truth." Flattery is effeminate in part because truth is hard and straight, while flattery is soft and bent. Truth is vir-
ile. Emerson regards flattery as effeminate because the very act of flattery
puts you in a dependent or subservient position. To be a man is to be self-
reliant; to be dependent is to be emasculated. "Nothing shall warp me," he
writes, "from the belief that every man is a lover of truth."

*   *   *

Emerson had beautiful manners, but no one would ever confuse him
with a courtier. "I shall hear without pain," Emerson writes in an essay on
manners, "that I play the courtier very ill." Emerson would say he was a
poor flatterer, but when it came to giving genuine and helpful praise, praise
that can change a person's life, Emerson made one of the greatest gestures
in literary history. In the summer of 1855, a slender, rather undistinctive-
looking volume of poems arrived from New York at Emerson's farmhouse
in Concord. It was called *Leaves of Grass* and Emerson read it straight
away. He promptly sat down to write a letter to its author.

"Dear Sir," began Emerson's famous reply. "I am not blind to the worth
of the wonderful gift of 'Leaves of Grass.' I find it the most extraordinary

piece of wit & wisdom that America has yet contributed. I am very happy in reading it, as great power makes me happy."

He continued, "I give you joy of your free & brave thought. I have great joy in it. I find incomparable things said incomparably well." And then, in the line that has come down to us, words which every young writer longs to hear: "I greet you at the beginning of a great career."

Walt Whitman was thirty-six when he received Emerson's letter. He had been knocking about for quite some time, and was then working in a downtown printing office and doing a little real estate speculating on the side. Emerson did not know him from Adam. His letter was an instinctive offering of support for a writer who was as yet unacknowledged. It was neither self-interested nor strategic; it was praise without strings attached.

Whitman's reaction to the letter was hardly self-effacing. The first thing he did was to get the *New York Tribune* to publish it. He then had it printed up as a flyer, which he distributed to bookstores. Whitman then got up a second edition of his book with "I Greet You at the Beginning of a Great Career / R W Emerson" printed in gold leaf on the cover. He did all this without Emerson's knowledge or permission. Whitman was the pioneer of the book jacket blurb. Whitman had immediately commodified Emerson's praise. He harnessed its economic benefit, not its psychological one. He saw immediately, it was an advertisement for himself.

Whitman's friend Horace Traubel tartly observed many years later that the letter was more important for Emerson to write than for Whitman to receive. Traubel meant that Emerson's own career was on the downward slope, and discovering Whitman made him feel vital again. As we have seen from La Rochefoucauld and others, we like the people whom we help and praise, because they make us feel better about ourselves. Perhaps, but I would guess that Emerson did not need Whitman's gratitude to feel good about himself.

In fact, Emerson never received much thanks from Whitman. It was not that Whitman was ungrateful; it was that he had used Emerson's praise not to boost his self-esteem but his book sales and reputation. Whitman had turned praise into the form it so often takes today, advertising. Advertising is often just paid-for flattery. It is not genuine praise, for it is never disinterested. Yes, it's nice to get a good review, but how quickly can you put it in neon on the theater's marquee? Whitman was inventing testimonial advertising. His use of Emerson's name on the outside of his book is like putting Michael Jordan's face on a box of Wheaties.

Flatter Me or Else

Alexis de Tocqueville was a spindly, rather sickly French aristocrat who came to America in 1835 when he was thirty years old. He traveled around the country for nine months, investigated America in places high and low. I can't help but imagine him shuddering and nearly collapsing when some ham-handed, broad-shouldered American clapped him on the back and bid him welcome. He was a contemporary of Emerson's—and as much as Emerson was an outsider even at home, it took a true outsider like Tocqueville to see what ordinary Americans were really like.

For years, I used to repeat the *mot* that Tocqueville was the most often quoted but least-read writer in America. I said this in part because I hadn't read him but I sometimes quoted him. But, now, having read Tocqueville, I can say that the man may have been a little precious, but he was extraordinarily perceptive about America. His views on race, for example—written twenty years before the Emancipation Proclamation—and how the racial divide would prove to be the great unhealed wound of American life, are clairvoyant.

His views of the nature of democracy were rather different from Emerson's. Emerson rarely thought about mankind en masse; Tocqueville always did. Like a good sociologist, he was able to see a culture's traits in an individual. He came initially to study America's prison system. Tocqueville had a love-hate relationship with America: He sometimes hated to love it, and sometimes loved to hate it. He was rather amazed that America was what it claimed to be, an essentially democratic country where equality was both an ideal and a reality.

America was re-forming and re-creating itself in the early nineteenth century. Millions of immigrants—2 million Irish immigrants alone—were flooding American cities. New York, Philadelphia, Boston were changing from sleepy towns to blooming, buzzing hubs of business. If money had not been important before, it was everything now. "I know of no other country where love of money has such a grip on men's hearts," Tocqueville observed. Industrialization was making life more impersonal. Ambition became the signature American trait; pride was no longer a sin but an essential virtue. "There is not a crowned head in Europe," Jefferson wrote Washington from Paris, "whose talents or merits would entitle him to be elected vestryman by the people of any parish in America." Mark Twain joked that the frogs in American swamps made more beautiful music than the symphony orchestras of Europe. And later, the critic Edmund Wilson praised what he considered the great achievements of American culture: "I have derived a good deal more benefit of the civilizing as well as of the inspirational kind from the admirable American bathroom than I have from the cathedrals of Europe."

Tocqueville coined the term "individualism," based on what he saw and described in America. He saw men shaking off deference and grabbing for the main chance. Old World servility was something alien in the new. The American ideal was the rejection of all artificial distinctions based on birth. Don't tell me who your ancestors were; tell me who you are.

One of the great engines of equality, Tocqueville says, was the ending of primogeniture in America. In one fell swoop, this strengthened democracy and undermined aristocracy. The second and third sons who settled America were determined not to have their own second and third sons deprived of an inheritance. There were comparativiely few great estates in America, Tocqueville observed, because they got divided up in the next generation.

This fostered a genuine equality, he says, and also an attitude that bitterly resented anything that smacked of inequality. One of the negative and unintended consequences of equality, he suggests, was a kind of national envy and a desire for leveling that undermined the purity of American democracy. "There is indeed a manly and legitimate passion for equality," Tocqueville writes (there's that *manly* thing again), "which rouses in all men a desire to be strong and respected. This passion tends to elevate the little man to the rank of the great. But the human heart also nourishes a debased taste for equality, which leads the weak to want to drag the strong down to their level and which induces men to prefer equality in servitude to inequality in freedom." Americans would rather be *un*free and equal than free and unequal. Tocqueville suggested that we are always looking over the hedge at what our neighbor is doing to see if he is getting ahead of us.

Societies that embrace equality, he contends, become societies of perva-sive envy. In an aristocracy, there is less jealousy even though there is more inequality because the inequality seems arbitrary and accidental. You can't help it if you were born a duke just as I can't help it if I'm born a chamber-maid. "Each citizen of an aristocratic society," he writes, "has his fixed sta-tion, one above another, so that there is always someone above him whose protection he needs and someone below him whose help he may require." In a democracy, he says, "the duties of each to all are much clearer," but that is all that is clearer. "Aristocracy links everybody, from peasant to king, in one long chain. Democracy breaks the chain and frees the link."

The result of this broken chain, he says, is envy. When people in democ-racies discover their neighbors, who do not seem any wiser or smarter or stronger, are doing better than they are—it bothers them. "They wonder how he who was their equal yesterday has today won the right to command them."

What Freud called the anxiety of little differences suggests that there is a greater jealousy between people who are similar than very different. We don't envy the billionaire in Switzerland who builds himself a castle, but let your neighbor across the street add a new porch—that brings out one's bil-ious competitiveness. It's like that humbling walk through the first-class cabin on the way to coach. First-class feels downright un-American. And if it *is* American, how come I'm not in it? A friend of mine has an idea for a talk show that would be called *The Fucking Lucky Show,* and would consist of her asking a single question to each well-known guest: "So how'd you get so fucking lucky?" Luck isn't democratic.

*   *   *

Equality, suggests Tocqueville, rather than making people content, makes them restless and insecure. Because people in a democracy have broken the chain that links a society, they feel unmoored and uncertain. As a result, Tocqueville says, America demands to be praised and doesn't much like being poked fun at. "The least reproach offends it [America], and the slightest sting of truth turns it fierce; and one must praise every-thing, from the turn of its phrases to its most robust virtues. No writer, no matter how famous, can escape from this obligation to sprinkle incense over his fellow citizens. Hence the majority lives in a state of perpetual self-adoration."

American self-regard is a curious mixture of insecurity and cockiness. If you really want to see the combination, he says, you need to be a foreigner, for American anxiety blossoms among people from abroad. Tocqueville really gets rolling on the subject:

> In their relations with strangers the Americans are impatient of the slightest criticism and insatiable for praise. They are pleased by the mildest praise but seldom quite satisfied even by the most fulsome eulogy. They are at you the whole time to make you praise them, and if you do not oblige, they sing their own praises. One might suppose that, doubting their own merits, they want an illustration thereof constantly before their eyes. Their vanity is not only greedy but also restless and jealous. It makes endless demands and gives nothing. It is both mendicant and querulous.
>
> I tell an American that he lives in a beautiful country; he answers: "That is true. There is none like it in the world." I praise the freedom enjoyed by the inhabitants, and he answers, "Freedom is a precious gift, but very few peoples are worthy to enjoy it." I note the chastity of morals prevailing in the United States, and he replies: "I suppose that a stranger, struck by the immorality apparent in all other nations, must be astonished at this sight." Finally I leave him to his self-contemplation, but he returns to the charge and will not stop till he has made me repeat everything I have said. One cannot imagine a more obnoxious or boastful form of patriotism. Even admirers are bored.

And Tocqueville is an admirer.

Tocqueville makes a clever and believable argument for why democracies breed flattery. (It's similar to Plato's.) He says that the relentless pursuit of equality changes the equation between people and their leaders. If the people are sovereign, every man and woman in a democracy must be played up to like a monarch. "In absolute monarchies," Tocqueville writes, "the king may often have great virtues, but the courtiers are always vile. It is true that American courtiers never say 'Sire' or 'Your Majesty,' as if the difference mattered; but they are constantly talking of their master's natural brilliance."

In a democracy, the courtiers are us. Everyone is a courtier and everyone is a king. "Democratic republics put the spirit of a court within reach of the multitude and let it penetrate through all classes at once." It is not a vertical court as in aristocracies, but a lateral court: Everyone is pandering to one another.

Politicians must go on bended knee before the electorate. "American moralists and philosophers are not obliged to wrap their views in veils of allegory, but before hazarding an unpleasant truth they say: 'We know that we are addressing a people so far above human weaknesses that they will always be masters of themselves. We should not use such language unless we knew that we were speaking to men whose virtues and enlightenment make them alone among all others worthy to remain free.' The sycophants of Louis XIV could not flatter more dexterously than that."

It is on those rare occasions that politicians have to tell voters something unpleasant that the news is couched in the most obsequious tribute to the people's ability to make difficult choices. (Which is patently untrue.) Here the politicians themselves will criticize the "don't-worry-be-happy" nostrums that they usually disseminate themselves. Before a politician says something that will be unpopular, he tells the public that he knows they are not swayed by mere popularity or motivated only by self-interest.

By definition, the people can do no wrong in a democracy. The *demos* has a kind of infallibility. If the people decide it, it can't be wrong. In a democracy, everyone is happy to take the boat over the falls as long as we all agree on it. Tocqueville makes this analogy: "Under the old monarchy, the French took it as a maxim that the king could do no wrong, and when he did do wrong, they thought the fault lay with his advisers. This made obedience much easier. One could grumble against the law without ceasing to love and honor the lawgiver. The Americans take the same view of the majority."

One of the by-products, he says, of this tyranny of the majority is a kind of intellectual tyranny that erases differences. Americans may have political independence, he says, but they do not have independence of mind. There is, he suggests, a kind of mass flattery of the conventional wisdom.

He says he knows of no country in which there is less independence of mind than in America. "In America the majority has enclosed thought within a formidable fence." Because people in a democracy are unmoored, they are too scared to venture very far from the familiar.

Tocqueville, as I've mentioned, is credited with coining the term "individualism." He saw individualism as a more narcissistic version of Emerson's independence and self-reliance. To him, individualism is what used to be known as egoism. And it is this egoism or individualism that makes Americans so hungry for praise. "The inhabitants of democracies love their country after the same fashion as they love themselves, and what is habitual in their private vanity is carried over into national pride. . . . This restless and insatiable vanity of democracies is entirely due to equality and the precariousness of social standing."

I realize that I'm making it seem as though Tocqueville had a low opinion of America, and that he found Americans themselves rather odious. That is far from the case. He has a curious, cheery regard for America, as though he is visiting a kind of Disneyland of democracy that he can't quite believe is really true. He has a good time in spite of himself. He marvels at American industriousness and resourcefulness, and he marvels at something else that is rather unexpected. In fact, after going on at great length about America's superiorities over the Old World, he chalks up the difference to a single factor. "If someone asks me what I think the chief cause of the extraordinary prosperity and growing power of this nation is," Tocqueville writes, "I should answer that it is due to the superiority of their women."

Tocqueville has a very simple explanation for why American women are superior. It is not genetics, or climate, or lack of makeup, or comfortable shoes; it is the fact that American women are not flattered the way women are in the Old World. And they wouldn't accept it if they were:

In Europe one has often noted that a certain contempt lurks in the flattery men lavish on women; although a European may often make himself a woman's slave, one feels that he never sincerely thinks her his equal. In the United States, men seldom compliment women, but they daily show how much they esteem them. Americans constantly display complete confidence in their spouse's judgment and deep respect for their freedom. They hold that woman's mind is just as capable as man's of discovering the naked truth, and her heart as firm to face it.

European male flattery reinforces the helplessness of women because that is what they secretly want, because they secretly hold women in contempt. For Tocqueville, American men of the nineteenth century create great, strong women because they treat them like, well—because they treat them like men. Which is to say, they treat them like equals.

The Confidence Man

Tocqueville found Americans to be a terminally restless people. He regarded the intensity of the American desire to succeed both amusing and dismaying. "It is strange to see with what feverish ardor the Americans pursue their own welfare," he wrote, "and to watch the vague dread that constantly torments them lest they should not have chosen the shortest path which may lead to it."

That short path often meant cutting corners. If success was the great goal, it became less and less important about how one reached it, just as long as one got there as soon as possible. The end not only justified the means; the end erased the means. Americans worshiped success, and its achievement camouflaged a multitude of sins.

The American of the mid–nineteenth century was on the move and on the make; the original free agent. "With all the parts of his universe, himself included, in erratic motion," writes Marvin Meyers in *Confidence Men and Painted Women* about the American man, "with no fixed terminus and no secure resting place, the democrat develops an acute awareness of loss and failure." The American was suspended between an unfixed present and a wished-for future, always concerned about whether he was succeeding or not.

One species of this American new man who emerged in the middle of the nineteenth century became known as the confidence man. The American confidence man is the descendant of the archetypal figure whom mythologist Joseph Campbell calls the Trickster, the deceiver who pretends to be one thing and turns out to be another, the moral seducer who leads the hero astray. The original confidence man of course is Satan, the prince of liars, the "false dissembler," in Milton's phrase, who could fool everyone, even the angels.

A swindler by the name of William Thomas has the dubious distinction of being the first official American confidence man. He was a well-dressed, well-spoken man who approached gentlemen on the streets of New York City in the late 1840s, lamented the fact that no one trusted anyone anymore, and then asked, Would the gentleman—who was obviously a man of honor—have "the confidence" to lend a stranger his watch? In this manner, he shamed a number of New Yorkers into parting with their expensive gold pocket watches. He might have continued in this fashion for a while, had not one of his victims seen him the next day and identified him to the police. The New York papers had a field day and dubbed him "the confidence man." Herman Melville's story of the same name, published eight years later, was probably inspired by Thomas's racket. By the 1860s, New York police estimated that one in ten criminals in the city was a "confidence man."

The technique of the confidence man was to pose as a man of means and substance and then flatter and cajole his way into your, well, confidence. Typically, he was a natty, charming, polished fellow who preyed upon the naive country youths who had just arrived in the big city. He was a pickpocket, a gambler, a pimp, a phony European nobleman, a racketeer, who would depict himself as a successful businessman and then befriend a lost youth by offering him help, only to get him drunk and steal his money, or debauch him and turn him into a kind of indentured servant in petty crime.

The rise of the confidence man was linked to changes in American society: the growth of cities, the increase in immigration, the new mobility of the young, the decline in social deference. He thrived in this new urban world of strangers, where no one knew or cared where a person was from, only where he was going; where young men and women were alone, without the buffer of family or sense of place that might have aided them in knowing whom to trust.

The dramatic expansion of the American economy also fueled the rise of the confidence man. It was an economy of risks and dangers, where speculators (who were a kind of confidence man) manipulated markets and consumers, where much investment was a financial three-card monte game. Speculators, too, made money by appearing certain and winning the confidence of their investors.

There were the older, countrified confidence men as well. The New England sharpster, the roving peddler man, the fictional backwoodsman Simon Suggs, whose motto was "It's good to be shifty in a new country." Tom Sawyer is a kind of endearing confidence man of a type that is familiar throughout American life and literature, soft-soaping his friends into whitewashing Aunt Polly's fence by making them feel important for doing the work. In the next chapter, we will see how Dale Carnegie says the secret to success is getting others to want to do what you want them to do. Tom Sawyer knew that without having to read *How to Win Friends and Influence People*.

The urban version of the confidence man ranged from the French valet who posed as a duke to the real estate swindler who pretended to be a man of property. What they all had in common, though, was a simulated sincerity, a pretended concern for the person being duped. In effect, the confidence man was cleverly following the principles of the most popular advice manuals of the day.

In the early to middle decades of the nineteenth century, there was what historian Karen Halttunen describes as a cult of sincerity in American middle-class culture. It grew out of the Puritan ethic of straightness combined with Emersonian authenticity. The etiquette manuals of this time counseled an abiding sincerity, "a perfectly transparent character." The secret to gentility, the manuals said, was ingenuousness of manner. True courtesy was right feeling from the heart.

Confidence men were masters of a false version of this etiquette of sincerity. They were parlor hypocrites who feigned a delicacy of manner and a sincerity of feeling. In fact, their success was due in part to the fact that the cult of sincerity disarmed those who embraced it. It robbed them of the skepticism that might have made them see through the confidence man. While the etiquette books deplored the "hollow-hearted courtesy" to be found in fashionable drawing rooms, they did not equip the earnest middle-class reader to discern it.

One of the broadway hits of 1845 was a play called *Fashion,* which was a satire of the "heartless manners" of a pretentious middle-class family who aspired to be American aristocrats. Mrs. Tiffany, the social-climbing matriarch, shamelessly flatters her usually ungrateful guests. She greets her visitors with a hearty "Bung jure!" (her mispronunciation of *bonjour);* hires a black handyman named Zeke who becomes a liveried butler called Adolph; and cultivates a titled Frenchman, the snobbish Count Jolimâitre, who of course turns out to be a valet by trade. The one honest character is a wealthy gentleman-farmer appropriately named Adam Trueman, who is the voice of sentimental sincerity and republican simplicity. "Deception is your house-hold God!" he exclaims at one point to Mrs. Tiffany. "Everything is something else from what it seems to be."

The play wasn't any great shakes, but it does record a change in American society. Adam Trueman was becoming a rare species. The earnest American was vanishing, to be replaced by a shrewder, more manipulative one. Success was becoming less about merit than about personality. The greatest promoter of the nineteenth-century success myth was Horatio Alger Jr.

A sensitive, rather frail Harvard graduate who was the son of a prosperous Unitarian minister, Alger wrote more than a hundred titles and they sold in the millions. They were not so much rags-to-riches stories, as is commonly thought, as rags-to-bourgeois-respectability stories. His young heroes became bank managers, not great industrialists. Nor were they a succession of Goody Two-Shoes. They tended to be canny young men who possessed in equal measure *Luck and Pluck,* which was the title of his 1869 best-seller. Alger, according to one scholar, had briefly been a Unitarian minister himself but was booted from the church when it was suspected that he was a pederast. It was only then that he began turning his friendships with street urchins into successful books.

Ragged Dick, Alger's first successful novel, published in 1868, features a fourteen-year-old orphan who lives on the street and works as a bootblack. Unlike his compatriots, Dick is a hustler with an "eye for business." "Shine yer boots, sir?" Dick calls out to passersby with a smile and a joke. He flatters his customers, calls servant girls "Queen Victoria," and generally ingratiates himself with everyone around him. He's an urban Tom Sawyer with even less of a conscience.

One day, he hears the respectable Mr. Whitney telling his nephew Frank that he is too busy to show him the city. "Being an enterprising young man

. . . [Dick] thought he saw a chance for speculation, and determined to avail himself of it." He becomes Frank's tour guide and is rewarded by the grateful Mr. Whitney with a fiver and a new suit. A short while later, he rescues a young boy off the Brooklyn Ferry, and the lad's father repays him for what the boatman calls his "pluck" with a clerkship in his counting room. Ragged Dick ascends not to riches but to middle-class respectability. God helps those who help themselves—and Dick helped himself to anything he could get his hands on.

By the early twentieth century, the confidence man was metamorphosing into another American archetype, the salesman, a grown-up Ragged Dick in a Paul Stuart suit. The ambitious young man had to have, as one magazine article of the time put it, "a tinge of charlatanism." He needed to have a shoeshine, a smile, and a flattering word for everyone. The etiquette books were becoming less drawing-room handbooks than success manuals. The success manuals were turning away from the character ethic of nineteenth-century manuals and embracing the personality ethic of the twentieth century. As small businesses were giving way to great corporations, getting along in a big bureaucracy began to take precedence over getting by in a small town. Handling people became a more marketable skill than handling tools.

The books were selling the efficacy of sincerity, not as a virtue but as a tool. And the greatest salesman of sincerity was Dale Carnegie.

Chapter 8

How Flattery
Won Friends and Influenced People

Just a Barefoot Missouri Boy

Dale Carnegie, the most successful "success" writer of the twentieth century, was the ideal Dale Carnegie student. He was an awkward man wholly without small talk. He kept the punch lines of jokes on index cards. He used dozens of corny or inappropriate conversational openers like, "Do you know what prevents you from being an idiot?" *No, Mr. Carnegie.* "Five cents of iodine secreted by your thyroid gland!"

Charming.

The Dale Carnegie course in human relations promised to make you a better conversationalist, something Carnegie longed to be. His course also promised to help you win friends quickly and easily—something else that Carnegie craved. All his life, Carnegie said he felt like the most unpopular kid at school. And while the grown-up Dale Carnegie had thousands of acquaintances (whose names he had committed to memory and would repeat over and over, mantralike, while talking to them), he had very few real friends. His course promised to make you a better salesman, and indeed, Dale Carnegie had failed at selling everything but the one thing that he deemed most important: himself.

He turned himself into a brand even before we had the term for it.

In one sense, Carnegie's whole career and message was about helping others overcome the weaknesses that he had discovered in himself. He became a success only when he figured out a way exploit those same weaknesses in others. His logic was, If I feel insecure and worthless, so must millions of others—and they will be hungry for the positive message I give them. I can flatter them into learning my method and then they can flatter their way to success. For his whole life, Carnegie had the drive and ambition of the insecure and was never really at ease with himself or with others. He was the original "people person" who was not really comfortable with other people.

Carnegie was more than just the quintessential American salesman. His life and work signal a change in the American persona. For Carnegie was both a cause and a symptom of the shift away from the signficance of "character" in the American makeup to the importance of "personality." He straddled an era that moved from the rough-hewn individualism of the frontier to the nervous and ingratiating style of the modern cities and suburbs. Almost forty years ago, David Riesman talked about the transition from the *inner-directed* individual of the nineteenth century—who did not particularly care what others thought of him—to the *other-directed* personality of the twentieth century, who cared about little else. Riesman described this transformation as the shift from the "invisible hand to the glad hand."

In this new era, as Willy Loman informed his son Biff in *Death of a Salesman,* "It's not the way you say it, it's how you say it—because personality always wins the day." It was not what you were selling, but how you sold it—because you were always selling youself. Personality, with all its smile and dazzle, was replacing character, with its more stolid virtues. The national persona Carnegie helped form was manufactured from the outside in, not from the inside out. Self-esteem was based on what others thought of you, not what you thought of yourself. It was the age of "impression-management," of appearance before reality. The transition was seen not only in business but in politics, where television made impression management the cornerstone of every presidential campaign.

The other-directed personality, said Riesman, was sensitized to the expectations and preferences of others. The psychoanalyst and philosopher Erich Fromm described this as the persona of "commercialized friendliness," the "have-a-nice-day" perkiness that is the essence of today's service economy. It ushered in an era, says Christopher Lasch, when "the management of interpersonal relations came to be seen as the essence of self-advancement."

*   *   *

Dale Carnegie was a slight, short man with an aquiline nose and a reedy voice that never lost its strong Midwestern twang. Like his fellow Missourian, Harry Truman, Carnegie was a natty dresser who fancied bow ties, red vests, and pocket squares. He idolized men he thought were great, and sought help from them whenever he could. He was aggressive and opportunistic. The most dangerous place to be in any room was between Dale Carnegie and the most important person in that room.

His involvement with public speaking came early. Carnegie was born in 1888. His father was an unsuccessful farmer and hog breeder in Warrensburg, Missouri. His mother was a strict Methodist (she kept an antidance tract called *From the Ball-Room to Hell* on a side table in the front hall) and yearned for Dale to be a minister. She tried to turn him into a boy preacher by taking him around to different Sunday schools where she made him stand on a chair and spout poetry. But what really inspired Carnegie were the secular versions of the minister, the peripatetic Chautauqua lecturers who came into town for one night, wowed the local folk, and then were off on a train to the next town. Young Dale yearned for the applause and he liked the idea of travel. He would eventually become a different kind of preacher than his mother wanted, a preacher of success.

He attended the nearby State Teachers College, but couldn't afford room and board, so he rode his horse each way. At college, Carnegie felt himself to be unpopular and inferior to the other students and had thoughts of suicide. "I wanted to prove to them that I was just as good as they were," he once wrote. The way he would do that was through public speaking. By the time he graduated, he was the star debater in the school.

Career prospects for college orators were not all that good, so Carnegie became a traveling salesman in the new age of traveling salesmen. It seemed like a perfect fit. Like the Chautauqua speakers, he came and went by railroad, made his pitch, and then left town. Salesmen were performers; they were sharply dressed, had the latest jokes and off-color tales, and won people over with a smile and a wink. The traveling salesman was the star in his own show of consumer attractions.

Until the power of mass advertising displaced them, salesmen were the most important marketing force in the early twentieth-century economy. Before the wide use of telephones, they linked consumers to merchants to wholesalers to manufacturers. Face-to-face selling helped them create the new American persona—upbeat, earnest, confident, a little aggressive. C. Wright Mills wrote that the salesman was at the heart of the "personality market" of middle-class American culture. The salesman tailored his personality to his customer. "He is all things to all men," wrote the novelist Asa Green, "in order to gain some."

But Carnegie wasn't gaining many. He proved unsuccessful as a salesman of International Correspondence courses to farmers—he only managed to sell one in two years—and then he failed at selling bacon and lard for the Armour Company. But he did manage to save $500, and with that he journeyed to Boston to study oratory. A teacher told him he'd make a good actor, and the impressionable Carnegie promptly went to New York and enrolled in the American Academy of Dramatic Art. He eventually landed one acting job: that of the small-town doctor in a road company of a now-forgotten play called *Polly of the Circus*. Howard Lindsay, a veteran actor in the cast, recalled that Carnegie was "quite a talker." "But I would not say he had any gift for conversation," said Lindsay. "He made speeches." Even while acting, Carnegie moonlighted as a salesman, carrying a heavy suitcase of neckties to try to sell to haberdashers while he was on the road.

In 1912, he gave up the theater, rented a cheap furnished room on West 56th Street, and got a job in New York selling trucks for the Packard Motor Company. He was again unsuccessful. But that same year, he got the notion of teaching public speaking to businessmen at the YMCA at 125th Street in Harlem. He auditioned for the job by reciting James Whitcomb Riley's "Knee-Deep in June" and "Giddyap, Napoleon, It Looks Like Rain," both to piano accompaniment. He was hired, but the manager refused to pay him the $2 a night that he wanted. Instead, he had to work on commission, which turned out to be a financial blessing.

He was very nervous before his first class, and by his own account, he spluttered to a halt fifteen minutes into it. He had run out of things to say. Then, inspiration struck, and he called on one of the businessmen in the audience to stand up and talk about something that made him angry. It was like opening a dam, and one by one, the businessmen got up. He asked everyone in the class to speak, a practice that would become standard in all his classes.

Within two years, he was speaking at other Y's in other cities and pulling in $400 a week. He lined up stellar speakers for his classes, including an address by the then assistant secretary of the navy, Franklin Roosevelt, to a Carnegie graduating class in Baltimore.

It was around this time, the 1920s, that he changed his name from Carnagey (with the accent on the second syllable) to Carnegie (accent on the first). Carnegie was more familiar, of course, from the name of Andrew Carnegie (to whom Dale's father claimed a distant connection) and Carnegie Hall, which Dale had started booking for classes and speeches. In light of what Carnegie says in *How to Win Friends* about the importance of a man's name ("the average man is more interested in his own name than all the other names on earth put together"), his decision is revealing. He pooh-poohed the change, saying that it was simply a matter of convenience, but he never spurned the implied connections to Andrew Carnegie or Carnegie Hall. Americans traditionally adopted new names in order to get a clean slate, but Carnegie wanted a slate that was already written on.

You Have Nothing to Fear but Fear of Public Speaking

In an age of salesmanship, Carnegie was the guru for those who were having trouble selling themselves.

Carnegie always said that he created his course to help people conquer what he regarded as the number-one fear in America. Not death or bankruptcy or the loss of a loved one—the top of the list, he said, was fear of public speaking. The students who enrolled in his classes were in his own self-image: men in their thirties who had not succeeded as they hoped, middle-level managers who quaked if they had to give a toast, salesmen who couldn't remember a joke, country club ladies who wanted to be able to get up and recite a poem at the spring luncheon. He was the pied piper of the anxious and ambitious. His course would have been perfect for Richard Nixon and a waste of time for John Kennedy.

Carnegie was not a naturally charming man, so in his course he deconstructed charm, breaking it down into what he saw as its constituent parts—lots of smiling, agreeing, listening, and many small flatteries. Each man could then learn to be his own Cary Grant. The principal exchange in the course was enthusiastic approval. After a speech, Carnegie or an instructor would always find something to praise and to praise lavishly. Carnegie helped give his students confidence, but he also did something more: He gave them a place where they could fail and not be humiliated. In that sense, his course was a precursor of twelve-step programs that incubated people in a warm and supportive environment.

*   *   *

Carnegie was a curious mixture of the modern and the old-fashioned. As a teacher of public speaking, he cast aside the stiff theatricality and stylized gestures of nineteenth-century prairie oratory and urged his students to embrace a more natural, colloquial style. He counseled them against formal diction and fancy language. Wordsworth had defined poetry as men speaking to men; Carnegie was teaching businessmen to speak to businessmen.

Carnegie was always more interested in style than content. Strike that: Carnegie was never really interested in content at all. He cared only about the *how* of things, not the *why*. (In that sense, he was in the great tradition of American basement tinkerers who are more interested in creating a new gadget than in figuring out how the universe works.) To him, it didn't matter whether you were speaking for or against socialism, whether you were advocating faith or atheism, just as long as you were engaging and smiled a lot. For Carnegie, you could give a great speech and never smile and lose your audience, or you could give a lousy one, smile a lot, and win your audience over.

In this sense, Carnegie helped usher in the age of what we now call communications, a subject that college students can now major in. He helped bring about the day when a president of the United States could be called the Great Communicator and people would regard that title as comparable to being the Great Emancipator. To Plato, the notion of communications would be no different than rhetoric, just a neutral means of packaging content.

Within twenty years of the start of Carnegie's course, four hundred of the nation's largest five hundred companies had paid for their employees to take it. By the late 1950s, three million Americans had taken it. Today, the Dale Carnegie Institute is a $100 million company.

* * *

By the early 1930s, Carnegie had crafted a lecture that he called "How to *Make* Friends and Influence People." One evening, Leon Shimkin, an editor at Simon & Schuster, attended Carnegie's talk and saw the possibilities for a book. He signed Carnegie up and they changed the "Make Friends" in the title to the catchier and more upbeat "Win Friends." The rest was publishing history. Carnegie, as he himself would be the first to tell you, was the classic overnight success who had worked a lifetime for it. In the year that he published *How to Win Friends and Influence People,* he had been teaching his course for nearly a quarter century.

How to Win Friends and Influence People quickly became a publishing phenomenon. It was for many years the best-selling nonfiction book of all time—depending of course on whether you consider the Bible fiction or nonfiction. When the book came out in 1936, it went through fourteen editions in a few weeks. It was the number-one best-seller of 1937, according to *Publishers' Weekly,* and was among the top three for the next three years. Coming out at the tail end of the Depression, the book helped restore faith in traditional American notions of success. Carnegie and Roosevelt both advanced the notion that there was nothing to fear but fear itself.

Carnegie's timing was perfect. His book came out at a time when the growth of corporate bureaucracies placed a premium on social skills. The key to success in corporations was not character but personality, and Carnegie was molding the latter, not the former. He was creating the organization man just at the time organizations needed them. He was making employees safe for the service economy.

People Are Not Very Nice

Dale Carnegie begins *How to Win Friends and Influence People,* not with one of his many folksy anecdotes about famous statesmen, successful salesmen, or corporate titans, but with a story about a notorious criminal. Carnegie tells the tale of the manhunt and sensational capture of the killer "Two-Gun" Crowley at his girlfriend's apartment on West End Avenue in New York City in 1931.

Crowley was a bank-robber who would "kill at the drop of a feather," according to the New York City police commissioner. He had eluded capture for months, but, finally, after a stakeout and a wild gunfight, he was arrested at his lady friend's flat. There, according to Carnegie, the cops found a note from the killer which read as follows: "To whom it may concern. Under my coat is a weary heart, but a kind one—one that would do nobody harm."

Carnegie then says—well, I think I'll let Carnegie himself explain why he begins his book with an anecdote about a bank-robber and cop-killer.

"The point of the story is this," Carnegie writes, " 'Two Gun' Crowley didn't blame himself for anything.

Is that an unusual attitude among criminals? If you think so, listen to this:

"I have spent the best years of my life giving people the lighter pleasures, helping them have a good time, and all I get is abuse, the existence of a hunted man."

That's Al Capone speaking. Yes, America's erstwhile Public Enemy Number One—the most sinister gang leader who ever shot up Chicago. Capone doesn't condemn himself either. He actually regards himself as a public benefactor.

Carnegie then goes on to quote Dutch Schultz, a few other gangsters, and various inmates at Sing-Sing to similar effect.

If Al Capone, 'Two Gun' Crowley, Dutch Schultz and the desperate men behind prison walls don't blame themselves for anything, what about the people with whom you and I come into contact?

Well, what about them?

Here is the lesson the author of *How to Win Friends and Influence People* draws from his example: "Criticism is futile because it puts a man on the defensive, and usually makes him strive to justify himself. Criticism is dangerous because it wounds a man's precious pride, hurts his sense of importance, and arouses his resentment."

As best as I can figure it, Carnegie's logic goes something like this: If the worst among us such as Al Capone or Two-Gun Crowley don't see themselves as bad, the rest of us, who are not nearly so bad, will never be able to see ourselves self-critically either. So don't bother criticizing anyone for anything because no one likes to be criticized and no one will cop to it anyway. And, furthermore, don't bother trying to change people—simply indulge their weaknesses so that you can triumph over them.

Well, perhaps I'm getting a little ahead of myself there.

Carnegie would strenuously disagree with my interpretation of his philosophy. He would insist that his outlook was a moral one, and at the very least, his book advocated a rather sunny, unthreatening regimen of self-improvement. Carnegie seemed unconscious of the darker interpretations of his philosophy. (He seemed unconscious of the unconscious altogether.) In fact, the Dale Carnegie philosophy was a coldly practical one based on a view of human nature that was as dark as that of Thomas Hobbes and more cunning and unsentimental than Machiavelli.

Here is a brief summary of Carnegie's view of human nature, as extrapolated from *How to Win Friends:* People are deeply irrational. They are not just self-absorbed, they are consummately self-absorbed. No one is really interested in anyone but himself or herself. People are easily duped. Humans are incapable of self-criticism. They desperately crave esteem and appreciation. And, as a result, they are easily won over by the simplest devices of paying attention, offering appreciation, and the giving of small flatteries.

Early on in *How to Win Friends*, Carnegie tells the reader that a recent study at the New York Telephone Company came up with the word used most in conversation; it was, he says, "I." "I." "I." "I." "I." (Yes, he repeats "I" five times.) Which leads him to sum up his view of humanity:

> People are not interested in you. They are not interested in me. They are interested in themselves—morning, noon, and after dinner.
>
> When you see a group photograph that you are in, whose picture do you look for first?

If you think people are interested in you, answer this question: If you died tonight, how many people would come to your funeral?

And then a little later, he waxes positively Stalinesque.

A person's toothache means more to that person than a famine in China which kills a million people. A boil on one's neck interests one more than forty earthquakes in Africa.

Not only are people selfish, he suggests, they are also deeply superficial. He cannot imagine anyone who has concerns any different from his, which are (1) to be liked, or, as Willy Loman put it, "well-liked" and (2) to be "successful," which seems to mean being well-liked *and* rich. Nowhere does Carnegie ever try to win people away from their selfishness. His approach is always to exploit it.

In fact, what Carnegie recognized is that one of the simplest and most effective forms of flattery is *listening*. If everyone is self-absorbed, then everyone will be pleased if you become absorbed in their self. He cites the Latin writer Publilius Syrus: "We are interested in others when they are interested in us." Listening and not interrupting is the way to ingratiate yourself with people. Carnegie quotes a young man who had a date with a woman who barely talked the whole evening as telling his friends that she might not have been pretty, but she was a "great conversationalist." (Men think talking is the way to flirt, but women know that listening is the more effective way to go.)

The "Secrets" of Success

From the start of *How to Win Friends,* Carnegie tips off the reader that he is not advocating the good old all-American Protestant work ethic in which industriousness and perseverance are the keystones to success. Carnegie had been guided by the psychologist H. A. Overstreet's *Influencing Human Behavior,* which suggested that even among engineers, only 15 percent of financial success was due to technical knowledge, but 85 percent was due to skill in human engineering. The cliché of the Protestant work ethic (as enunciated by Thomas Edison) is that genius is 99 percent perspiration and 1 percent inspiration. In fact, Carnegie was selling the no-sweat 1 percent solution. His techniques, he boasts, "aren't mere theories or guesswork. They work like magic."

Magic, not merit or hard work or skill. Merit plus 25 cents will get you a ride on the subway. Carnegie had discovered that the race goes not to the swift or the able, but to those who know how to handle people. And it is the only skill you'll ever need. "Say to yourself over and over: 'My popularity, my happiness and sense of worth depend to no small extent upon my skill in dealing with people." Part I in his book is titled "Fundamental Techniques in Handling People." (Problems, like people, are always *handled,* not solved.)

From the beginning, Carnegie depicts his techniques as a science. Human relations can be "engineered," he says, but you don't have to be an engineer to do it. In fact, when Carnegie's book came out, most libraries shelved it in the science section. (Plus, there was no self-help nook in libraries in those days.) He was seen as a kind of William James for the Everyman.

Handling people is a skill, Carnegie suggests, precisely because it is *un*natural and must be learned. "Whenever you are confronted with some specific problem," Carnegie writes, "hesitate about doing the natural thing, the impulsive thing. This is usually wrong." This puts Carnegie squarely in opposition to the Emerson and Whitman strain in American consciousness of following your instinct, of embracing your passions. Don't follow your instincts, he says; purge yourself of them, for they will only get you in trouble.

In essence, Carnegie's advice can be boiled down to the following: Never find fault, never argue, flatter people at every opportunity, appear sincere, and smile, smile, smile.

Let's look at how he supports each of his tenets.

~ *"Don't Criticize, Don't Argue"*

As a pseudo–social scientist, Carnegie theorizes only from anecdotal evidence. The source of his anecdotes is a mixture of stories from the high and mighty (Lincoln, Ben Franklin, Samuel Johnson, John D. Rockefeller, Andrew Carnegie) and everyday incidents from the ranks of the anonymous salesmen, mid-level executives, and housewives who have taken his course. Thus, he cites Ben Franklin saying, "I will speak ill of no man . . . and speak all the good I know of everybody." And then cites a Mr. W. P. Gaw of the Wark Company of Philadelphia (he sounds suspiciously like a made-up person) who has learned to keep his mouth shut and flatter his boss. For Carnegie, the great and the unknown, the famous and the anonymous, all merge, for Carnegie never lets on that Benjamin Franklin's task at the Constitutional Convention in 1787 (where Carnegie says he refused to criticize anyone) was any different or more important than W. P. Gaw's job of closing a real estate deal in downtown Philadelphia.

For Carnegie, the techniques are all the same and the ends don't seem to matter. In a way, this is a paradigm for all self-help movements; they don't distinguish between a genocide in Rwanda and a pitch meeting in Denver—it's how important the problem is to *you*.

In general, Carnegie is preaching the opposite of the Greek idea that the difference between a flatterer and a friend is parhesia, or candor. Carnegie's philosophy is, Never be candid, never be frank. Don't ever tell your friend something he won't want to hear or he will no longer be your friend.

The Greeks say that if he is your friend you owe it to him to tell him things he does not want to hear. But since Carnegie doesn't prize friendship enough to jeopardize it, and friends are really only business contacts anyway, why bother? There is no wrong so great, in his mind, that is worth being unpleasant about. When Carnegie says "You can't win an argument," what he really means is that you can't sell someone something if you get in an argument. The sell is all.

⌒ *"Flatter at Every Opportunity"*

For Carnegie, anything important is always labeled a "secret." Thus, he has chapter headings such as "The Big Secret of Dealing with People," or "The Secret of Socrates." He recounts that whenever he meets celebrated individuals, he asks them, "What is the secret to your success?"

The use of the word "secret" is a familiar advertising come-on, and is a vestige of his own adolescence, when he was forever trying to learn the "secret" to popularity. It plays into the childhood notion that there is some kind of open sesame or alchemy that will magically change your situation. Such concerns are once again the manifestation of the shift from character to personality in the American psyche. Character believes in hard work and perseverance. Personality is always looking for an angle, a silver bullet.

Carnegie again and again suggests that his "secrets" are effortless and work like "magic." This is reflected in other chapter titles such as "How to Make People Like You Instantly," "A Formula That Will Work Wonders for You," "Letters That Produce Miraculous Results." Everything is a snap—just like all the household cleaners from the 1950s that worked in a jiff. No elbow grease is required.

So, what is the Big Secret of Dealing with People? The secret is: "There is only one way under high Heaven to get anybody to do anything. . . . And that is by making the other person want to do it." And how do you make the other person want to do something? You flatter them and make them feel important, that's how. He quotes John Dewey as saying the deepest urge in human nature is "the desire to be important." You can get people to do what you want them to do by bribing them with praise, by making them feel important.

Here he cites the real exemplar of his book, the executive Charles Schwab, the first "hero bureaucrat," as the author Donald Meyer calls him. Carnegie seems to have a crush on Schwab, so giddy is he when talking about him. Schwab, according to Carnegie, was paid a million dollars a year to run U.S. Steel by Andrew Carnegie, not because he knew how to make steel, but because he knew how to manage people. Carnegie writes that Schwab understood "instinctively that [people] hungered for recognition; so he gave them praise and appreciation." He quotes Schwab as saying that his principal talent was the ability to arouse enthusiasm, and that he accomplished this with a simple formula: "If I like anything, I am hearty in my approbation and lavish in my praise." This phrase becomes a leitmotif in the book. For Carnegie, it is the mantra of success that he repeats over and over.

But Carnegie is shrewd enough to know this advice might seem hackneyed, or obvious, or hypocritical. "Some readers," he writes, "are saying right now as they read these lines: 'Old stuff, flattery seldom works with discerning people. It is shallow, selfish, and insincere.' " Besides the fact that he is flattering the reader ("Of course, [it] seldom works with discerning people" *like you,* dear reader), he is practicing one of his usual tricks, which is simply denying, denying, denying. In fact, after protesting too much, he tells a succession of stories to illustrate the success of his technique, all of which involve straight-from-the-shoulder flattery.

The first example he gives is of the "much-married [and now long forgotten] Mdivani brothers." "Why were these so-called 'Princes' able to marry two beautiful and famous screen stars and a world-famous prima donna and Barbara Hutton with five-and-ten-cent-store millions?" The screen actress Pola Negri furnishes the answer: "They understand the art of flattery as do no other men I have ever met." "That, I assure you, is the secret of the Mdivani charm for women. I know." Reader, she married one of them.

Finally, Carnegie tells the story of how Napoleon created the Legion of Honor and then distributed fifteen thousand of these medals to his soldiers. Napoleon, he says, was criticized by some for giving "toys" to hardened veterans who had risked their lives for him and France. "Napoleon replied," according to Carnegie, " 'Men are ruled by toys.' "

For Carnegie, flattery is the toy that rules men.

"Try to Seem Sincere"

Carnegie offers another argument as to why he is not simply advocating flattery. He makes a sharp distinction between praise and flattery. Praise, he says, is sincere; flattery is not. "One comes from the heart out; the other from the teeth out. One is unselfish; the other selfish. One is universally admired; the other is universally condemned."

It is a clever definition, but once again, he violates it even as he enunciates it. For in the very next breath, he asserts that there is no such thing as an unselfish act. "Every act you have ever performed since the day you were born," he writes, "was performed because you wanted something. How about the time you gave a large contribution to the Red Cross? Yes, that is no exception to the rule. You gave the Red Cross the donation because you wanted to lend a helping hand; you wanted to do a beautiful, unselfish divine act."

Carnegie insists on the notion of sincerity, but every bit of praise he recommends is strategic. Later, he does give one recommendation for how to make praise *seem* sincere. "Everybody likes to be praised," he says, "but when praise is specific, it comes across as sincere." But, of course, it only seems sincere because it is specific.

Carnegie cites England's King George V and the set of maxims displayed in his study at Buckingham Palace. One of them reads, " 'Teach me neither to proffer nor receive cheap praise.' That's all flattery is: cheap praise," adds Carnegie. But that's precisely what Carnegie advocates again and again. He tells a long story about how he goes out of his way to compliment a dour-looking bank teller by remarking on how abundant his hair is. And he does it just to see if he can get a smile out of the fellow. George V's maxim reminds me of the lovely Noël Coward line, "Extraordinary how potent cheap music is." And that is the point about flattery—it's extraordinary how potent even cheap flattery is.

It is precisely because praise disarms us that we tend not to think about whether or not it is genuine. There is no polygraph test for praise. Carnegie's notion of sincerity is that, if you are sincere in the result you want, your praise is sincere. If you tell the boss that his memo was brilliant because you want a raise, you won't be lying, according to Carnegie, because you *really, really* want the raise. Carnegie's point seems to be that if you want the result badly enough and begin to believe in your insincere praise, it will no longer be insincere.

At the end of the George V section, Carnegie writes, "If all we had to do was to use flattery, everybody would catch on to it, and we should all be experts in human relations." That would be terrible, disastrous even, for then everyone would be an expert. Don't forget, it is he, Dale Carnegie, who is the expert in human relations. If you could take his fairly elaborate theories and summarize them with the maxim "flattery works," then why would you ever need to buy his paperback or take his course?

*   *   *

Carnegie has very little to say about friendship in *How to Win Friends and Influence People*. In fact, he's less interested in friendship than *having* friends, and by having friends he means making others think you have lots of friends. Carnegie never seems to have outgrown the high-school view of the world. He spent the rest of his life trying to figure out how to be the most popular boy in school.

In *How to Win Friends,* Carnegie nowhere describes what a friend is, or what it means to be a friend. He is concerned only in how to *win* them. He does not ever refer to a personal friend of his—everyone is either someone he admires, and brown-noses, or some average Joe whom he's using as an example. For Carnegie, a friend is not someone he goes to dinner with, a friend is someone *who likes me*.

For Carnegie, friends are a commodity. They are names to put in an address book, connections, contacts, people to invite to dinner, people who can give you testimonials for your book or class. A friend, by his definition, is somone who can help you. And making friends is just another learned and useful skill.

*   *   *

In Part II of the book, Carnegie proposes "Six Ways to Make People Like You." His first rule for "making people like you" is, "Become *genuinely* interested in other people." (The italics are mine.) Very sensible, really. And here is how Carnegie follows his own advice:

For years I have made it a point to find out the birthdays of my friends. How? Although I haven't the foggiest bit of faith in astrology, I begin by asking the other party whether he believes the date of one's birth has anything to do with character and disposition. I then ask him to tell me the month and day of his birth. If he says November 24, for example, I keep repeating to myself, 'November 24, November 24.' The minute his back is turned, I write down his name and birthday and later transfer it to a birthday book. At the beginning of each year, I have these birthday dates scheduled in my calendar pad, so they come to my attention automatically. When the natal day arrives, there is my letter or telegram. What a hit it makes! I am frequently the only person on earth who remembers.

As ever, Carnegie proposes a trick of ingratiation, a small ruse that will help him convey genuineness or sincerity. It is never actual sincerity, just the verisimilitude of it. Carnegie's notion of what is sincere or genuine is whether he himself is sincere or genuine in wanting to cultivate someone. The birthday story is another example of what we might call the flattery of small attentions. Another example is the use of names.

Carnegie tells the story of Jim Farley, who became postmaster general of the United States under FDR, Carnegie says, all because he could remember people's names. Farley didn't have a high-school education, Carnegie tells us, but he was a gregarious man who could recall the first names of 50,000 people. "Jim Farley discovered early in life," Carnegie says, "that the average man is more interested in his own name than he is in all the other names on earth put together. Remember that name and call it easily, and you have paid him a subtle and very effective compliment. But forget it or misspell it—and you have placed yourself at a sharp disadvantage." Powerful men, Carnegie says, will block the mergers of companies if their name is not in the title, and wealthy people will blithely give away millions just to have their name on a hospital or a museum. "Remember," Carnegie says, "a man's name is to him the sweetest and most important sound in any language."

The technique—of repeating a person's name in conversation—is well known among salesman and politicians who make a fetish of remembering people's names. Bill Clinton is said to remember the names of thousands of people, and George Bush's administration was once known as "the thank-you-note presidency" because he was so punctilious about writing thank-you notes for every occasion.

*   *   *

The simplest and easiest trick of all to winning friends, according to Carnegie, is to smile. Charles Schwab, Carnegie says, had a "million-dollar smile." Why? Because it was his smile that got him his million-dollar job.

What does a smile do? (I'm sounding like Carnegie myself now; he has that effect on you.) "A smile says, 'I like you.' " In the nineteenth century, a smile might have made people a little wary ("Why is that fellow smiling at me?"), but in the new age of the big impersonal corporation, when employees began to feel like the proverbial cogs in a machine, Schwab's toothy grin made people feel special. It warmed the cold corridors of the heartless new American corporation. He was the first of the great corporate face men.

Carnegie's golden rule, his version of reciprocal altruism, is "Smile unto others and they will smile unto you." We've come a long way from Chesterfield's counsel to be *agréable*—by which he meant to be charming and witty and gracious, and know how to waltz. For Carnegie, it all comes down to putting on a happy face. He counsels smiling even when you don't feel like it, smiling every hour on the hour, smiling when you're low, smiling at strangers, just to get in the practice of it. In fact, he's again scientifically correct, for studies have shown that the physical act of smiling, regardless of any circumstances, can brighten your mood by raising the level of serotonin in your brain. As Carnegie says, "Act as if you were already happy, and that will tend to make you happy." That just happens to be one of the basic principles of all the twelve-step therapies as well. As Lincoln said, "Most folks are about as happy as they make up their minds to be."

Carnegie tells the story of a grouchy stockbroker whom he induces to start smiling. The fellow shocks his wife and his employees with his new sunniness. His wife becomes more cheerful. His employees are happier. Business improves. "I find that smiles," the stockbroker says, "are bringing me dollars, many dollars every day." A smile, ultimately, is another commodity. It helps you sell what you want to sell and buy what you want to buy. If you smile at the woman making sandwiches in the cafeteria, Carnegie says, she'll put more bologna between your bread. But remember, it must be sincere, for it is the *sincere* smile, he says, "that will bring a good price in the marketplace." So ring up that sale.

Making the World Safe for Corporations

God does not even make a cameo appearance in *How to Win Friends and Influence People. Poor Richard's Almanack,* which in many ways is the antecedent to *How to Win Friends,* seems like a religious tract compared to Carnegie's book, and Franklin was an agnostic at best. Franklin at least said that God helps those who help themselves; Carnegie simply said, *Help yourself.* Carnegie is preparing people not for heaven but for the new American marketplace.

Carnegie seems to be telling his readers how to achieve greater autonomy, but as Michel Foucault, the French philosopher, might suggest, it is an autonomy that is a cover for the exercise of power. It is an autonomy that is not autonomous. Foucault would say that Carnegie is just making the exchange of money and corporate power easier; he is just creating a docile and cheerful labor class, a kinder, gentler managerial class. Foucault would probably say that the change from nineteenth-century uplift manuals to Carnegie's how-to-ingratiate textbook represents an increasing colonization of the interior self, the self being hijacked by commerce.

Ultimately, what Carnegie is selling is the new style of capitalism in America. Part of that new style is the necessity for the selling of the self. You are your own number-one product. Men and women will increasingly be working in big corporations where it is better to listen and smile, than be an ornery iconoclast. Corporations don't really want inner-directed individuals, they want other-directed personalities. It is a world where flattery and ingratiation gets you promoted, not reprimanded.

Carnegie is not really advising anyone to shoot for the top. He's saying that this is how you get to the next rung of the ladder. Most of the people who would take his course or read his book were people who had hit a glass ceiling. Carnegie is telling them how to break through and get to the next level, not how to rise to get to the penthouse corner office. He is not telling them how to be Charles Schwab, but how to be one of the innumerable vice presidents below him.

Mostly, he seems to be advocating a kind of ingratiating passivity that will seem to others to be helpful. In the introduction to the book, he proudly quotes John D. Rockefeller as saying, "The ability to deal with people is as purchasable a commodity as sugar or coffee. And I will pay more for that ability than any other under the sun." By the same token, Carnegie advises that the way to get a job is to go to the boss and say, "I believe I can help you get even richer." So, it's a closed circle. John D. can pay any amount to land you and you can make him even richer.

*   *   *

On one level, *How to Win Friends and Influence People* signaled a move away from Depression-era pessimism to a restoration of American optimism. But it also symbolized, as we have seen, a change in the American persona itself. For Christopher Lasch, this represented a shift from an age of individualism to an era of narcissisim. "In earlier times," wrote Lasch, "the self-made man took pride in his judgment of character and probity; today he anxiously scans the faces of his fellows not so as to evaluate their credit but in order to gauge their susceptibility to his own blandishments. He practices the classic art of seduction and with the same indifference to moral niceties, hoping to win your heart while picking your pocket." Lasch could be describing Carnegie himself.

The personality era was represented by what William H. Whyte called the *Organization Man,* who existed in a corporation where conformity, not individuality, was the order of the day. The jovial, hail-fellow-well-met salesman had to learn to tone things down a bit. In the salesman ethos, your personality was your capital. But in the modern era of the soft sell, you weren't supposed to be the life of the party; you were a mirror, not a lamp, and you aimed to reflect the desires of your customer—or your boss.

As America shifted from the character era to the age of personality, Americans seemed to require more praise, more reassurance, more positive reinforcement. And they got it from books like *How to Win Friends* and from the unconditional positive regard of the postwar self-help movements, which used Carnegie's work as a springboard.

The American quest for enlightenment has traditionally taken the form of either old-time religion or new-fangled self-help. The idea, of course, is to have it both ways. You can be rich *and* get into heaven. You, too, can succeed and not feel guilty about it. It was the power not of positive thinking but of wishful thinking.

How to Win Friends, Find Inner Contentment, and Tighten Your Buns in One Easy Lesson

Carnegie was neither the first nor the last of the great American self-help gurus. Self-help is older than the republic. Puritan self-help tomes emphasized the basic virtues of work, diligence, and thrift. This theme was continued through the McGuffey readers for children of the nineteenth century, which sold over 100 million copies and suggested that if you worked hard and played by the rules you could grow rich with a good conscience.

After the Civil War, a new idea took root: Mind Power, or the Mind Cure, which was the idea that positive thinking controlled everything, from health to wealth. Phineas P. Quimby, one of the fathers of Mind Cure in America, preached the idea that disease was an unfortunate mental delusion. "I deny disease as a truth," he wrote, "but admit it as a deception handed down from generation to generation until they believe it." One of his patients was a Mrs. Mary Patterson, who as Mary Baker Eddy would found Christian Science. There is nothing more self-flattering than thinking that you yourself control absolutely everything that happens to you. Another Mind Power author, Orison Swett Marsden, asserted in his 1921 book, *Masterful Personality,* that "You Can Compel People to Like You!" The magic formula of all of these books was that there was in fact a magic formula.

In the ideology of Mind Power, the unconscious was seen not as Freud's miasma of sex drives and death instincts but as a benevolent source of power and creativity. The authors simply took Freud's thought and Hollywoodized it, giving it a happy ending. This optimistic approach to psychology was the precursor to the don't-worry-be-happy pop psychology and self-actualization movements of America in the 1970s and 1980s. What Carnegie did was take the basic idea of Mind Power and purge it of any spirituality.

After World War I, the rise of psychology and psychiatry relegated the pseudoscience of mind-healing and New Thought to the realm of the kooky. But the importance of positive thinking seemed to increase. In 1923, the upbeat message of a visiting Frenchman named Émile Coué captivated

America. Within months, millions of Americans were starting their day repeating his self-flattering formula: "Day by day, in every way, I am getting better and better." Carnegie proudly acknowledges having been influenced by Coué. Coué's philosophy was meant for mental healing but it also appealed to the sensibilities of American businessmen. "He has the right idea," said Henry Ford, one of Carnegie's idols. Coué's spiritual philosophy was quickly transformed into a kind of American fast-food success formula with books like S. A. Harrington's *Success Nuggets: "Pep" in Capsule Form.* Take one a day.

Napoleon Hill's 1937 book, *Think and Grow Rich,* which came out just after *How to Win Friends,* had an even more magical formula than Carnegie's. He claimed that there was a universal ether that carried "vibrations" of wealth and poverty, success and failure, and that you must learn to attract the right vibrations through positive thoughts. He advised his readers that at least once a day they should close their eyes and fix their minds on money for twenty minutes. David Riesman called its central idea "economic Couéism." His book was reprinted in paperback as late as 1961.

Positive thinking reached its apotheosis with the book of a failed journalist turned Methodist minister named Norman Vincent Peale. Peale combined the Carnegie ethos with old-time religion to create a theology of success. His 1952 book *The Power of Positive Thinking* was at the top of the best-seller list for nearly four years and became a familiar American mantra. ("Paul is appealing," said Adlai Stevenson, "but Peale is appalling.") Peale, like Carnegie, saw what he called a national "inferiority complex" and sought to remedy it. Want to be happy? Peale asked. Well, then think happy thoughts. It was Emerson, infantilized.

Like Carnegie, Peale seemed more interested in achieving outer esteem than inner virtue. He preached faith, but it was a faith that would, as he said, make you "a more popular, esteemed and well-liked individual." And as if the commercial significance was not clear enough, Peale counsels his readers to have "a merger with God." Like so many of the ministers of positive thinking who would follow him in movements as various as Alcoholics Anonymous, est, and Scientology, Peale contended that the greatest human problem of all was a negative state of mind.

Carnegie tried to tap into this shift with his next book, *How to Stop Worrying and Start Living,* in which he tried to mirror the change from the chase of outer achievement to the pursuit of inner contentment. It was a primer for the new age of anxiety. But *How to Stop Worrying* misses the boat, for while Carnegie sensed the uncertainty in America, his remedy is only skin-deep. It is neither spiritual nor psychological. It's a kind of salesman's behaviorism. Put your worries in airtight compartments, he said, and only think about today. It is meant to be inspirational, but it comes across as deeply nonintrospective and simplistic.

The shift over the last thirty years to a greater concern with inner than outer is in part a reaction to the Dale Carnegie view of the world. The political activism and concern with nonmaterial pursuits that erupted in the 1960s was in part a reaction to the bland conformity of the 1950s, which Carnegie helped create.

Carnegie would have understood the rise of victimhood that has been going on since the 1970s and seen it as a need for attention. Leeza Gibbons, with her showcase of all manner of victims, is a kind of more soulful Dale Carnegie. Remember how Carnegie started? Asking people to get up and talk about what made them angry. After all, it's better to be a victim on *Leeza* than a sap that no one pays attention to.

Victimhood then becomes a form of recognition and a modern type of celebrity, however fleeting. The flattery of the modern self-help and recovery movement is that it recognizes that your problem is more important to you than anyone else's. But the scale is off. As Wendy Kaminer, an astute critic of self-help, writes, "Recovery gives people permission to put themselves first, partly because it doesn't give them a sense of perspective on their complaints." That is a form of modern flattery.

But in the late 1990s, some of the shine has been taken off of victimhood. An overcharged economy and a new gilded age have made people more assertive if not more confident. What we are seeing in the 1990s is a kind of ingratiating individualism, where the ruggedness and inner direction are gone, but not the unrelenting pursuit of success and self-interest. The obsessive pursuit of self-interest is camouflaged by a surface of bland and ingratiating friendliness. Wealth has become the ultimate measurement. There is no achievement anymore that is outside the commercial.

In a sense, things have come around again to Dale Carnegie's mechanistic view of human relations. He was allergic to the spiritual; he understood Pavlov and would have been deeply confused by Deepak Chopra. In *How to Stop Worrying and Start Living,* his sequel to *How to Win Friends,* Carnegie recalls that he just didn't feel right becoming a preacher as his mother wanted. In a moment of rare introspection, he says he couldn't do it because he couldn't get himself to believe in something that was so, well, intangible. "I believed that life was planless and aimless," he wrote. "I believed that all human beings had no more divine purpose than the dinosaurs that roamed the earth two hundred million years ago."

Carnegie was never deceptive. He didn't pretend to a spirituality or deep insight that he did not possess. He figured out a few basic rules that seemed to work, and he taught people to follow them. In fact, he tells us he learned the way to be happy and successful when he was just a boy. His guru was his—and man's—best friend.

When I was five years old my father bought a little yellow-haired pup for fifty cents. He was the light and joy of my childhood. Every afternoon about four-thirty, he would sit in the front yard with his beautiful eyes staring steadfastly at the path, and as soon as he heard my voice or saw me swinging my dinner pail through the buck brush, he was off like a shot, racing breathlessly up the hill to greet me with leaps of joy and barks of sheer ecstasy.

Tippy was my constant companion for five years. Then one tragic night—I shall never forget it—he was killed within ten feet of my head, killed by lightning. Tippy's death was the tragedy of my boyhood.

Then Carnegie addresses his departed friend:

You never read a book on psychology, Tippy. You didn't need to. You knew by some divine instinct that one can make more friends in two months by becoming genuinely interested in other people than one can in two years by trying to get other people interested in him.

The humble canine, says Carnegie, is "the greatest winner of friends the world has ever known." At last, Carnegie has found his one true expert in human relations, and it's an expert he does not have to fear as a potential rival. Just study Tippy's technique, he says. Tippy's wagging tail is the most sincere smile of all. And that cannot be taught.

Chapter 9

The Science
of Ingratiation

All the World's a Stage

In 1959, the great sociologist Erving Goffman gave a talk as a visiting university lecturer in which he described his theories of human behavior in his extraordinary book, *The Presentation of Self in Everyday Life*. Goffman's theory has come to be known as the "dramaturgical approach" because he essentially says life is like a play in which we are all actors who portray ourselves to other actors who are portraying themselves. He says that in every encounter we attempt to present ourselves in the best possible light, that we all try to control the impression we make, and that there is a tacit social agreement, "a working consensus," that we allow each person to perform as himself however he chooses.

At the end of the lecture, a graduate student rose and asked a question in a rather supercilious tone. *Isn't your theory,* he asked, *just the all-the-world's-a-stage-and-we-are-merely-players-on-it cliché that Shakespeare used four hundred years ago?* Goffman, who was a rather introverted man, stumbled a bit, and then replied, *Ah, well, let me ask you, except for the fact that there is no audience, can you tell me how life is fundamentally different than that?*

In many ways, Goffman was more an artist than a social scientist. He had a Proustian eye for the subtlest details of human relations, though he expressed his insights in the rather dry and mechanical prose of social science.

Goffman saw social behavior as a giant and unspoken conspiracy. Everyone is in on the game, and the game is deception. We are all, says Goffman, just "harried fabricators of impressions." Every day, with the tacit approval of everyone else, we practice myriad deceptions small and large that make society function. Without them, the polite veneer of civilization would drop and we'd have a nasty situation on our hands. Instead, we all do what we can to get through every social encounter without creating a "scene."

Everyone in society, Goffman says, has a double role: "A defensive orientation toward saving his own face and a protective orientation toward saving the other's face." Tact was the only thing standing between us and the primal horde. "Much of the activity during an encounter," he writes, "can be understood as an effort on everyone's part to get through the occasion and all the unanticipated and unintentional events"—without making anyone uncomfortable. Goffman notes, for example, how we all tend to gloss over a person's shortcomings or failures when in his or her presence. In this way, we also protect ourselves—for we know that someday the shoe will be on the other foot.

At the same time Goffman was describing the dramaturgical approach, another sociologist by the name of Edward E. Jones began to test it. Goffman's work was observational; Jones's was empirical. Jones set out to see if he could demonstrate the things that Goffman observed about everyday behavior. Jones's own preoccupation was how we decide what people are "really like," and how we all control our own presentation of what we ourselves are "really like."

Like Goffman, Jones believed that we all try to manage the impressions we make on others. Even when we say "Please pass the pepper," we have some goal of self-presentation that we are trying to make. We may whisper it because we don't want the hostess to think the dish requires more seasoning, or we may say it loudly to give the impression that we are forceful, or we may say it softly to suggest that we have lovely manners.

In ways both conscious and unconscious, we all use strategic self-presentation to create the impression we want to convey. The type of strategic self-presentation that Jones studied and tested for over forty years was ingratiation. What Freud was to psychoanalysis, Jones was to ingratiation. Jones described his own work with ingratiation as taking a phenomenon that had had a long literary and cultural history and attempting to put it in "the domain of systematic psychological inquiry." Ingratiation, said Jones, was a ubiquitous strategy that we all use to manipulate and control our own "outcomes," to use the sociologist's term. Every interpersonal encounter, Jones suggests, involves some opportunity for "social rewards and punishments," and ingratiation is one of our primary tactics for getting the rewards and avoiding the punishments.

For all practical purposes, Jones viewed flattery and ingratiation as interchangeable. He called them "sister" terms. The distinction he made is that the goal of ingratiation is merely to secure attraction, while the goal of flattery is to secure a benefit. Jones also coined the phrase the "ingratiator's dilemma," by which he meant that flattery is going to be least effective when the ingratiator's overtures are most transparent—which is likely to be when the ingratiator is most dependent. In other words, the more desperate we are, the more transparent our goals are likely to be and the lower our probability of success.

Jones's studies also helped give rise to a term that Goffman first used: "impression management." Goffman's use of the term was basically descriptive; he meant the behavior and strategies we used to try to control the impressions we make ("Spin control," is the more popular term for it these days). Since Goffman and Jones, "impression management" has become a term used almost exclusively by management professors, authors of business handbooks, and industrial-organizational psychologists. It is used today to describe everything from what kind of tie to wear to a job interview to how a CEO conducts himself in front of his board to what kind of public relations effort an airline should make after a very public crash. In business studies, ingratiation is deemed a subset of impression management.

.   .   .

At the outset of his classic 1964 book *Ingratiation,* Jones notes that "ingratiation" and "flattery" are both "mildly pejorative." This is a long way from Dante's eighth circle of hell. Flattery long ago lost much of its moral sting. He observes, for example, that when a critic describes an actor's performance as "ingratiating," he means the actor is perhaps trying too hard, or is a little oleaginous. The reason people do not like ingratiation or flattery in everyday life, he suggests, is that they both involve "manipulative intent and deceitful execution."

Jones calls flattery and ingratiation a "subversive masquerade" and says they are "illicit." The reason they are "illicit" and "subversive" is because they violate Goffman's social contract, which is that in every social occasion we all help each other save face. "Ingratiation," he wrote, "exploits the logic of social exchange while subverting it" at the same time. The ingratiator sends out signals that he accepts the basic social contract, and then privately violates it.

Instead of saving face, what ingratiation does, says Jones, is to allow a person to leave an interchange "with a better face than when he entered." It is a way of seeking to shift the power relationship between the ingratiator and his or her target. It is "non-normative behavior under a normative guise," he says, and therefore "illegitimate."

Jones posits another model for how flattery and ingratiation work and how they rend the social fabric. He cites the sociologist George Homan's notion of "distributive justice," the idea that in any regular social interaction, the reward and benefits are distributed justly. This is the assumption that we operate on all the time. But flattery and ingratiation, Jones suggests, stack the deck in the flatterer's favor, so that an ingratiator is trying to get a greater reward based on a minimal extra cost. He wants something for nothing. "The ingratiator," Jones says, "is ultimately concerned with creating feelings of obligation which will redound to his benefit."

Jones, like many others, says the basic reason that flattery works is that we like people who seem to like us. Jones cites the work of the psychologist Fritz Heider in suggesting that if one person perceives that the other likes or respects him, that person will have a tendency to reciprocate the feeling. Heider suggests that one reason we do so is that we feel uncomfortable if there is an imbalance in affection. We don't like *not* liking people who like us. So, we raise our opinion of the flatterer. It is not so much reciprocal altruism as reciprocal congeniality. And as Jones notes, "it is the perception of being liked, not the actual *fact* of being liked," that makes us like in return.

One of the staples of social psychology is that human behavior is ambiguous and that it is an unreliable indicator of internal states. In other words, we are just not very good at figuring out what others are really thinking or feeling. One of the reasons for this, suggests Jones, is that we all conceal our true feelings much of the time. And we are very poor decoders of deception. Every experimental study of lying has shown that we can spot it with no better odds than winning at roulette. Jones once pointed out that if by some evolutionary quirk we had all evolved with CRT screens in our foreheads that allowed everyone to read what we were thinking and feeling, none of us would have any friends at all.

Jones notes that ingratiation is particularly ambiguous behavior. He calls it "cognitively inaccessible." A compliment can be a strategic ploy or just an act of politeness. Much of our daily behavior, he notes, is just the ritual exchange of scripted pleasantries. But what makes ingratiation especially murky is that we are deceptive both about its goal and its content. Moreover, the ingratiator often conceals his ulterior motive from himself so that it is almost impossible for the scientific observer to "distinguish between genuine admiration and false praise." We are taken in by our own performances. We do this in order to avoid what sociologists call "dissonance arousal"—that queasy feeling of being a hypocrite.

Toward the end of his life, Jones concluded that much of what he originally thought was consciously strategic was in fact unconscious and automatic, what he called a "reaction tendency" to certain cues in the social environment that indicated one's momentary dependency. In other words, we did a lot of it without thinking. That does not mean that the goals or effects of ingratiation are any different, only that it is even more deeply ingrained than he had originally believed.

A Taxonomy of Tactics

Let's abandon the abstract theorizing and look at how Jones looked at ingratiation. First, his working definition: Ingratiation was "a class of strategic behaviors illicitly designed to influence a particular other person concerning the attractiveness of one's personal qualities." Jones examined ingratiation from three angles: from the point of view of the actor or ingratiator, from the point of view of the subject or "target," and from the perspective of the observer or bystander.

Jones tested four major types of tactical behavior: what sociologists call "other enhancement," that is, compliments or praise; "opinion conformity," agreeing with everything; "self-presentation," which can take a variety of forms from boastfulness to name-dropping; and finally, "rendering favors." Jones notes that there are many other social tactics to gain favor and power, such as self-promotion, exemplification (trying to be seen as saintly), intimidation, and supplication, but that ingratiation is the most prevalent. In fact, ingratiation, he says, is an ingredient in almost every other form of strategic behavior.

Other Enhancement—or, You Look Marvelous!

One day when I was in college, I was strolling across campus and crossed paths with a professor I greatly admired. I greeted him and he turned to his companion, another professor, and said, "Here is one of our brightest young men." My heart swelled. That evening, I saw him again at a lecture where I overheard him introduce a student to a different colleague by saying, "Here is one of our brightest young men." My heart sank.

Now, of course, there are a number of possible explanations: that we two were in fact two of the university's "brightest young men"; that he used the same line about all of his students; or, he did it just to ingratiate himself with me and the other fellow. Jones notes that there are a myriad of potential explanations for a compliment like that, only one of which is that the person saying it actually believes it.

That professor had used what Jones calls "other enhancement," which comes closest to what we think of as the everyday meaning of flattery: giving compliments. Jones calls this "directly enhancing, evaluative responses to the target person," in other words, telling someone that he is handsome, or that she has done an excellent job, and thereby conveying the general impression that "You're the cat's meow" or "I really think highly of you." The compliments may be exaggerated or made-up, or they can even be genuine. "Direct duplicity," Jones notes dryly, isn't necessary.

Jones gives the example of a young man telling a young woman during a date that she is a "beautiful, sensitive person." Jones suggests that there are at least five responses on the woman's part: (1) he wants something from me; (2) he is the kind of person who always makes positive comments; (3)

it is an appropriate comment for the occasion (let's say, a senior prom); (4) he's trying not to hurt my feelings; (5) he actually means it. If she concludes that it is (1), her estimation of the date goes down; (2) it probably stays the same; (3) the same; (4) some increase; (5) major increase.

Thus, in complimenting people, you should avoid seeming like you want something; avoid giving the same kind of compliment to more than one person; make the compliment not contingent on the occasion; and don't seem like you're pitying the person and trying to boost her confidence.

In general, Jones also counsels against outlandish or extreme compliments because (a) they will seem unwarranted and (b) they will embarrass the target. I would add another caveat, which is, don't use abstract superlatives, such as "You're the greatest." Its extreme form and lack of specificity make the praise lack plausibility. Lavish praise requires a delicate act, says Jones: "The communicator must deliver compliments which are more lavish than the recipient expects or thinks he deserves, and yet he must convey the impression that he himself believes them to be justified."

So how do you establish credibility? That is, how should an ingratiator structure his flattery to make sure the target person will accept it and not see through it? Jones offers several suggestions.

Don't give a compliment and ask for a favor at the same time. For instance, You know, Professor Flutesnoot, this is the best course I've ever taken. Could I have an extension on that paper? As Mark Twain once said, "A compliment that is charged for is not valuable."

Flatter people behind their back. Jones notes that one way to establish credibility is through a rather devious method: third-party compliments. That is, flatter a person to someone else, and when the praise gets back to her, she will think it genuine. Lord Chesterfield advised his son to do this, saying, quite correctly, that "of all flattery, it is the most pleasing and consequently, the most effectual." It is the perfect crime because it leaves no evidence.

Make the compliment plausible. It's probably not wise to say to your obese uncle Elmo that he's looking svelte.

Don't flatter the obvious. Jones cites Lord Chesterfield advising his son to flatter people not for what they obviously do well but for what they want to do better.

Jones advises that when we are considering flattery, we must think of what the target person wants to hear and whether or not he will believe it. This brings up the interesting issue of the self-esteem of the target. It would seem that you would flatter the person who hungers for reassurance while you avoid flattering the person who already thinks he hung the moon and stars.

There have been quite a number of studies that deal with how one's self-esteem affects one's response to flattery. Some researchers assumed that those with low self-esteem were more susceptible to flattery than those with high self-esteem. But, in fact, many studies found that the opposite was true.

Jones cites a UCLA study which suggested that we like those who seem to like us only if we like ourselves. The study suggested that when you flatter someone with high self-esteem you are only confirming what that individual already thinks about himself. A young man walks into the office of his manager at the firm and says, "Mr. Smith, I thought the work you did on the XYZ account was brilliant." Inside Mr. Smith's head: Yes, I am a brilliant fellow, aren't I, and this young man is quite clever to perceive it. As Samuel Johnson said, "Every man willingly gives value to the praise which he receives and considers the sentence passed in his favor as a sentence of discernment."

By the same token, if he said precisely the same thing to a Mr. Smith who, as it turned out, had very low self-esteem, Mr. Smith's inner voice might respond this way: Hmm, we all know I'm not brilliant—my work on the XYZ account was mediocre at best—so why is this little sycophantic weenie trying to worm his way into my good graces? Low self-esteem, the study suggested, often makes us more skeptical of praise directed our way.

This same study suggested that sometimes disliking begets liking—if the target has very low self-esteem. Deutch and Solomon suggested that if a person has a very low opinion of self, he will like or respect someone who seems to share that opinion. As a woman friend of mine once said, "My boyfriend and I only have one thing in common: we both hate me."

Jones recounts a study in which a young woman evaluated a group of young men. Each young man was permitted to read the woman's evaluation of him and then was asked to indicate how he liked her. If the men were rejected by the woman, low-self-esteem individuals disliked her more than those with high self-esteem. When the message was ambiguous, high-self-esteem men liked her better than low self-esteem men. When the subjects were liked by the woman, they all seemed to like her back equally. The researchers suggest that people with low self-esteem interpret neutral or ambiguous comments to be negative, while high-self-esteem people interpret them as positive.

Jones comes up with a commonsense theory regarding self-esteem that echoes Chesterfield's earlier points. He says if a person is quite certain that he is lousy at singing, he will find compliments directed toward his voice to be not credible. If, however, he is *uncertain* about the quality of his singing voice, and may want or need reassurance as to its quality, he will respond better to praise. Shrewd ingratiators, he says, will follow what he calls the "uncertainty reduction principle."

To sum up, even the studies with different conclusions about low and high self-esteem suggest that praising people generally has a positive reaction no matter what they think of themselves. The difference is that people with high self-esteem rarely question the praise because it is congruent with what they already think, while people with low self-esteem are more likely to be skeptical.

In general, Jones says, other enhancement works well as long as the target doesn't think the ingratiator has an ulterior motive. Virtually every study shows that a positive evaluation engenders liking as long as the target believes the ingratiator has nothing to gain by it. As soon as the target perceives the subject as seeking some benefit, the positive evaluation declines.

The rules, then, according to Jones, are: avoid complimenting the target in a way that makes it clear you want a reward; make sure the compliment is plausible; praise an attribute about which the target is uncertain; and don't leave the impression that you are a promiscuous praiser. So, for example, if you're a man who's trying to impress his date, don't go around telling every other woman at the dance that she is ravishing.

*   *   *

Jones suggests a number of ways in which the ingratiator can obscure ulterior motive. One way is to mix in some minor criticism with the praise. Praise first, and do it big, then add a cavil or two: *I thought your novel was magnificent, but I thought that one scene with the horse might have been unnecessary.* Don't be uniformly positive. Avoid relative comparisons ("You're a much better writer than Jay McInerney"). Another way is to be cool or neutral in the beginning and grow warmer and more complimentary over time. We tend to regard such a person as discerning. One experiment cited by Jones shows that we feel more warmly toward people when they seem to grow to like us rather than when they like us right away.

Jones cites two other situations that affect the effectiveness of "other enhancement" and what to do about them.

Ritual compliments. Jones notes that certain occasions seem to require a compliment, and if you want to get the benefit of your flattery, you must make sure your praise does not come across as perfunctory or obligatory. When, for example, we visit a mother and her new baby, we are pretty much obliged to say the baby is adorable. You must say something. The danger here is in not complimenting.

Thus, in situations that demand a compliment, don't be neutral. When I was in high school, my mother told me never to say to a woman, "Hey, you got your hair cut!" Say either "I like your haircut" or say nothing at all. Better yet, be specific: "You look great with bangs!"

How's my hair? Beware when people ask your opinion. So, how did you like the play? Or, I just redesigned the living room, what do you think? Or a person asks for your opinion on some even more sensitive subject, such as, do you think I'm smart? "By and large," as Jones and his sometime collaborator Camille Wortman note, "when people ask us what we think of them, they do not necessarily crave the truth." Not necessarily? They absolutely don't want the truth if the truth is going to hurt. Jones suggests they want compliments, not candor; support, not criticism. A self-aware person may understand that he is nullifying whatever praise he may receive by avidly seeking it. That, however, is rare. I've had friends who are writers say to me, "I'd like you to read this piece, but only if you tell me it's good." And if I do read it, I will. And as Jones says, the "devious ingratiator" will learn from such inquiries just what areas of uncertainties to exploit in the future.

* * *

Is there a downside to an undeserved compliment? Is Chesterfield right that there is no harm? For one thing, suggests Jones, it might make the person think she is more competent or appealing than she really is and such a perception may spur her to compete for a job or a place for which she is unqualified and thereby be disappointed. It may actually cause people to enter situations in which they are bound to fail. A student may get falsely praised by his teachers, and then set his heart on Yale, and be crushed by his rejection. Praise can be dangerous if it inspires someone to do something he isn't able to do, like fly a small plane under nonoptimal conditions.

There is also the annoyance of dealing with people who have too high an opinion of themselves, people who overestimate their own competence and attractiveness. What's so annoying is the same problem that we have with hypocrisy—the discrepancy between appearance and reality. We don't like anything that is overvalued, even people. A friend of mine is fond of saying, "If only idiots knew they were idiots."

Opinion Conformity—Yes, I Couldn't Agree More

The second tactic that Jones examines is what sociologists call "opinion conformity"—or, in layman's terms, agreeing with everything. There were a great many studies of conformity after World War II, but nearly all of them focused on conformity as a result of social pressures rather than conformity as a tactic of social influence.

The strategy has a very simple rationale: Just as we like people who appear to like us, studies show that we like people whose values and beliefs appear to be similar to our own. In short, we like people who are like us and we like people who agree with us—and we assume that they will very often be one and the same.

Opinion conformity takes a variety of forms, everything from simple agreement ("Yes, Ray, that's a terrific idea for the pitch meeting") to imitation (if the boss always wears a red turtleneck on casual Friday, you do too) to more elaborate attempts to articulate positions you imagine someone else has ("Now if I hear you correctly, I would say your idea about raising the payroll tax is a profound one").

Many of the same caveats apply to opinion conformity that apply to giving compliments: You shouldn't be a toady, or too dependent, or obviously seeking some benefit. You shouldn't appear to be someone who just agrees for the sake of agreeing. One should always avoid slavish agreement, which comes across as indiscriminate. And don't just agree only at the times that you are looking for a raise.

Jones suggests that one way of not being seen to be a suck-up is to anticipate what the boss's opinion will be and then state it before she does. Call this preemptive conformity. So, you notice your boss is impressed with a coworker and you suggest to her that she ought to give him the job that just opened up in marketing. Good thinking, Smith.

To avoid the appearance that you are the kind of person who always agrees with everybody, allow your target to see you disagree with others. If you're trying to impress your boss, don't agree with others who are at the meeting (unless of course the boss does first). You don't want your boss to think that you're just one of those people who end up agreeing with the last person they talk to.

Another way to demonstrate that you're not just an echo, Jones notes, is to make it seem that you are gradually persuaded to agree with the target's views. Show a little resistance to change and then slowly be won over to your target's point of view.

What makes a difference, according to Jones, is agreeing with someone in a way that reduces the target's anxiety and uncertainty. One study suggested that an ingratiator is better off agreeing with the target after someone else has just disagreed. Another study suggested that it is better to agree when an opinion is unverifiable ("Yes, I agree that Michael Jordan was the greatest ever") than when the opinion can be verified ("Yes, the national debt is more than $3 trillion"). When there is no objective verification, the person making the claim is a little more uncertain and agreement thereby becomes a more effective ingratiation tool. Opinion conformity is also more effective when the target has taken an unusual or unpopular opinion than one that is more common ("Yes, Sir, I agree that we need to tell the American people that we are going to raise their taxes").

The downside of opinion conformity is that you are liable to be thought of as someone who has no ideas and lacks independence. Or that you are deceitful little kiss-ass. Studies show that we like people who don't slavishly agree. And we especially like people, according to a number of studies, who do not agree too closely even in situations where they are seen to be dependent. We give such people "extra credit," according to Jones. We interpret a refusal to conform as integrity.

I Don't Like to Brag, But . . .

Self-presentation is a tricky strategy. Studies show that we don't like self-promoters. But when individuals are told to seek approval from targets, they do it by promoting themselves. (This is slightly less true of women than men, by the way.) Many studies show that when individuals are instructed to make themselves attractive to another person they describe themselves much more favorably than when they are told to just "be themselves." The Self-Promoter's Dilemma is that we can alienate the person we're trying to impress by making our self-enhancement too transparent. So, don't be too full of yourself.

Jones looks at self-presentation as both an overt and a covert activity. He examines the way in which we make statements about ourselves ("You know, I'm the sort of person who gets along well with other people") and the way we imply or suggest that we possess certain characteristics (a groaning bookcase implies that we read a lot).

The idea of course is to present yourself in a way that enhances your interpersonal attractiveness, that makes the other person want to have you as a friend or colleague. Thus, you don't try to convey what a mean-spirited and self-absorbed human being you are, but what a cheerful, generous, and faithful person you are. But Jones suggests there is a kind of binary choice: You can portray yourself as a generally all-around great guy or gal, or you can be a chameleon and tailor yourself to what you know the target person likes.

Chesterfield confesses that he was a chameleon: "With the men I was a Proteus," he wrote to his son, "and assumed every shape to please them all: among the gay, I was the gayest; among the grave, the gravest." For this strategy to be a success, you have to correctly divine what the target person likes, and this is not as easy as Chesterfield implies. The gravest person might actually prefer the life of the party as a companion, not another dour fellow like himself.

If you choose to tell someone else about yourself as a way of ingratiating yourself, it's better to be a little discreet. If you tell a colleague that you were a high-school all-American football player, you run several risks: (a) he may think you're lying or exaggerating, which won't impress him at all, or (b) he may think you're trying to impress him or intimidate him, neither of which is very ingratiating. (Except, perhaps, that it indicates that you think him worth impressing.)

There is also the self-promoter's paradox, which is that we think that truly competent people do not have to boast about their competence. They let their performance speak for them.

The best strategy is to have someone else tell your target, "Hey, did you know Kelly was a high-school all-American football player?" (This is the self-presentation version of third-party compliments.) Jones also suggests maneuvering your target into a position that she asks about your achievements. In this way, you don't have to blow your own horn.

There are a variety of other direct and indirect forms of ingratiating self-presentation.

Background. "Hey, you old Delta Beta Gamma rugrat you." One familiar tactic is to emphasize some shared experience. "You know, I was in the National Guard during the Vietnam War, too." This is generally a no-brainer as a strategy. If you learn that your new boss is from a small town in West Virginia, are you not going to tell him that you went to the same high school?

Ask advice. Another sly way of ingratiating yourself with someone, suggests Jones, is to ask her for her advice. "You know, I'm thinking of going to law school, Ms. Frith, and I was wondering what your thoughts on that might be?" Or "Tell me how you got started as a writer because I want to try to become a writer, too." Such a request implicitly suggests that we value the target's judgment and expertise.

Tell a secret. Revealing something intimate suggests we trust the other person and that we would like the relationship to deepen. Jones notes that some studies suggest that if you reveal something too personal or too early, it can boomerang. You might not want to tell your new boss right away that you like cross-dressing.

Name-dropping. One tactic is to convey just how gosh darn important and popular you are, and one way to do that—especially in New York and Hollywood—is to name-drop. "Oh, I was just having lunch with Bobby De

Niro the other day, and he said . . ." Or, "George Soros was just telling me yesterday that . . ." This is a similar form of self-aggrandizement to boasting and the same rules apply. The target may assume that you're making it up, but he also may think, Hmm, I'd like to meet De Niro, maybe he'd be interested in my script idea? Or, he may think, if this guy is a friend of De Niro's, he's probably pretty interesting. The people who use name-dropping tend to be individuals with relatively low self-esteem and whose self-image is improved by their proximity to the famous.

Be modest—up to a point. If self-aggrandizement is alienating and unattractive, what about its antithesis, self-deprecation and humility? Jones notes that many studies have shown that a judicious humility is very appealing. Jones suggests being humble about things that seem trivial ("I can't sew a button to save my life") to give the impression of modesty, and then be more forthright about real achievements. The problem with modesty is that it only really works if you have a certain amount of success. If you have a lot to be modest about, it's not the wisest strategy.

Dale Carnegie was right. Jones lists some small things about one's self-presentation that are ingratiating. Smile. Look people in the eye. Don't look over someone's shoulder while talking to him at a party. Ask questions. Use conversational reinforcers like, "Really!" or "Interesting," or "Good point." Nod your head. Call the person by his name. Jones cites an amusing study in which a very attractive woman interviewed pairs of men. With one man, she said his name at the beginning of the interview and never again, while with the other, she repeated his name a number of times over the course of the session. The men whose names were cited frequently liked the interviewer significantly more than those whose names were uttered only once.

I Can Get It for You Wholesale

The rationale for the tactic of doing favors is that we like people who do nice things for us. Jones cites the work of George Homans, who beautifully explains the quid pro quo of the favor exchange: "We influence others to give us the things we want more than they do, by giving them the things they want more than we do."

The dynamic of favor-giving has a lot in common with giving compliments. But there is one big difference: Favors are more than just words. A favor usually involves some action, not just some applesauce but some actual apple polishing. Favors are the least subtle of all ingratiation tactics. And more than any other of these activities, a favor can make the ulterior motive of the ingratiator all too clear.

Jones notes that the ingratiator must always avoid giving the impression that he is performing a favor because he wants some benefit in return. "The trouble with favors, from the ingratiator's point of view," writes Jones, "is that they make so salient the questions of obligation, reciprocation, and exchange." Unlike the strategy with compliments or opinion conformity, it might actually be useful to let the target see you perform favors for others; in that way, he might be persuaded that you are in fact a kind and considerate person rather than a conniving pickthank.

The effectiveness of the favor rests in part on whether or not the circumstances are appropriate. Jones suggests that when a favor is done under inappropriate circumstances, it alerts us to the possibility of ulterior motive. If someone stops to help us fix a flat tire, that is one thing, but if someone wants to give us what seems to be a stolen car, that is another. Too great a favor from someone we know too little can make us feel awkward, not grateful. The costlier the favor, the more intimate the connection needs to be. Your brother can give you a car, not the fellow who sits across the hall from you at work. Jones cites studies which suggest that a favor is regarded as inappropriate in formal or highly structured situations. You don't expect an IRS agent to offer you some tax breaks during your audit—though it might be nice.

Status Differences—The Way Up and the Way Down Are Not the Same

The study of ingratiation, Jones notes, is closely connected to the study of power. In any society, he says, where there are power asymmetries, strategic sucking up. Yes, some forms of ingratiation involve only a desire to be liked, but most involve some exchange between people of different power and status.

When it comes to flattery, Jones suggests, status colors everything.

In general, the greater the discrepancy in status the more subtle the ingratiation must be. The greater the similarity, the less subtle it needs to be. Lateral flattery is the simplest. Flattery, like water, flows more easily downward.

High-status ingratiators can generally flatter low-status targets with impunity. It doesn't work that way in reverse.

Lower-status people who seek something from higher status individuals must be more oblique. For those flattering upward, conformity is usually the best choice. For one thing, agreeing with the boss doesn't necessarily raise the red flag of ulterior motive. The boss probably expects it. "Opinion agreement," says Jones, "bolsters the validity of the leader's views without raising obvious questions about devious intentions." The boss is not likely to suspect its tactical origins because, *Hey it's hardly surprising that my employers agree with what's right.*

Compliments, favors, and self-enhancement aren't good bets when ingratiating upward because they seem manipulative and even impertinent. And forget modesty. You already have low status.

If you have any doubt which direction flattery normally takes, look at the two following statements and tell me which is more likely to be successful.

1. "You're doing a great job. You're a good man to have around. I'm glad you're working for us."
2. "You're doing a great job. You're a good boss to have around. I'm glad I'm working for you."

Try number 2, if you don't want to keep your job very long.

Upward flattery often violates the role prescriptions of low-status people. "It is presumptuous," Jones says, "for an underling implicitly to claim the capacity to appraise a superior." *Hey, who are you to tell me that I'm doing a good job?* As Jones notes, "To evaluate someone positively to his face implies that you are in a position to pass judgment." There is also the double-edged problem that a compliment conveyed by an underling might imply that she didn't think the boss was doing a very good job before.

High-status individuals who use downward ingratiation don't have to worry too much about the low-status target suspecting their motives. The low-status subject is likely to see it as part of the boss's job. The thing the high-status ingratiator does have to worry about is undermining his position and courting disrespect. High-status ingratiators can't use conformity as an ingratiation tool because it undermines their status. Jones notes that respect and likability are often inversely correlated. That is, the boss can lose respect in trying to be liked, or lose his likability in trying to be respected. If you're the boss, be careful about trying to be one of the boys.

One way for high-status individuals to be ingratiating without losing respect or likability is to be self-deprecating. Self-deprecation in a superior is winning. Jones cites studies by Blau and others showing that high-status people are more likely to emphasize their positive attributes in important areas and to deprecate themselves in less important ones. For low-status people, it is precisely the reverse: They deprecate their important abilities and play up their less important ones. Not a good strategy.

"The trick of the successful ingratiator," says Jones, "is to let modesty reflect the secure acceptance of a few weaknesses that are obviously trivial in the context of one's strengths." High-status people can afford to be modest. "Modesty is becoming to the great," noted the French writer Jules Renard. "What is difficult is to be modest when one is nobody."

In general, it is much easier to get people to like you than to convince them you're competent. But given two people of equal competence, the one who is liked will go farther. The ingratiator will go ahead and use flattery if, (a) he thinks he can get away with it, (b) he's not constrained by any moral qualms, and (c) the potential value of what he can gain is worth the risk.

*   *   *

High-status people do not need to worry as much about making mistakes. Jones notes that high-status people's popularity often goes up after an embarrassment or a blunder. He cites the fact that John F. Kennedy's popularity rose after the Bay of Pigs fiasco. Bill Clinton's numbers went up after the Monica Lewinsky scandal. The researchers reasoned that some evidence of fallibility of those in very high-status positions actually makes them seem more human and therefore likable.

The test that measured something akin to this was an experiment in which subjects were asked to listen to a tape recording containing an interview

with a candidate for the College Quiz Bowl. For half the subjects, the interviewee was depicted as an extraordinarily successful student. For the other
half, the interviewee was average. About halfway through the interview, half
the students in each situation heard the interviewee spill a cup of coffee all
over himself. The results showed that the individual who was liked the most
was the smart guy who spilled coffee on himself. The average Joe who
soiled himself was just considered a loser. The smart guy became more *sim-
patico*. So, if you're afraid your underlings perceive you as perfect and superior, drop your latte all over your Armani suit at the morning staff meeting.

Ingratiating the Ingratiator

How does one respond when one is fulsomely complimented?

You can be embarrassed. You can say "You flatter me," or you can say
"Thank you."

Really over-the-top praise is both embarrassing and a conversation-
ender. What do you say in response to "You're a genius"?

Under the circumstances, "Thank you" is not really an option.

Such praise is generally embarrassing and that embarrassment may turn
you against the flatterer.

When, in reply to a more normative compliment, someone says "You
flatter me," that is a double-edged reply. It can be interpreted as either positive or negative—positive in the sense that the person is being modest and
appreciative; negative in the sense that the person is saying, "Oh, you're
using some form of strategic or insincere praise on me." We generally interpret this reply more as a modest disclaimer than as an accusation of deceit,
but there is an undertone of the latter.

It would be extraordinarily unusual if someone made a scene or reacted
unpleasantly to being flattered. In fact, we usually make an effort to seem
appreciative, even if we are not. We pretend we consider it sincere. If you
seem appreciative, you will probably make the ingratiator believe that he
has been successful. He now thinks he has biased you in his favor, and it
may be in your best interest to let him think so.

Jones posits five basic responses to flattery that range along a continuum
between trust and liking, and mistrust and disliking.

1. *Affection, affiliation, attraction.* Flattery often simply yields these three feelings. Chalk up one for the flatterer.
2. *Reciprocal feelings / reciprocation.* The target feels either that he'd like to reciprocate or that he is obligated to reciprocate. This can even become slightly hostile, particularly if the reciprocal favor is a pain in the ass.
3. *Tolerance or forbearance.* This is what Jones calls the "minimally desired outcome." This gives the flatterer protection, which is perhaps what she desired. The flattery doesn't elicit attraction or affection, so much as a kind of patronizing or disdainful tolerance. You're a worm, but I won't fire you.
4. *Embarrassment and annoyance.* Jones calls this the "boomerang effect." You don't know what to say or do, and you find the feeling annoying.
5. *Disgust and indignation; reprisal.* This is rare. Few people want to actually punish the flatterer. "Obsequious flatterers are often discussed critically behind their backs," says Jones, "but rarely subjected to open criticism." Or termination.

Goffman proposes the most Machiavellian response to flattery. As Goffman notes, it is polite to acknowledge someone who praises us with cheerful thanks. We do this, Goffman notes, even if our internal reaction is negative. But this is actually quite shrewd, for we are ingratiating ourselves with the ingratiator. We ought to make agreeable noises so that the ingratiator feels that he's been successful, and therefore likes *us* more. The idea is, *Hmm, since you're only pretending to like me, I'll simply pretend to like you, and when reward time comes around, you'll see whether your smarmy flattery gets you any results.* Since the ingratiator has been making a conscious effort to gain approval, he generally views some positive feedback as evidence that he was successful. Jones notes that as a result, the ingratiator may actually come to believe the things he has said about the target person. This is particularly true if the ingratiator is feeling a little guilty about his flattery. We want to persuade ourselves that we don't have ulterior motives. Jones notes we become more sympathetic to that which we conform to. Yes, that's a little scary.

When to Hold 'em and When to Fold 'em

In 1994, an experimental social psychologist named Randall Gordon at the University of Minnesota at Duluth did what is known as a "meta-analytic" review of all the empirical studies that had been conducted by social and industrial psychologists on ingratiation over the previous forty years. A meta-analytic review is a statistical summary of all the results. Gordon looked at 155 articles, and the study itself is based on 69 of them.

The results bear out almost everything Jones said. (A good number of the studies, of course, are Jones's.) The studies showed that with the exception of rendering favors, all of the other categories of ingratiation—other enhancement, that is, compliments, opinion conformity, and self-presentation—all had a positive effect on perceptions. Only self-promotion had a negative effect. Men were both more affected by ingratiation than women and more critical of it when they perceived it as observers. All directions of ingratiation yielded positive effects, but downward and lateral attempts were significantly more effective than upward. Downward ingratiation produced the greatest affection. As status differences increased, so did the dangers of upward ingratiation. All forms of lateral ingratiation were positive. For upward ingratiation, opinion conformity was a more successful tactic than compliments. (But compliments also did well, as some upscale targets simply regarded opinion conformity as normal behavior.) For downward ingratiation, compliments were more effective than opinion conformity. In confirmation of Jones's point that one shouldn't be too transparent or too opaque about ingratiating, the study showed that low-to-moderate levels of transparency produced the most positive results.

All the studies show that ingratiators are judged more positively by their targets than by bystanders. No one likes a flatterer—except when you're being flattered. A number of studies showed the interesting result that ingratiators form positive opinions of their targets when the target reacts with opinion conformity, while observers develop more positive opinions of targets who resist the ingratiator's appeals. In other words, we like people who seem to agree with us and we like people who don't agree with flatterers. The studies confirmed Jones's ingratiator's dilemma, and showed that the more obvious the ingratiation, the less likely it is to succeed. It also confirmed the wonderful little wormhole in his theory, which is that if an ingratiation tactic is seen as entirely normative, it will fail to work. Thus, some transparency is better than none at all, or too much. So, don't be too subtle—or too obvious.

* * *

By the end of his life, Jones came to the conclusion that most ingratiating overtures are not really conscious or the result of deliberate strategic planning. Most of the behaviors he describes, he wrote, are "overlearned responses to the condition of dependence." What Jones means by that is that much of what we do consists of automatic or unthinking reactions that are the result of a lifetime of socialization. We never even consider complete openness and frankness as a response in social situations. We have all learned to nod and smile and hold our tongue and murmur approval and say thank you.

It is just as well, for modern business studies are trying to do away with the idea of ingratiation altogether. As the model of so many corporations these days is collegial rather than hierarchical, upward and downward ingratiation are not what they used to be. The old chain of command is dying. "It's not PC anymore in the workplace to say superior or subordinate," says Fred Luthans, author of the classic business handbook, *Organizational Behavior.* "We don't use that anymore. It is just not compatible with the new business environment." Luthans says that ingratiation is passé; what is necessary, he says, is "recognition." A manager no longer says, "You're doing a good job"; he says something like, "I saw that you stayed here till midnight working on that report." Luthans adds, "I wouldn't even say, 'Thanks a lot, we appreciate your good work.' That last part is equated with phoniness these days."

I suspect Jones and certainly Goffman would say that ingratiation merely needs to become more subtle. When Sam Walton called his employees his "associates," that was a form of flattery.

Ingratiation, Jones notes, is a social lubricant. It hides and camouflages what is really going on within. Transparency is dangerous. "The benefits of information clarity," says Jones, "would be purchased at a cost that might be intolerably high from the point of view of maintaining the social system." In other words, candor is dangerous. A little bit of ingratiation in social interaction gives us all more leeway and breathing room. It allows us to maintain our illusions. It is kinder and gentler. It makes everyone happy, for when successful ingratiation occurs, the target feels happier and more secure and the ingratiator feels successful. Everyone gains.

In his last book, published shortly before he died, Jones quotes one of the wisest observers of human nature in history to the effect that flattery is not always strategic and not always such a bad thing. "To charge all unmerited praise with the guilt of flattery," wrote Samuel Johnson, "and to suppose that the encomiast always knows and feels the falsehood of his assertions, is surely to discover great ignorance of human nature and human life. In determinations dependent not on rules, but on experience and comparison, judgment is always to some degree subject to affection. Very near admiration is the wish to admire."

It's not a bad wish. And anyway, what's so terrible?

Chapter 10

The Capitals
of Modern Flattery

The Very Model of the Modern Flatterer

Every era has its characteristic flatterers. Plato's Gorgias was a shallow orator who smoothly pandered to his audiences. Molière's Monsieur Jourdain buffoonishly tried to insinuate himself into the aristocracy and was comically unconscious that they were taking advantage of him. Dickens's unctuous and hypocritical Uriah Heep flatters himself and others by pretending he is " 'umble."

For me, the model of the modern flatterer was Eddie Haskell.

Eddie was a character on the classic 1960s sitcom *Leave It to Beaver*. The show depicted the Cleavers, an all-American suburban family consisting of two good-natured parents, Ward and June, and two boys, Wally, the earnest older brother, and Beaver, the mischievous younger son. Wally's friend was a skinny, curly-haired, hatchet-faced fellow named Eddie Haskell.

When Eddie walked through the Cleavers' front door, the first thing he would do was turn to Mrs. Cleaver and in his most courtly twelve-year-old manner say, "You're looking lovely today, Mrs. Cleaver," to which a slightly unsettled June Cleaver would say, "Well, thank you, Eddie." If Mr. Cleaver was there, Eddie would compliment him on his business or how buffed his brogans were. Eddie called his own parents by their first names.

With adults, Eddie was all smarminess and elaborate good manners.

With his peers, he was a scheming little weasel. Eddie was the model of the miniature backyard Machiavelli, the smooth-talking garden snake in the suburban Eden. Flattery was mother's milk to him. He used it reflexively to disarm people, to distract them from whatever plot he might be hatching. And he was unblushing about it.

At the time, I detested Eddie for the way he played up to grown-ups, finding in it a betrayal of what I thought of as the necessity of youthful rebelliousness. Eddie was not the sort of kid that other kids much liked. Now, as an adult, I see that Eddie was in fact smart and precocious, and that his chameleonlike ways were good preparation for a successful career.

Mark Twain once observed that it's only natural to be liberal when one is young and conservative when one is old. To the adolescent's mind, Eddie seemed unnatural because he was a kind of young fogy, a prematurely savvy twelve-year-old boy. As an adolescent, you figure Eddie will get his comeuppance; as an adult, you know that it's unlikely.

Eddie Haskell was the child of Dale Carnegie, the offspring of the new American era of smiles and salesmanship and the service economy. And Eddie grew up. You see him today in corporate offices, at advertising agencies, in boardrooms, in the late-night commercials by earnest self-esteem gurus, and in Washington and Hollywood. Like Eddie, they are strategic flatterers, though often without a particular strategy in mind. They are promiscuous flatterers, those who sprinkle praise on everyone in order to boost their own shaky self-esteem. Bill Clinton is an Oval Office Eddie Haskell, the smooth charmer who says whatever he thinks people want to hear, and then does whatever he wants.

The Halo Effect

Eddie is the face of interpersonal flattery. But there is another type of flattery that is characteristic of our age. Eddie is small potatoes; the macro face of flattery today is what we see in the culture of celebrity.

In the 1930s, the American psychologist Edward Thorndike coined the term "the halo effect." Thorndike, who had studied animal behavior under William James at Harvard, and later become a professor at Columbia, was a pioneer in determining that reinforced learning forms neural connections in the brain. The halo effect is defined by social scientists as a process by which we associate positive characteristics with other positive characteristics, even though there may be no connection. The classic example of this is research that shows that we unconsciously assign favorable traits such as intelligence, kindness, and honesty to people we think are good-looking.

A whole range of studies have shown that we do this without realizing our bias. Research with elementary schoolchildren suggests that adults view aggressive acts less negatively when they are performed by good-looking children and that teachers make an unconscious assumption that attractive children are more intelligent than unattractive ones. In another study, researchers in Pennsylvania rated the physical attractiveness of seventy-four different male defendants in local criminal cases and found that handsome defendants received significantly lighter sentences, and were twice as likely to avoid jail, as unattractive defendants.

I believe we give the same sort of positive bias for fame in our society, and that there is a pervasive halo effect that surrounds celebrity. We give unthinking approbation to celebrity. There is an automatic flattery of the famous, which constitutes a kind of societal praise where praise is not due. We are conditioned to think that anything associated with celebrity is smarter, sexier, happier, more fun, more interesting—*better.* Advertising has been using this aspect of the halo effect for decades. When General Mills slaps a picture of Mia Hamm on a box of Wheaties, the positive feelings we have about Mia give us positive feelings about the cereal. As sociologists say, this "taints" the product positively. This is not so much a new type of flattery, but an epidemic of an old type, due to ubiquity of the mass media. Yes, celebrity often means people who are famous for being famous, but we also think and assume that they are better and more deserving *because* they are famous.

In New York City, where I live, there is rampant celebrityophilia. Many people derive much of their self-esteem from their proximity to the famous. The positiveness we associate with celebrity rubs off on them in a way that makes them feel more positive about themselves. There is so much worship of celebrity that there is even a mini-celebrity in being friends with a celebrity. One of Andy Warhol's less well-known observations was that you can use other people's fame to enhance your own. Thus, the rationale: I may not be famous myself, but I can get my fifteen minutes for being friends with someone who is. Borrow that halo. It is a more self-conscious version of that strange phenomenon of people grinning manically and waving crazily when a television camera focuses on them at a sporting event or in an audience or standing outside Rockefeller Center during the *Today Show.* If a Martian observed this, he might think the cameras were shooting mysterious invisible rays at these unfortunate people, causing them to act erratically.

This is how people are often introduced in New York: "I'd like you to meet Samantha. She's a friend of Al Pacino's." Now, this is a very curious formulation. Usually, when someone is introduced to us as a friend of someone else's, that someone else is someone we know. Thus, "I'd like you to meet Samantha—she's a friend of Jake Gibbs's, who used to live down the street from you." "Ah, hi, Samantha," we might then say, "what's Jake up to these days?" The introduction fulfills the familiar and traditional hostly role of explaining how two people who don't know each other actually have some connection that is not at first apparent.

I'm not friends with Al Pacino; I've never met the man. But of course, I know Al Pacino in the way that we all know people who are famous. In fact, I know far more about what he's doing these days than about good old Jake Gibbs. But I wouldn't dream of asking Samantha, "So how is Al these days?" Because the point of the introduction is not really to establish a connection, but to impress you with the fact that this person you are meeting is a friend of someone famous.

For most people, celebrity and fame is refracted through the media. We consume celebrity through television, newspapers, and magazines, and the media project the halo effect on a great big screen for everyone to see. The media have helped create this whole phenomenon by reflexively lionizing people who are famous. It is a vertically integrated economic system, for the media manufactures fame and then sells us stories about the famous people they have created. The media giants produce a movie, promote it on their television or cable network, and then stick the stars' faces on the cover of one of their magazines. Now that's synergy.

This tradition isn't new, but it's never been more pervasive. It can be traced in part to the Henry Luce dictum that personalities are what drive the news. This is the modern media-lite version of Carlyle's Great Man theory of history, the idea that great men make history, history doesn't make great men. Whether or not we agree with Carlyle—and I don't—the point is that it is much easier to write and read and consume stories about personalities than complex and impersonal historical forces. The halo effect was then fueled by the even more frivolous versions of the Luce idea: the *People Magazinization* of journalism and the *Barbarazation* of television (from the "Barbara Walters interview"), which almost single-handedly influenced all television journalists to ask their subjects what they *feel* rather than what they *think*. All of which have contributed to the erosion of analytical thinking and abstract thought. We don't analyze ideas anymore in the media, we analyze personalities.

This Carlyle-lite tendency is aided and abetted by what sociologists call "correspondence bias." Correspondence bias suggests that we all have an intrinsic tendency to explain the behavior of others by who we think they are, rather than by what the circumstances of a given situation are. (We do this in relation to others, not ourselves. We make plenty of excuses for ourselves.) For example, when we see a person trip, we automatically think that he fell because he was clumsy, not because the floor was slippery or he stepped in a small rut that we couldn't see. We naturally imagine human error to be the cause of most accidents.

Correspondence bias often causes us to make fundamental errors in explaining events. We say a certain senator passed a bill. Or a certain player led his team to victory. Or a certain movie director created a film. When we know that no one individual was responsible for any of these things. And that each example represents a group effort with complex causes. It's more than just a shorthand we find convenient. It reflects a combination of correspondence bias and our bias toward fame. In an age when Freud has been discarded, popular culture attributes almost everything to personality. It causes us to give some people much too much credit—and others much too little.

Fame and celebrity are now the greatest common denominator in our society. Magazines these days seem to display only celebrities on their covers. Even staid shelter magazines like *Architectural Digest,* which used to put beautiful homes on their cover, now put John Travolta and his wife standing in front of their beautiful home. The late John F. Kennedy Jr. started a monthly political magazine, but virtually every cover image was of a movie star. The celebrity profile is a debased form; it is flattering by its very nature, even when the writer thinks he's being objective or even harsh.

Television news once featured stories about events; now they mostly profile famous people, or people they will make briefly famous. The television series *Biography*—a word which once suggested a certain gravitas—offers profiles (a word which suggests shallowness) about Candice Bergen and Tom Hanks. (By the way, when did biographies of *living* people start being taken seriously? Once, you had to die before getting a "serious" biography.) The television newsmagazine shows are not so much about news but about what used to be known as "human interest" stories. The most vital staff person at one of these shows is not the producer or the host but the bookers, those people with bulging Rolodexes (or overloaded Palm Pilots) and lightning dialing fingers. They are the ones who snare the famous guests that every other show is seeking. Sought-after guests are not known as newsmakers but "gets." To entice the "gets," the shows flatter the subjects by making dinner reservations, as one show did for the annoying Lewinsky lawyer William Ginsburg, or giving them little gifts, as Barbara Walters did one day for Mr. Ginsburg when she hand-delivered him a shopping bag of bran flakes and milk for his breakfast.

These famous "gets" are courted as assiduously as any romantic quarry. Here is what Walters wrote to Colin Powell when she was trying to lure him into being a guest: "Dear General Powell, I hope that the book is coming along well and that we might start thinking about when we might do an interview based on your book. We would give it an enormous amount of time and attention, as well as a huge audience. I promise it will be a wonderful send-off for the book." Pre-emptive flattery. When Sam Donaldson tried to book Brenda L. Hoster, the first woman to accuse fellow army sergeant Major Gene C. McKinney of sexual harassment, he sent her lawyer the following letter. "We think what happened to her is both shocking and, sadly, all too common. We aren't just 'after the ratings' but after a change in attitudes toward sexual harassment." Pandering words. He got his "get."

Journalists often cite "the public's right to know" as an all-purpose excuse for their own sometimes hysterical behavior and their routine invasion of privacy. But this rationale is both self-flattery and flattery of the public. What journalists are really saying is, *The public's right to know is whatever we sell and whatever the public will buy.* There is a great difference between the public interest and what the public's interested in. What the public often wants to know is personal trash, but that does not mean that they have the right to know it. In fact, it seems to me that one of the few things the public does have a right to know is the "source" of unsourced stories in the news, but this is precisely the thing journalists shield from the public. It is in the journalist's interest to do so, not the public's.

In order to court fame from the media, all kinds of people in all kinds of professions now routinely hire publicists and public relations firms to "get their name out there." Surgeons and dentists and divorce lawyers and real estate magnates have publicists. People hire spokespeople on the assumption that because famous people have spokespeople they will become famous too. And then of course, spokespeople glom on to their famous charges so that they can bask in fame's reflected halo.

One of the great attractions of modern celebrity is that it offers the promise of continual forgiveness to anyone famous. One of the great wrongheaded remarks of the twentieth century was F. Scott Fitzgerald's observation that there are no second acts in American lives. In fact, there are third, fourth, fifth, a seemingly infinite number of acts just as long as you are famous you can always, as the media says, "reinvent" yourself—whatever that means. Nowadays, fame and success excuse all, especially the pushiness, shamelessness, and the neurotic single-mindedness that is so often required in order to achieve it.

The halo effect also works in reverse; it's called demonization. We are even more assiduous in attributing bad things to individuals. We can't analyze what we don't like in any abstract way, so we call it evil and personify it in individuals. We were not invading Iraq; we were bombing Saddam. We were not trying to defeat the Serbs, just Slobodan Milosevic. Cuba *is* Castro. We have the childlike attitude, fostered by the media, that if we just remove one person, the entire complex problem that has grown up over hundreds or even thousands of years will be solved just-like-that. We used to smirk when Iran under Khomeini turned America into the Great Satan, but that is precisely what we do with our enemies.

Part of this quest for fame and the halo effect can be attributed to what the French postmodern philosopher Jean Baudrillard describes as the erosion of actual lived experience. The reason is that we consume so much vicarious experience through our twenty-four-hour access to all kinds of media. We experience so much through television and the movies and the Web, that this secondhand experience becomes more immediate and vital

to us than much of our lived experience. Fame and celebrity become more
real to us than actual experience. Thus, I'm more excited to meet a friend of
Al Pacino's than one of Jake Gibbs's.

*   *   *

In this new Gilded Age, there is also a halo effect around great wealth.
Great wealth now automatically commands great fame, and the combination yields great obsequiousness. There is nothing new about this. Jesus
found the adulation of wealth to be one of the signature sins of his time.
But today we see the flattery of wealth in a way that is new. People once rationalized the pursuit of wealth as a means to an end not an end in itself.
We seem persuaded, though, that the pure pursuit of wealth is a pure pursuit. A 1998 poll of college students revealed that the number one reason
for attending university was in order to make more money when they got
out. Bumper stickers that read "He who dies with the most toys wins" is an
ironic acknowledgment of this idea. Yes, there does seem to be greater consciousness of charitable giving, but as with Bill Gates, it is often mixed
with a continued frenzied and rapacious pursuit of even greater wealth at
the same time. The idea is, *I can give away half my toys and still have more
toys than you.*
    The fantastic wealth of the cyber-barons and dot.com billionaires has
created a halo around their style, or lack of it. *Geek chic* reigns. Since most
of these billionaires are self-described "nerds"—and proud of it—nerd-
dom itself has become cool. They are the new role models of instant upward mobility. They are pictured with virtual halos around their heads on
magazine covers. Their wealth and new financial clout has changed the etiquette of the marketplace; thus, Gerry Levin, the head of Time Warner, a
creature of the old business ethos, affects the uniform of the new dot-com
style—khakis and a sport shirt without a tie—at the press conference an-
nouncing the takeover of Time Warner by AOL. These new consortiums always begin their existence with very public flattery: *We're merging in order
to better serve you, the consumer.*
    The television corollary to what seems like the instant wealth generated
by dot-com IPOs is the proliferation of shows that revolve around the idea
of instant riches, the prototype being *Who Wants to Be a Millionaire.* But,

of course, the dot-com IPOs only seem as if they're instant. (At the same time, investors flatter their inflated conceptions of themselves by showering them with wealth even though their companies don't yet make money.) The television shows instead flatter our avarice and our sense that as Americans we are not just entitled to pursue happiness but to have it, which at the turn of this century means instant wealth. The simple equation of money as the key to happiness is a throwback to Tocqueville's observation that in no other country did money have such a grip on people's hearts. Some things don't change.

The habitual American obsession with youth culture has become even more commercially driven in the cyber age. These are not just kids with web pages, they're kids with credit cards and software companies, to whom an ever larger percentage of advertising and TV programming and moviemaking is directed. Boomer execs are tripping over themselves to pander to the cyber generation, flattering their micro-attention spans, creating mean-spirited loathe-anyone-over-thirty ads, all in the hope that they can cash in on the new wealth created by the cyber generation.

But cyber-youth are different. They are a throwback not to Dale Carnegie self-advancement but a new kind of Emersonian self-reliance. They are the children of Benjamin Franklin, whose test for every form of behavior was not its morality but its efficacy. Far more than boomers, they are self-directed, indifferent to the world's opinion of them, and immune to the flattery that is bestowed on them. It comes in part from the fact that more than any other generation, they have been able to live inside their heads due to the mouse/keyboard/dialpad existence of computers, videogames, and online-everything. It has made them more insular but less insecure. It is not the kind of moral confidence of the nineteenth century, but the cocksure confidence that they are the future and they know it. They are jaded and cynical about the ads and programming directed at them, but at the same time it boosts their sense of being at the center of this new universe. Emerson would recognize their spirit though not their values.

A hallmark of the halo effect is the distortion it causes in judgment and how we render those judgments. There are a myriad of such examples, one of which is the inflation of language we use to describe the famous and near famous. This has made the language of flattery a rather worn-out currency that needs to remake itself. Language inflation has undermined the meaning of ordinary praise. The ancient Greeks saw flattery as a distortion of language and an abuse of rhetoric for the purpose of exaggeration. We see the same thing in the promiscuous overuse of words such as "visionary," "genius," "charisma," and "gifted."

Once, the word "genius" was reserved for people of towering intellect or unimaginable ability. Genius was rare and almost magical. Nowadays, one reads about makeup artists and magazine editors and TV commercial directors who are "geniuses." Stories in business publications routinely describe executives as "gifted." The same inflation is seen in the use of the word "visionary," a term that was once even rarer than genius and was reserved for geniuses who altered the course of history. But I noted in my *New York Times* the other day that a real estate developer who is converting some industrial building in Brooklyn to residential use is a "great visionary." (Not just a visionary, mind you, but a *great* one.) If a Brooklyn developer is a "great visionary," what does that make Robert Moses or Frederick Law Olmsted or Baron Hausmann, not to mention the likes of Luther or Darwin or Freud? The word "charisma," whose origin comes from an ancient Greek term for a rare and divine gift of grace, used to refer to the magnetic power of phenomenal individuals. But now charm-free billionaires like Ronald Perelman and Donald Trump are routinely referred to as charismatic. Everyone these days is "gifted." Once, a gift meant some extraordinary artistic talent, but I read in a profile of a Hollywood manager that he is a "gifted protégé," which sounds like an oxymoron, unless it means that he is a sycophant *extraordinaire,* a brownnoser of genius.

Aren't there more standing ovations these days than ever before? They seem to have become mandatory at plays, at assemblies, at speeches, at conferences. As a boy, I remember a standing ovation as being something exceedingly rare and used to mark a truly memorable occasion. But now, if speakers or performers don't get a standing ovation, they seem to feel the audience is indifferent and their performance has been mediocre.

Names for things also show this inflation. Not too long ago, American businesses, like the federal government, had one president and one vice president. Now big corporations have literally hundreds of vice presidents. There are senior vice presidents and executive vice presidents of marketing and public relations. These titles no longer have a descriptive function; they are signs of status. The awarding of such corporate titles is not unlike the meretricious titles that were once handed out at court.

On television news today, there are no more "interviews"—everything must be a "conversation." On the *Lehrer NewsHour,* David Gergen doesn't *interview* his guest, he has a "conversation." Charlie Rose welcomes us every night not to watch him interview his guests but to have a "conversation." An interview is between people of different status; a conversation is between people of the same status. Interviews are *declassé.*

Euphemism is also a form of flattery. On the Web, advertisers are now known as "partners." An "advertorial" in a magazine is of course just a fancy name for an advertisement with a little more information in it. During the Monica Lewinsky scandal, Representative Henry Hyde flattered himself when he called an adulterous affair he had a "youthful indiscretion": he was forty-one at the time. Corporations try to calm workers and stockholders through euphemism: firing people became downsizing, which is now known as "rightsizing."

The self-help and recovery movements distort language in their effort to flatter people into taking up their sometimes ersatz spirituality. The oft-heard claim among such groups that "there is no death" may be the greatest flattery of all. Gurus always offer the tautological flattery of telling people that they can prove their own divinity by being open to the guru's teaching—and by shelling out $24.99 for the guru's video.

Person-to-person commercial flattery is also on the rise. I've noticed lately that if I happen to order a bottle of wine in a restaurant (a subject about which I know next to nothing), the waiter smiles and says, "Excellent choice!" I momentarily feel relieved before realizing that he would have said the same thing had I requested a bottle of Thunderbird. These days, sales people in department stores speak only in exclamation points: "That looks *super* on you!" Stores offer personal shoppers who are in fact your own private flatterer. It is the commercialization of strategic praise. In fact, more and more, the concept of point-of-purchase selling has become the shopping philosophy of the entire store—perhaps, the entire nation. Everything is displayed and promoted in a way to make you want to buy on impulse.

In some respects, flattery has also become less personal. Technology is shaping cultural forms. Increasingly, flattery seems analog, not digital. E-mail amputates salutations and valedictions. As a medium, it is less formal and more direct. There is no room for the coyness and suggestiveness of old-fashioned epistolary communication. The principal rhetorical innovation of e-mail is flaming—the hysterical insult—not flattery. Old-fashioned flattery would seem out of place in an e-mail; it would be too formal, too stylized, too earnest. Chat rooms prize quickness and directness; flattery in chat rooms is more like a wolf-whistle than a compliment. Cyber-kids are into "rude truths" from their friends. Not telling you what you want to hear but what you need to know. This is the twenty-first-century version of parhesia.

Finally, there is actual grade inflation as a form of flattery. If I give you an A when you deserve a B, it is false praise; it is giving more praise than is due. When $B-$ is the minimum acceptable grade, as it has become at most liberal arts colleges, that is a kind of guaranteed flattery. As in Lake Wobegon, all students are "above average."

All of this flattery inflation has produced a kind of necessary and required flattery exchange. There is the unspoken notion that flattery establishes a debt in the receiver. In so many circumstances if we don't flatter someone it seems closer to an insult than benign neutrality. It reminds me of a game we used to play in my house when I was growing up. It worked like this: Someone, usually my mother, would say to either my father, my sister, or myself, "I have a TL for you." (TL stood for "trade-last.") What she meant was, I have a compliment for you that someone else said. The trick was, in order to receive it, you had to give a compliment back. It was a kind of enforced mutual flattery that in fact made everybody feel a little better. But it was not disinterested praise. It was a flattery exchange that was appealing in part because it was so transparent. The debt was declared and repaid instantly.

A City of Northern Charm and Southern Efficiency

The sociologist Edward Jones observed that some subcultures are havens for flattery and ingratiation, while others have a dearth of it. He noted that there are organizations and social settings where ingratiation is officially sanctioned. There are two particular American subcultures where flattery does flourish and is officially sanctioned: Washington and Hollywood.

When it comes to flattery, Washington, D.C., is in some ways closer to the courts of Renaissance Europe than it is to our modern era. The president is the king, and he is surrounded by all manner of nobles and gentry, ranging from senators and congresspeople to lobbyists and the permanent Washington establishment. In the same way that dukes and barons recapitulated the royal court in their own domestic establishments, each congressional office, be it that of a senator or a congressperson, mirrors that of the presidential court. Every senator and congressperson likewise has a chief of staff, a press secretary, an appointments secretary, and the like. The only difference is that he or she doesn't live above the shop the way the president does.

Just as the lesser aristocracy in royal courts looked to dine off the monarchy, the lesser cast of characters in Washington live off of these executive courts. The city's lawyers and think-tank intellectuals and journalists are all looking for scraps from the executive table. The K Street lobbyists are in a sense professional flatterers; they wine and dine officials, wheedling and cajoling their way into offices, offering baubles and often more than that in the way of campaign contributions and PAC money. At the same time they must flatter their own corporate bosses, because the success or failure of a lobbyist is almost completely subjective. They must persuade their employers that they're worth the hundreds of thousands of dollars that they make.

From outside the Beltway, the Washington press corps is perceived as having an adversarial relationship with both the president and Congress. But if you saw up close how Washington journalists in their ill-fitting suits and bad shoes attempted to ingratiate themselves with elected officials and their staffs, you wouldn't think so. There is a Goffmanesque equation, a mutual saving of face, that generally exists between reporters and their subjects. It works like this: The journalist never writes or says what he really knows about the subject, perhaps how dumb, assholic, or scary the politician is; and the politician never lets on how little the journalist knows about what he or she is writing about.

By far the easiest and silliest job in Washington journalism is being a White House reporter. Although they preen and show off for the cameras at presidential news conferences, they are relegated to a nasty warren of tiny cubicles off the press office, where they wait all day for handouts in the form of press releases or news in the form of leaks that the press secretary doles out to them. It's more a stenographer's job than a journalist's. The competition is over scraps of gossip that pass as news.

The single most excruciating Washington ritual involving the press and their quarry is the annual White House Correspondents Dinner. Journalists from the nation's news organizations put on their rented tuxedos and compete with each other to invite the most interesting celebrity guest, usually a second-tier movie or TV actor. The queasiest moment always comes when the president himself hands out awards to various journalists who may have won for their criticism of the president. The proud but slightly sheepish journalist is handed the award by the president and then poses for an official photograph with the leader of the free world. Later, after the president has given his amusing speech in which he gently tweaks the assembled fourth estate, the journalists all rise and give him a standing ovation.

•   •   •

In Washington, rituals of obligatory adulation still abound. The rounds and rounds of standing ovations that the president gets at his State of the Union address every year seem more and more anachronistic. (Only in the year of Clinton's impeachment did some ornery Republicans sit on their hands.) Politicians will say such a reception is merely veneration for the office, but no other office ever gets such lusty cheers and huzzahs. It makes one yearn for the days when the State of the Union message was delivered to Congress on paper and read aloud by a clerk.

George Washington rejected becoming a president for life and the honorific of "Your Excellency." Although he had a taste for fine living, he would be dismayed by the elaborate trappings of the modern imperial presidency. No one travels heavier than an American president. Two 747s: one for him, and one to hold his various armored limousines. Presidential motorcades sometimes stretch for half a mile, forcing the life of any town or city he passes through to come to a standstill so that the president can get to where he's going, usually a fund-raiser. We've come a long way from the time when the newly elected president Thomas Jefferson had to wait for a seat at the dinner table at his boardinghouse.

Every Renaissance courtier would recognize the stiff and instantly responsive postures of White House and congressional staffers in the presence of their respective bosses. Senators and congresspeople stride along the great polished marble hallways of the Capitol with their aides walking an obligatory step or two behind them. "Staff" is the all-purpose name for the people who serve our representatives.

The history of how ministers have used flattery to control leaders did not begin with Henry Kissinger's relentless and unctuous toadying to Richard Nixon. It was Disraeli who famously said that when ministers use flattery, they must not stint at all. "Everyone likes flattery," he told Matthew Arnold, "and when you come to royalty you should lay it on with a trowel." Cardinal Richelieu was a famous user of flattery to manipulate weak kings, and he was a famous sucker for it himself.

Nixon was the recipient of much flattery, not only from Henry Kissinger but from, of all people, Daniel Patrick Moynihan, who astutely understood the role of the courtiers. Moynihan once recommended a scholarly tome for Nixon's perusal, saying that only an intellect like the president's would truly appreciate it. A few days later, a presidential aide said to Moynihan that Nixon was devouring the book and particularly enjoyed a certain chapter. Moynihan replied he wouldn't know, as he'd never read it. It was said during the Carter administration that the key to Joseph Califano's success was his ability to work the phrase "Mr. President" into an English sentence more times than anyone thought possible. Dale Carnegie would have been proud.

One of the secrets to Dick Morris's long-time success with Bill Clinton was that he flattered Clinton's cherished image of himself as a world-historical figure. Alone of Clinton's aides, Morris would discuss with Clinton where he might rank among American presidents. You can't be among the Lincolns, Roosevelts, Wilsons, or Washingtons, Morris said, only because you haven't presided over a war, but you surely rank in the next tier.

Flattery is even more appreciated when the president is beleaguered. One of the most extraordinary examples of such flattery was the day of President Clinton's impeachment, when dozens of members of Congress gathered on the White House lawn to give paeans of praise to the man who had just become only the second impeached president in American history. Clinton was introduced by Vice President Gore, whose job is roughly equivalent to that of Ed McMahon's duties on the old *Tonight Show*. He must laugh loudest and longest at the president's jokes. In words that he will someday regret if he does not already, Gore introduced his boss by saying, "I'm proud to speak for a man that history will regard as one of our greatest presidents."

.   .   .

Some small insight was rendered into the kind of personal flattery a president gets when the Clinton White House, in an effort to discredit Kathleen Willey, a former White House staffer, released her private notes to the president. Willey had recently appeared on the program *60 Minutes* to accuse the president of having groped her in the Oval Office.

Willey was the attractive widow of a financial supporter of the president, and had worked in the social office of the White House for three years. Her job was to answer letters and help plan parties. She had two children and was not a college graduate.

In November of 1993, she dropped the president a handwritten note.

Dear Mr. President,
What a wonderful week you have had! Congratulations on all your well-deserved successes.
    I would very much like to have a few minutes of your time to discuss something of importance to me.
    I will wait to hear from you.

                                                              Fondly, Kathleen

Obviously, she does not know Mark Twain's dictum not to give a compliment and ask a favor at the same time. But apparently President Clinton is not aware of it either because he meets with her shortly afterward.

A few months later, she writes to the president to tell him that she "would like to be considered for an ambassadorship," as her two sons are now away in college and she has more free time than she used to. She ends by saying, "Please accept my best wishes for your historical trip to the Mideast next week—I don't need to remind you of my willingness to help you in any way that I can. Fondly, Kathleen."

In June of 1994, she writes again.

Dear Mr. President,
I just wanted to take a moment to tell you how caring and heartfelt your
speech was on D-Day.
*   While you have had many shining moments, that day was for me, the*
proudest I have had that you are our President.

Kathleen

In the meantime, she has another meeting with the president, and then a meeting with several staffers about her quest for an ambassadorship. She wants to meet with Leon Panetta, the chief of staff, but Mr. Panetta is too busy to see her.

In the meantime, she tells the president that he was "hilarious" at the White House Correspondents Dinner. She also sends him a tie. He writes back to say, "I love the tie."

In December of 1994, she writes:

Dear Mr. President,
You have been on my mind so often this week—there are so very many
people who believe in you and what you are trying to do for our
country.
*   Take heart in knowing that your No. 1 fan thanks you every day for*
your help in saving her wonderful state. [Virginia was her state.]

With appreciation, Kathleen

Three months later, she writes to him to say that she understood that the position of U.S. representative to the International Union for the Conservation of Nature is vacant and that she "would like to meet with you at your earliest convenience to discuss this appointment."

He does. But alas, she doesn't get the job.

The American People Are the Greatest

Flattery, as we know, is a two-way street. In many ways, the more interesting direction is not the flattery directed toward the president, but the flattery the president directs toward us, the wise and just and fair—and gullible—American people. If patriotism, as Samuel Johnson once said, is the refuge of a scoundrel, then the flattery of the people is probably that scoundrel's first tactic.

People in democracies want and need to be praised. We need to be praised because, heck, it's a free country, and we just might not feel like paying our taxes or fighting a war or fulfilling whatever a given president thinks is our civic responsibility. Democratic governments, as Jefferson tells us, "[derive] their just Powers from the Consent of the Governed." Flattery is often how democratic governments cajole our consent. Leaders tell us how wise we are, which makes us less guilty about the fact that fewer than 50 percent of eligible voters turn out even in presidential elections. It seems that as the percentage of participation has declined, the praise of the public's virtue has increased. In his book *Time Past, Time Present,* Bill Bradley referred to this ritual as "the mindless puffery of American virtue."

The Greeks derided this kind of puffery as the foulest sort of demagoguery and the surest way to weaken the foundations of democracy. Evidently, our recent presidents have not been reading their Plutarch. Jimmy Carter's signature mantra, "I want a government as good as the American people," worked on two levels. It flattered the public by extolling all of us as the gold standard of goodness and decency, and it suggested, as well, that smiling Jimmy was as good and decent as us because he knew it. But I wonder if the American people really want a government as good and decent as themselves. Do they want a government that watches the *Jerry Springer Show* during the day, that doesn't know the name of the president of Pakistan, that is apathetic about democracy?

In some ways, Ronald Reagan based his whole political career on the flattering of the American people. "I have never failed when I trusted the wisdom of the American people," he often said. He constantly sang odes to America's virtue and essential goodness. But like so many other visions of

Reagan's, it was an image of America that he had formed not so much from experience as from popular culture. He hearkened back to a Norman Rockwell vision of America that only existed in our fantasies.

Bill Clinton has been a promiscuous invoker of American virtue and wisdom. On the day the House of Representatives voted to open an impeachment inquiry, Mr. Clinton said, "I trust the wisdom of the American people. They almost always get it right, as they have done for the last two hundred years." In his eloquent defense of Mr. Clinton, former Arkansas Senator Dale Bumpers quoted another president: " 'Trust the people,' " he says, " 'they can handle it.' Harry Truman once said that to me." What Clinton trusted was in fact the weary tolerance of the American people, their good-natured willingness to cut him some slack, and their unwillingness to switch horses in the middle of even a polluted stream.

Clinton, in fact, has always demonstrated the opposite of what the Greeks said was necessary in a democracy, that is parhesia, or candor. If candor is the telling of unpleasant truths, Clinton perfected the art of sugarcoating or obfuscating any truth that was even slightly unpleasant. His regular use of legalisms and euphemism and evasion is a textbook example of what the Greeks considered the abuse of rhetoric. But, of course, that depends on what your definition of *is* is.

Clinton's other tool of flattering the people is his ability to be perceived as an interested listener. For a politician, it is much more important to be perceived as a listener than to actually listen. In 1992 and ever since, reporters described Clinton as "listening deeply," or as an "active listener," or as someone put it at the time, an "aerobic listener." His campaign people cleverly promoted the notion that he was listening so hard that he seemed to draw the words out of you. Clinton perfected the public art of making it seem that the voter he was talking to was the single most important human being in the world at that very moment. (It is also one of the seducer's great arts.) During the 1992 campaign, he cultivated the pose of himself hunched over, his chin resting on his fist: The Listener. The First Lady paid attention. When Hillary Clinton traveled around New York State in 1999 to gauge and stimulate support for her run for the senate, she labeled it her "listening tour."

One new accessory in the art of chief executive flattery is the Presidential Point. I believe it was started by Ronald Reagan, and it undoubtedly has its origins in show business. Reagan would come onstage for a speech, and, as he and Nancy were waving to the crowd, Reagan would see—or, more likely, pretend to see—a familiar face and point at that person, often nudging Nancy so that she could smile and point, too. The idea was that it humanized the president, making him seem like someone who actually has friends. It was picked up by George Bush, who did it more awkwardly than his predecessor but used it even more frequently. Clinton has picked up the Point as well and uses it dexterously. He has also plagiarized another Reagan trick—one of Nancy's this time. It is very public flattery masquerading as private communication, which he did by mouthing the words "I love you" to his wife up in the balcony, which he did during his State of the Union address in both 1999 and 2000. Somehow, I can't imagine any of the presidents to whom Clinton likes to compare himself—Lincoln, FDR, Wilson—miming the words "I love you" to their wives before a speech.

But the greatest presidential rhetorician in American history actually set the bar of flattery very low. When Abraham Lincoln said you could fool some of the people all of the time, all of the people some of the time, but you couldn't fool all of the people all of the time, he was not offering a very high estimation of American wisdom. If some people can be fooled all of the time and all of the people some of the time, you have a goodly percentage of the American people who are being duped at any given time. Even a broken clock is right twice a day. Lincoln did not think these United States should have a government as gullible as the American people.

Tinseltown

Earlier this year, *The New York Times* reported that acting is on the rise as an occupational choice of young people in the United States. In a 1998 poll of their own, *USA Today* reported that 51 percent of the men surveyed said they would prefer their child to grow up to be a Hollywood actor rather than a U.S. senator. We live in a very different time from when acting was considered a profession on a par with bootblacks and actors were not allowed to be buried in public graveyards. But it's the perfect profession for a narcissistic age, for only to the actor is the part greater than the whole.

The Hollywood culture is fueled by flattery. Of course, everyone flatters movie stars, and they flatter themselves, but there are elaborate hierarchies of flattery around other bastions of power. Directors flatter producers, producers flatter studio chiefs, and agents flatter everybody. Whoever is the flavor of the month, the hot actor, producer, director, agent, gets flattered by everybody. And everybody except actors thinks actors are ridiculous, but no one would ever think of telling them so.

A producer who has had a string of well-received movies over the last decade puts it this way. "The adulation of actors is extraordinary," he says. "They're narcissistic children who are often aberrant in their behavior, which is fostered in part by all that adulation. Two hundred years ago, they couldn't have a proper burial. Now they're idols and heroes."

And does this producer treat actors like narcissistic children? "You *have* to flatter a movie star," he says. "If you don't, you're stupid. The thing is, though, they often don't think you're flattering them. If you tell them they're brilliant, they think you're just saying the equivalent of '2 + 2 = 4.'" The best way to flatter them, he says, is to play up their intelligence. This is our old friend, the seducer's credo. "You say, 'Hey, that was great what you said the other day about screenwriters,' or 'the deficit,' or 'the price of bread,' whatever, even if it was the most inane thing you've ever heard. No one tells them that something they say is anything less than brilliant even if it is breathtakingly stupid."

The lowest rung on the flattery food chain in Hollywood is the D-girl. "D-girl" is short for "development girl" (there don't seem to be any development boys). A technical job description would be that a D-girl works for a star or a producer and is meant to ferret out ideas for movies and scripts. But in practice they are also a mixture of secretary, gofer, arm candy, chauffeur, and schmoozer. In a book called *Development Girl: The Hollywood Virgin's Guide to Making It in the Movie Business,* Hadley Davis lists some of the jobs of a D-girl: "Clean his house? Trim his beard? Remove a dead mouse from his office? Buy her birth control? Retrieve his fat analysis from an obesity doctor? Go through her garbage in search of a favorite felt-tip pen?" The list goes on and on.

Her principal advice for success is to lie. Lie to pump up, but also lie to protect. "An inflated sense of self-importance is epidemic in the entertainment business," she writes. "Don't tell your boss that his name did not mean enough to get a table. After all, there is always an available table and there is always an extra fifth-row-center seat for a VIP." And try not to alienate anyone, she says; you must guard other egos from being bruised as well. She gives an example of talking to someone the boss doesn't particularly want to talk to. Say, " 'I know he's dying to talk to you—he's going to be soooo upset,' rather than, 'Oh, he's in, all right. He's sitting in his office thumbing through *Vanity Fair,* and he doesn't want to talk to you because you aren't important enough. And by the way, he's not calling you back today, tomorrow, or ever.' "

In the 1980s and '90s, the media's anointing of the agent as the key player in Hollywood was an acknowledgment that flattery was what really drove Hollywood. (It also suggests the rise of the middleman in the service economy, where delivery, not content, is the important thing.) The glorification of the agent was personified by the deification of Michael Ovitz, the founder of the Creative Artists Agency, who was universally described as "the most powerful man in Hollywood." One of the traditional functions of an agent is to hold the hand of the client. Flattery became such a necessary and important part of the way Hollywood worked that the professional flatterers rose to power.

The veneration of Mike Ovitz was extraordinary. The reverential tones in which his various attributes were spoken of. His appreciation for fine art. His sleek Armani suits on his boxy little frame. His hiring of I. M. Pei to design the Creative Artists Agency office. The fact that he read Sun-Tzu. His fuzzy and unoriginal thinking about new media. All of this was described as if one were watching a great artist at work. He was routinely described as a visionary.

Yet after all the mumbo-jumbo about Ovitz, his power seemed to come from one thing, his connections to movie stars. He was their guru. He oiled their self-esteem. And since movie stars are able to "open" movies, as they say, Ovitz was powerful. His other secret, of course, as described by Michael Eisner in the Disney chairman's autobiography, is that Ovitz was a relentless flatterer, plying his clients and everyone else with gifts and compliments.

CAA was famous for giving lavish gifts to their clients. In fact, gift-giving is one of the traditional forms of ingratiation in Hollywood. Every year at Christmas, the studios try to outdo each other in sending expensive and interesting gifts to others in the community, like producers, screenwriters, even journalists. But the gifts the movie companies give their stars aren't chopped liver: on one film, Steven Spielberg gave each of his stars a Miata sports car. Now, if an actor is making $5 million for five weeks' work on the film, a $100,000 sports car is actually a trinket, but it is like the extra little 25-cent stocking stuffer you get for a child that she adores much more than the bigger more expensive ones.

Even though the more subtle flattery of movie stars is to flatter their minds, the minimum flattery, the entry-level flattery throughout Hollywood has to do with appearance. Even men in Hollywood flatter each other's appearance. "You look good" or "Hey, you look great" has replaced "How are you?" as the universal greeting. There is no sense that complimenting someone on their appearance may be gauche or a little bit vulgar, or out of line or even presumptuous. It's not seen as an invasion of space or privacy. In Hollywood, it is merely the price of admission. Every person is a walking billboard presenting himself or herself for admiration. Going into last year's Oscars, Dustin Hoffman turned to Joan Rivers, who was interviewing the procession of stars, and said with as much animation as you've ever seen on screen, *"God,* you look good!" *You look good* is so ubiquitous, so common, that you must imbue it with real enthusiasm for it to register. He should have received an Oscar nomination for that one line.

The unnamed producer I mentioned earlier has great reverence for a partner of his whom he describes as a "great flatterer." "Now there's this studio executive," he says, "and she's so ugly she could chase a dog off the back of a truck, and my friend said to her, 'Hey, what have you been doing lately, you look great!' But he said it with such enthusiasm that it seemed genuine, and she smiled." But, he noted, there are people you just can't flatter. "You can't tell the Elephant Man, 'Nice haircut!' "

If Washington journalists are often on bended knee, Hollywood journalists are doing a full grovel. Granted, there is no particular reason to be adversarial with an actor. The stakes are just too low. But even the occasional tough question makes actors uneasy. Here is a lovely example of the genre of mutual flattery between journalist and subject in a Q and A between Sharon Stone and a reporter in *Elle* magazine.

INTERVIEWER: How do you see yourself in ten years?
STONE: Oh, more like you, I guess. I'm writing short stories.

INTERVIEWER: Are they good?

STONE: Your guess is as good as mine.

INTERVIEWER: Have you let anyone read them?

STONE: Only people who love me enough to lie. [laughs]

Stone reveals a subtle understanding of the art and science of flattery. First, she ingratiates herself with the interviewer by saying that she wants to be "more like you." Then she acknowledges that since she is uncertain about the quality of her work, she only gives it to people who will flatter her—which, in her case, is probably pretty much anyone. Why hear an unpleasant truth when you can hear a pleasing lie?

But even this type of questioning is not good enough for many stars these days. We now have the phenomenon in journalism of actors interviewing actors, actors playing the role of journalist. *Jane* magazine only has stars interview other stars. In *Harper's Bazaar,* Ellen Degeneres interviews Elizabeth Hurley. (At least it's not billed as a "conversation.") And apparently no interviewer is any longer good enough for Sharon Stone, because in a later issue of *Harper's Bazaar* she interviews herself. Once magazines airbrushed only the pictures.

The show business parallel to the flattery of the *demos* is the flattery of the audience. It's a pleasing form of demagoguery. When the great Jackie Gleason used to come onstage in Miami Beach to open his television variety show, he would bellow, "The Miami Beach audience is the greatest audience in the world!" And the Miami Beach audience would cheer itself. This is so common in show business as almost not to be noticed. The last time Billy Crystal hosted the Oscar broadcast, he told the audience in Los Angeles, "You're the best!" When Aretha Franklin sang at the VH1 divas concert last year in New York, she also said, "You're the best!" and then added, "Only in New York"—to which the New York audience cheered. This is, of course, reciprocal flattery; in exchange for the performer flattering the audience, the audience rewards the performer with even more exuberant ovations.

One of the great examples of a show business institution of flattery was that of the talk-show sidekick, as personified by Ed McMahon. Every night, Ed sat next to Johnny's big desk and was the perfect hearty show business lapdog. After Johnny's monologue, Ed would mime an elaborate salaam to the king of late night. He was a jovial one-man claque: He laughed first and loudest at Johnny's jokes, he laughed even louder when Johnny teased or made fun of him, and he earnestly alerted the audience to any praise or award that Johnny had recently received but was far too modest to mention.

The institution of the talk-show sidekick seems to be ebbing away. Both David Letterman and Jay Leno use their good-natured bandleaders as their comic foils. (It does save money on salaries; Johnny had Ed *and* Doc Severinsen.) Only Conan O'Brien has a late-night copilot. It's probably a sign of show business maturity that this role is dying out. The host who doesn't need a lackey seems to stand more firmly on his own two feet.

One of the last places for the putative sidekick is in show business interviews, where the movie star almost always is accompanied by a nervous publicist who is there to monitor the star's remarks, make sure the journalist doesn't ask any untoward questions, and order room service. Having a publicist (like a bodyguard) suggests (a) that you are important enough to require such protection, but (b) that you can't really protect yourself.

The earnestness of the talk-show introduction has also subsided into a kind of ironic haze. So much public praise, these days, has descended into the ironic, as though the person is ashamed to say something nice or something undeserving. Whereas Johnny's introductions tended to be rather serious, the contemporary intros are a mixture of adulation and irony. Old-fashioned earnestness is often satirized. In an appearance not too long ago with David Letterman, the comedian Bill Murray announced, even before he sat down: "Dave, I just want to thank you for all the great entertainment you have given North America. Not just North America, Dave, the world."

Hollywood has also popularized the flattery of insult, better known as the roast. This show business ritual was originally headquartered at the Friars Club in New York, where comedians were "roasted" by their pals at lunches or dinners. Now the idea of the roast has become universal; mid-level TV stars have prime-time roasts on the networks. A roast is mock mockery; the idea is that I would only make fun of someone I hold in the highest esteem. I'm doing you the honor of ridiculing you. As Edward Jones noted, this form of ingratiation takes its cue from the traditional masculine habit of poking fun as a sign of affection. It is the verbal equivalent of a cuff on the neck. If a coach needles you, you know he likes you. In Don DeLillo's novel *Underworld,* he paints a scene of Jackie Gleason playfully insulting his buddy, Toots Shor, the old New York restaurateur. Shor, writes DeLillo, "loves the insults, the slurs and taunts, and he stands there beaming with balloonhead love. It is the highest thing that can pass between men of a certain mind—the stand-up scorn that carries their affections."

Another iteration of Hollywood and show business self-flattery is the proliferation of cheesy award shows. Once there were the Oscars and the Tonys and the Grammys, but now there are the MTV Video Music Awards, the VH1 Fashion Awards, the People's Choice Awards, and the silliest of them all, the Golden Globes. They all have an air of self-absorption mixed with self-congratulation. The spirit of, *We only care about ourselves, but everybody else cares about us, too.*

For years, the Golden Globes were a show business punch line. They were started by a group called the Hollywood Foreign Press Association, a collection of a few dozen foreign hack reporters who wanted a boozy lunch with a few second-rate movie stars. They were the only voters, and not one of them had a byline in an American publication. When it came to stars, the notion was, if you come, we'll give you an award, which is how Tom Selleck once won best actor. In 1982, the association honored Pia Zadora with the New Star of the Year award after her husband, the Israeli industrialist Meshulam Riklis, wined and dined all the voters. The price wasn't very high.

But Hollywood saw it as another way to generate free publicity, and as Jack Nicholson so beautifully said of getting an award at the Golden Globes last year, "It's great when people like you." The tipping point came when NBC started broadcasting them. Now, A-list actors and directors like Julia Roberts and Steven Spielberg are there in their gowns and tuxes. Yet it's still just a few dozen journalists with no particular specialty in show business who do the voting. Now, the actors flatter the Golden Globes. Backstage at the 1998 awards, Matt Damon said after receiving an award for best screenplay: "This is the most amazing thing that's ever happened to me." (Uttered without irony.) Chris Carter, the creator of *The X-Files,* called his Golden Globe "as high an honor as there is." One journalist who attended last year's Golden Globes said he heard the sentence "I love your work" more times than he could remember.

The default celebrity story these days is how the famous have struggled with both fame and the media. Fame sob stories. These are more flattering even than upbeat puff pieces. But most of those who complain about media attention have already reached their highest trajectory of fame. No one ever complains of media attention when they are on the way up. In the beginning, there is a clear unanimity between the rising star and the press: We both want my name in the paper. But the point, as Heraclitus said almost three thousand years ago, is that "the way up and the way down are the same." It all depends on where you are on the ladder.

The rule is: *The first time is always positive.* No television show or magazine introduces a new person or celebrity to their readers or viewers by saying, "Here is an untalented jerk you haven't heard of before." If you introduce the reader or viewer to someone they don't know about who is an asshole, the viewer or reader says, "Then why are you introducing me to this person?" Stories about new celebrities are always positive.

Don't get too high. Once a celebrity has reached a certain level of fame or notoriety, some media outlet will be itching to be the first to take him or her down a peg. All journalistic coverage of an issue or a person has a narrative arc, and a rise is almost always followed by a fall. It's much less interesting to keep praising someone who has already been praised to the skies than to say, Actually, she's overrated.

But Hollywood is not about sad stories or even moviemaking, but the joy of selling, and I don't just mean movie tickets. We're talking about all the paraphernalia now associated with movies: T-shirts, CDs, games, dolls. Salesmanship, as we know from Mr. Carnegie, is about ingratiation and pleasing everybody, and so Hollywood looks not so much for great actors but great salesmen. They have created one in the extraordinarily likable and ingratiating Will Smith, who is now perhaps the highest-paid star in Hollywood. As Ned Zeman wrote in a *Vanity Fair* cover about Smith, "The only thing you can really, truly hate about Will Smith is that he is not your best friend and never will be." Dale Carnegie, eat your heart out.

Like his hero, Michael Jordan, Smith knows that the trick is to flatter the public into thinking that you are their friend. The modern salesman is a master of the soft sell that is now called "attitude," a little bit of cheekiness while all the time embracing and reaffirming the values of consumerism. Smith's easygoing middle-of-the-roadness in all mediums epitomizes this. We flatter him, he flatters us by being so ingratiating, and then he flatters himself. "I absolutely believe I could be president of the United States," he says in that *Vanity Fair* cover story. "I believe that if . . . that's what I wanted to do with my life, I could win."

It's Like Chicken Soup—It Doesn't Hurt

As we've noted before, Montaigne argued that flattery flourishes in times of uncertainty. In ancient Rome, he notes, rhetoric was at its most elaborate when political unrest was at its highest. The idea is that in times of upheaval, people are less secure, and that manifests itself in a clinging to power and a need for reassurance.

Our times are uncertain not so much because of political upheaval but because of societal change. In science, medicine, electronics, and computers, change seems to be coming at a much faster rate than ever before. Biological engineering is changing the nature of what it means to be human. We are living in a hypertext universe. The Internet is annihilating distance, making time the only variable in work and communication. Image has become reality.

Once philosophy broke down into a series of opposed propositions— God exists or God does not exist. But now, all binary opposites are true. Modern reality contains both the thesis and the antithesis without the necessity of a synthesis. Technology will set us free / Technology will enslave us. Activism is on the rise / Apathy is everywhere. Jerry Lewis is absurd / Jerry Lewis is a genius. All of these contradictory propositions are true. As subatomic physicists have shown, an electron can be in two places at once.

All of these new ideas cause us to seek reassurance in the familiar. So much flattery these days is about seeking reassurance, about the understandable quid pro quo of mutual flattery. There is a kind of society-wide TradeLast game like I played at my family's dinner table. *I'll tell you something nice about you if you tell me something nice about me.* At the opening of her film at the Toronto Film Festival, the poet Maya Angelou told her audience, "If you hate the film, don't say a word." If you don't have something nice to say, don't say it. Flattery works on the premise that we all promise to believe.

But we are sometimes uncertain about flattery because it seems to point to an incongruity between our inner and outer selves. Are we being hypocritical in flattering this other person? Are we being dishonest in accepting and enjoying the flattery we receive? But these questions seem less vexing today in an era when we are more sophisticated about social interaction and when our outer selves seem to have overtaken our inner selves. There is less incongruity between outer and inner because outer and inner have blended.

The point about the kinds of modern flattery that we've been talking about is that there is too much undeserving public praise. I worry that the pervasiveness of such public flattery undermines the authenticity of private praise. It would be sad if private praise were to become as phony as so much public praise. But I don't really think we are in danger of that yet. In private, people find the language that is appropriate to convey their meaning. If it mirrors public praise, so be it; if we have to find our way to a new language of private praise, so much the better. It is when we fail to praise privately that we are in trouble.

Ultimately we must embrace flattery to redeem praise. Small flatteries are part of the mortar that holds society together. It is one of the daily rituals that help make civil society what we want it to be. Flattery is one of those little things which, even if it is insincere, makes everyday life pleasant in tiny, incremental ways. I am not talking about strategic manipulative duplicity that gets people undeserved credit. I am talking about the praise that we exchange with each other as a means of keeping the social peace.

Transparency is not the thing that will make society more decent and livable. Rampant insincere flattery is not either, but there is surely a happy mean. The tactical omissions of everyday life are what make society possible. Out of both compassion and convenience, we don't contest other people's depictions of themselves. Is that a form of flattery? I think it is. Is it harmful? I don't think so. As Lord Chesterfield said, if some men and women want to think themselves a little brighter, a little more attractive than they actually are, what is the harm? The benefits outweigh its costs. If telling someone that he or she is brighter or more attractive than they are makes them feel a little brighter and more attractive, that will probably make them a little brighter and more attractive. And nicer. It's social amelioration. It's making life a little pleasanter. I trust, I hope, I pray that you, wise and gentle reader, will agree—or, at least, not dispraise the effort.

Epilogue:
How to Flatter Without
Getting Caught

~ *Be specific.* Forget one-size-fits-all compliments, like "You're the best!" Better to say, "I loved your first novel, which was only published in New Zealand, and is now out of print."

~ *Find something you really do like.* If you're a bit squeamish about making things up out of whole cloth, find something you honestly admire, and praise it. Maybe even a little more than it deserves.

~ *Never offer a compliment and ask a favor at the same time.* When you charge for a compliment you make the receiver wary.

~ *Know how far to go too far.* Don't overdo it. If you're over the top, you make people wary. Plus, if you sate your target's desire for flattery, you've used up your resources. Mark Twain once remarked that telling the truth made sense because there was less to remember. Same thing with flattery: Keep it based on the real.

~ *Be a little esoteric.* If you're flattering someone who is used to flattery, find something out of the way to praise. Don't tell Tom Hanks you liked him in *Forrest Gump,* but tell him that you admired that tracking shot in the opening scene in *That Thing You Do!*

~ *Don't be afraid to flatter people you think already get enough flattery.* If they get a lot of flattery, they need a lot of flattery. And they can always use more. It's a renewable resource. And it's free.

~ *Flatter people behind their backs.* The virtue of this is, they don't suspect you of flattery. It makes its way to them through a third party—"He said you were brilliant!"—and suddenly your target thinks much more highly of you.

〰 *Absolutely no absolutes.* If you tell someone "You're the greatest" or "You're the best," it seems hollow and meretricious. Only Muhammad Ali is "the greatest."

〰 *Comparisons are never odious.* Tell someone she is better than someone she knows and respects. That's alway very gratifiying and gives the compliment a sense of being based in reality. Just as we envy those people nearest to us in status, we are more complimented by being better than our neighbor as well.

〰 *Never say, You were so much better than I thought you would be.* Never give a compliment in a way that suggests you held a low opinon of the person before.

〰 *Don't damn with faint praise.* What do you say when your friend directed a movie that's lousy but you don't want to lie? You clap him on the back and say, "You son of a gun, you did it again." Saying something was "pretty good" is not going to endear you to your target.

〰 *Never give the same compliment to different people.* If you do, and they find out, it undermines the value of the compliment and makes you seem like a weasel who brownnoses indiscriminately.

〰 *Mix a little bitter in with the sweet.* In other words, blend a tiny criticism with huge praise, e.g., "I thought the play moved a little slowly in the first act, but apart from that I thought it was better than *Long Day's Journey into Night.*"

〰 *Never ever be candid when a person asks you to be candid.* They are seeking compliments, not candor; support, not frankness—so anything even mildly negative is interpreted as a harsh criticism.

〰 *Agree, but not with everything.* If you're going to use what psychologists call "opinion conformity," don't conform on every little detail. Find some trivial thing to mildly disagree with, and that will make your hearty agreement on the bigger things seem more genuine.

〰 *Smile when you say that, pardner.* Enjoy the giving of praise. That way you're less likely to be detected and more likely to seem sincere. Take pleasure in the feeling that you're giving pleasure.

〰 *Start slowly and build up.* Studies show that we tend to like people who gradually come to like us more than we like people who like us right away. We regard them as more discerning.

∼ *Tell a secret.* Reveal something intimate. (But not, for example, that you are a shameless flatterer.) This suggests you like and trust the other person, that you think she's understanding and discreet, and that you want the relationship to deepen. You're flattering her with your trust.

∼ *Ask for advice.* We like people who think we are authorities. "Gee, Mr. Green, I was thinking of using that factory in Wisconsin to make widgets. You have a lot of experience with that—what do you think?"

∼ *Tease and chafe.* The roast compliment. "You lazy old bastard, that was some deal you pulled off." This is generally a guy thing.

∼ *Ask a small favor.* As Plutarch and La Rochefoucauld suggested, we like people for whom we do favors more than people who do favors for us.

∼ *Locate a weakness and praise its opposite.* Compliment a cheapskate for his generosity. Tell the pretentious woman how down-to-earth she is.

∼ *Open a compliment bank.* That is, make little deposits of compliments and favors, particularly at times the subject doesn't think you're being a brownnoser. Then you can draw on the account when you really need a favor in return.

∼ *Don't tell the CEO he's a genius if you're just a lowly account executive.* The greater the status difference between you and your target, the more subtle your flattery should be.

∼ *But you can tell the account executive that he's a genius if you are the CEO.* Downward flattery always is easier and more effective. The recipient is more gratified and less suspicious because the downward flow seems more natural.

How to Receive Flattery: It's Not as Easy as It Looks

∼ *"You flatter me."* Only say this when you want to return the honey of flattery with a bit of a barb. On one level you seem to be thanking the person; on another you're accusing him of duplicity.

~ *"I'm flattered."* This can be said with a feeling of warmth, as though you are acknowledging the person's kindness, or it can be said with a kind of disengenuous modesty—that is, I completely agree with your evaluation, but it would be rude of me to say so.

~ *"That's very flattering of you."* This suggests in fact that you're actually rather impressed with the compliment. That you like it, and you're requesting more.

~ *"You're too kind."* This expresses a formal, old-fashioned Southern sort of graciousness, but it also has a slight flavor of haughtiness or superiority. On the other hand, it is also reciprocal. You're praising the other person in return.

~ *"I hope you'll speak at my funeral."* This is ironic; it acknowledges the compliment while showing that you don't take it all that seriously.

~ *"Cut the bullshit."* It all depends on how this is uttered. If done in a jocular way, no problem, it's kind of like a wink. But if it is said seriously, the sucking up has backfired.

~ *Silence.* Again, there is silence and there is silence. If you just let it pass over like rain on the ocean, fine. But if it's deliberate, charged silence, you are leaving the person hanging out there, unrequited. This is about as aggressive as one gets in rebuffing flattery. No one ever says, "You sniveling little suck-up, be quiet."

~ *"Oh, nonsense."* You don't even want to be seen to be going down that road; you don't even want to acknowledge that it might be true.

~ *Ignore it, but let the person know you received it.* This can be done with a smile or a knowing look, but you do not thank the person for it because you don't want to reckon with any implicit quid pro quo. It's the gift under the tree you choose not to open.

"I'm so pleased you thought You're Too Kind: A Brief History of Flattery *was one of the best books you ever read. Care to purchase another copy?"*

Appendix

The unusual thing about the word "flattery" is not its origin or its history, but the extraordinary variety and number of synonyms, slang terms, and colloquialisms for the word and the idea. I don't know whether it's true or not that the Eskimos have dozens of different words for snow, but the theory is the same when it comes to all the different words we have for flattery: people only think up lots of names for something that is a ubiquitous part of their lives. Based on the sheer number and variety of terms for flattery, it's something that we find not only omnipresent, but amusing, annoying, and even rather tasty.

Here is a partial list of words that suggest flattery, as well as slang terms and standard synonyms: adulator, adulation, apple-polisher, applesauce, ass-kisser, ass-licking, assentator, back-scratching, banana oil, beflatter, beslaver, beslobber, blandishments, blarney, blow smoke, boot-licker, boot-kisser, brownnose, butter, butter up, cajole, cajoler, candied, carney, claw, clawback, compliment, court holy water, curry favor, daub, dissimulation, dope, ear grease, earwig, elozable, expalpate, eyewash, fawn, fawning, feed, flannel, fleech, flummer, fulsome, fume, graver, glother, glaze, grease, grease job, guyver, hagiography, honey, honeyed phrases, incense, inflate, ingratiate, ingratiation, kiss up, kowtow, laud, laudation, laying it on thick, lickspittle, lipsalve, monkey-blower, obsequious, oil, oily, oily-tongued, paint, palaver, palp, pander, panderer, panegyric, parasite, pepper, phrase, pickthank, placebo, play up to, puff, puffery, roll over, roose, rose water, salve, sawder, schmeer, shine up, silver tongue, simonize, slaver, smarm, smarminess, smoodge, smooth, smooth-boots, smoother, smooth-tongued, snow, snow job, soap, soft-soap, soft-solder, soften up, soothe, soother, spreading it on thick, stroke, suckass, suck-up, sugar, sweet-mouth, sweet-talk, sycophant, taffy, tickle the ears, toad-eater, toady, truckling, trowel, tuft-hunter, unctuous, varnish, velvet, weasel, wheedle, whillywha, yes, yes-man, yessir.

The slang terms for flattery basically fall into four categories that roughly parallel our senses of touch, taste, smell, and hearing. The first cat-egory, which we'll call Stroking, roughly follows the original sense of the word "flattery," which had to do with touching or feeling, smoothing or ca-ressing. The second category, which is somewhat related and which we'll call Sucking Up, involves the placing of a certain organ, the mouth, near certain other body parts, mainly what we will discreetly call the derriere. The third category, Edibles, contains words that have to do with things you can eat or taste—most of which are sweet. And the fourth category, which we'll call Rhetoric, basically involves the idea of flattery as language or words that have been stretched or distorted in some way.

Stroking

The meaning of the verb to *smooth* (as in to smooth something down and a "smooth flattering tongue") obviously derives from the original sense of the verb *flater*. It also suggests, when followed by "up"—to *smooth up*—a smarmy sort of ingratiation that butters people up and makes them easier to handle or more sympathetic. A *smooth-boots* is a flatterer who uses sleek and ingratiating language. To *soothe* is to offer blandishments. A *soother*—not to be confused with a smoothie—is one who assents or agrees with an-other, someone who uses what sociologists call "opinion conformity." Shakespeare talks of a *soothing tongue*. To *stroke down* is to smooth some-one down with flattering language. To *salve* is also to soothe with palliative words, to calm with unctuous phrases. To *tickle the ears* is to gratify with agreeable and pleasing sounds such as soft compliments. An *earwig* was an eighteenth-century term for a flatterer or parasite who whispered sweet somethings into your ear.

The familiar term *currying favor* has nothing to do with spicy food but comes from the term *curry,* which means to rub, stroke down, or dress a horse with a comb. The modern expression comes from the Renaissance, *to curry favel,* an early word for favor, which meant to seek royal or aristocratic patronage through insincere flattery or toadying. When *favel* turned to *favor,* the sense also became more modern: to ingratiate oneself with another through officious courtesy.

The term *soap* is to address with smooth or flattering words. If someone is soaped up, he is oiled, covered with emollients. *Soft-soap* is another slang term from the nineteenth century. ("He and I are great chums, and a little soft soap will go a long way with him."—Thomas Hughes, *Tom Brown at Oxford.)* To *lather someone up* is to coat someone with soft soap. If a journalist soft-soaps his subject, he lets him off easily. *Soft-sawder* is derived from *soft-solder,* which came from a technique for uniting metals, and also became a metaphor for uniting in friendship or union through soft and ingratiating words.

Sucking Up

Ass-kissing describes a graphic form of ingratiation. It implies a puckering of the lips from an inferior posture toward a superior one. Using a much tamer term, sociologists call this *upward ingratiation*. It is the flattery between an underling and a boss, between someone who has lower status and someone who has higher status, or just between a person who really wants something and the person who has it. It suggests a form of ingratiation that is particularly unappetizing—and thereby even more flattering to the subject.

The first reference the *OED* has to this form of flattery is a quote from Henry Miller's *Tropic of Capricorn:* "Besides, I wasn't a good ass-licker." *Ass-licking* seems a little more servile than ass-kissing. Kissing seems to come from the more genteel practice of kissing someone's ring or kissing their feet, which are somewhat less unsavory forms of ingratiation. And, of course, there's *boot-licking,* which is to *boot-kissing* what ass-licking is to ass-kissing. *Sucking up* seems to be just a punchier and more shorthand way of saying ass-licking, though of course sucking and licking are two distinctly different activities. The act of sucking seems to connote an even more energetic and exhaustive servility. *Sucking around* suggests someone who is lurking or hanging around in order to be in a position to suck up.

The 1961 *Webster's Third New International Dictionary* defines the related term *brownnosing* with admirable directness: "from the implication that servility is tantamount to having one's nose in the anus of the person from whom advancement is sought." My sense is that brownnosers are even more weenie-ish and fawning than ass-kissers or suck-ups. A brownnoser is someone who does his ingratiating with a kind of enthusiastic obsequiousness, and generally without any real awareness that he himself is odious. Ass-kissers, suck-ups, and brownnosers all have a geeky quality, but brownnosers seem even more weaselly somehow.

Beslaver, beslobber, and *bedrivel* all have the same suggestion of salivating over someone, of covering them with a wet and fulsome form of flattery. The *OED* cites an example from a nineteenth-century biography of Bacon: "He was ready to beslaver Majesty." We occasionally see this usage today, when we say a critic *slobbered* all over a movie, for example. *Gush* is another verb that has the same damp roots.

Even the term *blarney,* which is defined as smoothly flattering or cajoling talk, has osculatory origins. Blarney is the name of a village near Cork, in Ireland, where there was a sacred stone that was in a hard-to-reach place. The local custom was to climb up and kiss it. Anyone who kisses the *Blarney Stone,* according to *The Lewis Topographical Dictionary,* will have "a cajoling tongue and the art of flattery or of telling lies with unblushing effrontery." Compared to the alternative, kissing a stone doesn't seem so bad at all.

Edibles

Applesauce has two distinct meanings: nonsense and insincere flattery. It was used in both ways by the beginning of the nineteenth century. It was also a term of good-natured contempt in reply to a flattering statement. If I said, for example, "You have beautiful eyes," you might reply, "Applesauce!"—a kind of variation on "Pshaw!" You can even *apple up* someone, which is to butter them up, an activity we'll get to in a moment. *Applepolisher* suggests a lackey who does you small servile favors, a flattery valet.

Butter is defined by the *OED* as unctuous flattery. *Buttering someone up* is to ply them with rich flattery. To make it even more unctuous, you might *lay it on thick.* The *OED* cites a quote from the newspaper the *World* from 1880 that combines the two: "A lavish interchange of compliments, the butter being laid on pretty thick."

Candied, or *sugared,* or *honeyed* words all imply pleasing or sweetly flattering speech. ("The honeyed tongue."—*Hamlet*) To *sugar someone up* was to ply them with sweet talk. *Sweet-mouth* is a slang verb for giving someone sugary compliments. In the eighteenth century, a *sweetener* was not an add-on to a contract but one who flattered or cajoled. *Sweet-talk* meant to flatter and persuade with dulcet words. ("Don't try to sweet-talk me."—Margaret Mitchell, *Gone with the Wind.)*

Soothing syrup is a colloquial term for empty palliatives that calm someone down. *Taffy* is early-twentieth-century American slang for a crude or vulgar compliment, the kind that construction workers have traditionally called out to a young woman walking by on the sidewalk. *Sweet nothings* are whispered sweetmeats in a lover's ear. To *edulcorate* is to soften, to cajole, to flatter; its root is from *dulcis,* the Latin word for "sweet." The word is used for a situation where you charm a sourpuss by giving her something that is literally sweet (a Mars bar) or figuratively sweet (a compliment).

To *schmeer,* from the Yiddish "to smear or *grease,"* is a phrase not only for the swipe of cream cheese on a bagel, but for bribery or flattery. Nourishment is not only involved in giving flattery but in consuming it: If someone is susceptible to flattery, they *eat it up.* A *parasite,* according to Samuel Johnson's definition, is one who sups at rich tables and repays the favor with flattery.

The most unusual form of eating is suggested by the origin of the familiar term *toady,* which we define as a servile, flattering parasite. The origin of toady is the *toad-eater,* who was the attendant or assistant of a charlatan. The toady was employed to eat—or pretend to eat—poisonous toads in order to allow his master to demonstrate his skill for neutralizing or expelling poison.

Rhetoric

The final category should be the richest, but it is in fact the most meager. Going back to the Greeks, flattery has always been seen as a form of exaggerated or illegitimate rhetoric. Plato inveighed against rhetoric in general, and flattery was seen as a particularly pernicious and dangerous form of it. While there are quite a number of standard synonyms for flattery that suggest speech—praise, palaver, panegyric, hagiography, compliments, blandishments, cajolery—there is relatively little slang.

To *echo* suggests to flatter with servile assent. This is what sociologists call *opinion conformity.* (OTHELLO: What do'st thou thinke? IAGO: Thinke, my Lord? OTHELLO: Thinke, my Lord? Alas, thou echo'st me.) To *gloze* is to talk smoothly if emptily. *Gloze* is a pretense, a false show, a dissimulation. To *wheedle* is to insinuate with praise. To *schmooze* someone in modern parlance often suggests to use ingratiating speech, to blow smoke their way. *Phrase* is Scottish dialect for flattery or gush. A *proneur* is an extoller or eulogist, another rhetorical term for someone who praises. To *puff* is to give inflated public praise, to write an extravagantly favorable review (which, *dear reader*—or perhaps I should call you *cher maître*—wise and perceptive reviewers sometimes do). *London Magazine,* 1732: "Puff is a cant word for the applause that writers and Book-sellers give their own books &c. to promote their sale." Oh, well.

Notes

A Word or Two on the Etymology of Flattery

26   The English verb: This sense is still current in modern French.

26   The origins all: The *Oxford English Dictionary* surmises that the Old French term may have come from the Teutonic word *flat* or *flach,* which means to dash to the ground, but that doesn't sound very convincing. Another guess is that the modern meaning of the word came from the native English *flatter,* an onomatopoetic word expressive of light repeated movements similar to words in Old Norse and MSw. ("The flattering of the tinsmith's hammer woke me early on Sunday morning.")

26   Somewhere in the history: In fact, one of the earliest definitions of flattery, going back to the Middle Ages, is of an animal showing pleasure or fondness by, wagging its tail or making a caressing sound. The *OED* cites Topsell, from 1607, in a work called *Four-f. Beasts:* "Dogges who would fawne & gently flatter vpon all those which chame chastly & religiosly to worship." Three hundred and fifty years later later, Dale Carnegie will cite the dog wagging—or *flattering*—its tail as the most winning creature on the planet.

27   "This was the place": Dante Alighieri, *The Divine Comedy, Inferno,* trans. Allen Mandelbaum (New York: Bantam Books, 1982), XVIII, 112–126, p. 167.

27   the more common Italian term: *Webster's Third New International Dictionary,* p. 30.

28   "When I tell him": Shakespeare, *Julius Caesar,* II, i, 208.

29   "Oliver said to him": *Oxford English Dictionary* (hereafter, *OED*).

Chapter 1: Everyone Has a Hierarchy

31   The modern notion of animal hierarchies: Robert Wright, *The Moral Animal* (New York: Pantheon Books, 1994), p. 239.

33   The collective noun for certain primates: Steven Pinker, *How the Mind Works* (New York: W. W. Norton & Company, 1997), p. 193.

33   "The social organization of chimpanzees:" Frans de Waal, *Chimpanzee Politics* (Baltimore: Johns Hopkins University Press, 1989), p. 19.

33   "never make an uncalculated move:" de Waal, p. 41.

34   The most frequent social activity: de Waal, p. 21.

35   Female bonobos, who are even: Eugene Linden, "Apes and Humans: A Curious Kinship," *National Geographic,* March 1992.

35   Another form of this "affinitive" behavior: de Waal, p. 45.

36   "The more scientists have studied primates:" John Mitani, "Review of Kanzi," *Scientific American,* June 1995, Vol. 272, no. 6.

37   Their concern with power: de Waal, p. 212.

39   the revenge of the nerds: Pinker, p. 187.

40   "If we have a friend who is:" Wright, p. 282.

42   In *Adaptation and Natural Selection:* George C. Williams, *Adaptation and Natural Selection: A Critique of Some Current Evolutionary Thought* (Princeton, N.J.: Princeton University Press, 1974), p. 94.

42   We carry out evolutionary logic: Wright, p. 88.

44   "Genes for mimicry:" Richard Dawkins, *The Selfish Gene* (Oxford: Oxford University Press, 1989), p. 32.

44   "If deceit is fundamental:" Wright, p. 256.

45   Natural selection may well favor males: Wright, p. 61.

45   "We evolved from apes": Wright, p. 54.

46   A recent study: Michael T. McGuire, *The Neurotransmitter Revolution* (Carbondale: Southern Illinois University Press, 1994), p. 140.

Chapter 2: You *Can* Take It with You

51   "Royalty is a good profession": Lionel Casson and the Editors of Time-Life Books, *Ancient Egypt* (Alexandria, Va.: Time-Life Books, 1978), p. 103.

52   "If you are one": Miriam Lichtheim, *Ancient Egyptian Literature: A Book of Readings,* vol. 1 (Berkeley: University of California Press, 1975), p. 65.

53   "If you are in": Lichtheim, p. 65.

53   "He who hears": Lichtheim, p. 74.

55   All play and no work: J. M. Roberts, *The Penguin History of the World* (New York: Penguin Books, 1995), p. 84.

55   Abiding by the same: Sinatra burial details in *New York Post,* May 24, 1998, p. 9.

57   "Thou art destined": Casson, pp. 15–16.

59   Ramses did know how: Bob Brier, "The Great Egyptians." Produced by The Learning Channel (BMG Video). Written and narrated by Bill Brier.

59   "excessively self-laudatory": Lichtheim, p. 4.

60   The inscriptions always: William C. Hayes, *The Scepter of Egypt: A Background for the Study of the Egyptian Antiquities in the Metropolitan Museum of Art* (Cambridge: Harvard University Press, 1965), p. 78.

60   It reads in part: Lichtheim, p. 19.

60   "Only I alone": Ibid.

60   "I was responsible": Lichtheim, p. 75.

62   The idea was not: Daniel P. Silverman, ed., *Ancient Egypt* (New York: Oxford University Press, 1997), p. 148.

62   For them, appearances: Silverman, p. 155.

62   This picture appears: Ibid.

62   This was a revolutionary notion: Brier, "The Great Egyptians."

63   His successor, who was: There were some other exceptions. A life-size granite statue of King Sesostris III shows him with enormous ears that stick out so that he looks like a taxi with two open doors.

Chapter 3: Flatter Me or Else

66   "Let us make": Genesis 1:24.

67   "So God created man": Genesis 1:27.

67   As Jack Miles writes: Jack Miles, *God: A Biography* (New York: Knopf, 1995), p. 89.

67   "sole and indispensable": As many scholars have noted, there are essentially two creation stories in Genesis. In the first, quoted above, God simply snaps his fingers and creates man and woman. In the second story, a few paragraphs later, God creates Adam from the "dust of the ground" and then brings forth Eve from Adam's rib. While the first Adam seems pristine and almost notional, the second Adam is, well, more earthy. This Adam isn't just from the wrong side of the tracks, he's from under the tracks.

67   Even the Koran: Karen Armstrong, *A History of God: The 4,000-Year Quest of Judaism, Christianity, and Islam* (New York: Ballantine Books, 1993), p. 229.

67   *So that's:* This is the reason that God tells the angels to bow down before Adam: because he is made in the Lord's image.

67   "Where are you?": Genesis 3:9.

67   "Who told you": Genesis 3:11.

67 "She gave me": Genesis 3:12.
67 "till you return": Genesis 3:19.
68 "has become like": Genesis 3:22.
68 "because he wished": Miles, p. 403.
69 "It is part of": Harold Bloom, *The Book of J* (New York: Grove Weidenfeld, 1990) p. 207.
70 "For you shall worship": Exodus 34:14.
70 "And the anger": 2 Samuel 6:6–7.
70 But they're outdone: Miles, p. 133.
70 "For a long time": Isaiah 42:14–15.
70 "How long will": Numbers 14:11–12.
71 "Look on every one": Job 40:12.
71 As Jack Miles writes: Miles, p. 408.
71 "That they might know": Ezekiel 20:26.
71 "rebelling against his": Bloom, p. 15.
71 "Surely this instruction": Deuteronomy 30:11–12.
71 "Go and tell my servant": 2 Samuel 7:4–7.
72 "I am the first": Isaiah 44:6–8.
72 "I, the Lord": Isaiah 41:4.
72 "The Lord, the Lord God": Exodus 34:6–7.
72 But Yahweh's great: And by "no one," of course, he means the Israelites because they are everyone and everything to him.
72 "Sons have I reared": Isaiah 1:3.
73 They're stubborn: What God wanted from the Israelites is what he got from his angels. The angels are like African praise singers calling out the virtues of the Lord before his arrival. "Holy, holy, holy is the Lord of hosts; the whole earth is full of his glory." Isaiah 6:3.
73 "If the anger": Ecclesiastes 10:4.
74 "If God will be": Genesis 28:20–21.
74 "The people found": Exodus 17:1–4.
75 "You will be torn": Deuteronomy 28:64–68.
75 "Hear, O, Israel": Deuteronomy 6:4–6.
76 "I will leave only": 1 Kings 19:18.
76 "The beginning of wisdom": Proverbs 1:7, 9:10, 15:33.
76 "A personal God": Armstrong, p. 55.
77 God became the self-esteem: Perceiving oneself as chosen is not unique to the Jews, of course. When the Crusaders of the Middle Ages rode east to stamp out Jews and Muslims, they called themselves the new Chosen People. All three monotheistic religions have seen theologies of selection in their histories. And not just religions, but nations. The French in the eighteenth century, the British in the nineteenth century, and the Americans in the twentieth have all thought of themselves as a kind of chosen people.

77 Yes, the goyim: Armstrong, p. 191.
77 "Whence, then, did this": Sigmund Freud, *Moses and Monotheism*, trans. Katherine Jones (New York: Vintage Books, 1967), p. 81.
77 "There is no doubt": Freud, p. 134 and passim.
77 "Whom best I love": Shakespeare, *Cymbeline*, V, iv, 71.
78 The Lord gives Moses: Exodus 25:1–9.
78 "You shall kill": Exodus 29:19–20.
78 All of a sudden: See Exodus 25:8–9.
78 "They shall make an ark": Exodus 25:8–9.
79 "And you shall make the robe": Exodus 28:31–34.
79 "And when the Lord": Genesis 20:20–21.
79 "I will give you a son": Genesis 17:15–17.
79 "No, but you did laugh": Genesis 18:9–15.
80 "This is my covenant": Genesis 17:9–12.
80 "Circumcise therefore the foreskin": Deuteronomy 10:16.
81 "After these things God": Genesis 22:1–2.
81 "Oh God said to Abraham": "Highway 61 Revisited," words and music by Bob Dylan (Warner Bros., Inc., 1965).
81 "Do not lay your hand": Genesis 22:12.
83 "I will not show": Job 32:21–22.
83 "What is man": Job 7:17–18.
83 "Who is this": Job 38:2.
83 "Where were you": Job 38:4–6,12.
84 "Shall a faultfinder": Job 40:2–5.
85 God was the Unnameable: By contrast, the Koran gives God ninety-nine names or attributes.
85 You cannot say: Paul is thinking along these same lines when he says, "God's foolishness is wiser than human wisdom, and God's weakness is stronger than human strength." 1 Corinthians 1:25.
86 "He who speaks": Armstrong, p. 412, n. 85.
86 "I have had enough": Isaiah 1:11–13.
87 "Cease to do evil": Isaiah 1:16–17.
87 "Behold, I am doing": Isaiah 43:18–20.
88 As Jack Miles suggests: Miles, p. 373.

Chapter 4: Flattery Is Undemocratic

93 "To win the people": All quotes are from Aristophanes, *The Knights*, online at the Internet Classics Archive at classics.mit.edu/Aristophanes/knights.html.
93 One of the problems of democracy: Plato, *The Republic*, trans. Benjamin

Jowett (New York: P. F. Collier & Son, 1901). See no. VIII, "Forms of Government" (Internet ed.).

94   In Plato's dialogue: All quotations from the dialogue are from Plato, *Gorgias,* trans. and with an intro. by Walter Hamilton (London: Penguin Books, 1971).

95   In the fifth century B.C.: See John T. Fitzgerald, ed., *Friendship, Flattery, and Frankness of Speech: Studies on Friendship in the New Testament World* (New York: E. J. Brill, 1996), p. 32.

95   The philosopher Isocrates: David Konstan, *Friendship in the Classical World* (Cambridge: Cambridge University Press, 1997), p. 93.

96   Asked what the most beautiful: Fitzgerald, p. 233.

97   They were not romantic: Konstan, p. 4.

97   The Stoics, on the other hand: Konstan, p. 113.

97   In Aristotle's famous doctrine: Aristotle, *The Ethics of Aristotle: The Nicomachean Ethics,* trans. J. A. K. Thomson (New York: Penguin Books, 1976), p. 106.

98   "To make themselves pleasant": *The Ethics of Aristotle,* p. 163.

98   His model of behavior: *The Ethics of Aristotle,* pp. 155–156.

99   After the death of Alexander: Fitzgerald, p. 10.

99   "Without friendship": *The Ethics of Aristotle,* p. 263–264.

99   Aristotle describes friends: Fitzgerald, p. 144.

105 Plutarch addresses his essay: Fitzgerald, p. 64.

106 "For the man who is spoken of": Quotes from Plutarch are from *Plutarch's Moralia I,* the Loeb Classical Library (London: Heinemann, 1986).

Chapter 5: The Invention of Romantic Flattery

111 "Real changes in human": C. S. Lewis, *The Allegory of Love* (New York: Oxford University Press, 1975), p. 11.

111 Dante, who often: Paul Zumthor, in *A Handbook of the Troubadours,* ed. F. R. P. Akehurst and Judith M. Davis (Berkeley: University of California Press, 1995).

112 "Young girl of": Anthony Bonner, ed., *Songs of the Troubadours,* (New York: Schocken Books, 1972) 3.V.54 (P4).

113 "For no one can": Bonner, p. 169.

113 "The day I first": Bonner, p. 190.

113 "The fairest woman": *Proensa, An Anthology of Troubadour Poetry, Selected and Translated by Paul Blackburn* (Berkeley: University of California Press, 1978), p. 30.

114 "But I can't go on": Proensa, p. 28.

114 "If no hope": Proensa, p. 17.

114 "Love, which way": Bonner, p. 90.

115 "Oh, if only": Bonner, p. 76.

115 "Oh, God!": Bonner, p. 98.

116 "I have so much": Denis de Rougement, *Love in the Western World* (Princeton, N.J.: Princeton University Press, 1983), p. 38.

118 "Whoever loves passionately": de Rougement, p. 281.

119 As one critic said: de Rougement, p. 98.

120 "It is no wonder": Bonner, p. 96.

120 ". . . a man without": Bonner, p. 77.

120 "For such was the": de Rougement, p. 178.

121 "He is dead": Bonner, p. 97.

121 "Through her": Zumthor, p. 66.

121 Indeed, as strict: Zumthor, pp. 96–97.

121 Capellanus was a chaplain: Andreas Capellanus, *The Art of Courtly Love* (New York: Columbia University Press, 1960), p. 7.

122 Three of Capellanus's: Capellanus, p. 107 (re jealousy).

122 "certain inborn suffering": Capellanus, p. 28.

122 "Blindness is a bar": Capellanus, p. 33.

123 "A true lover would": Capellanus, p. 30.

123 The idea, as C. S. Lewis: Zumthor, p. 63.

123 C. S. Lewis listed: Lewis, p. 2.

123 "A too ardent lover": Capellanus, p. 103.

123 *"Omnis ardentior amator"* : Lewis, p. 15.

124 Women, she says: Capellanus (both quotations), 107.

124 "This fault can be": Capellanus, p. 206.

124 "For women, particularly": Capellanus, p. 37.

124 "When the Divine": Ibid.

124 "If the woman": Capellanus, p. 44.

125 "It doesn't seem": Capellanus, p. 54.

125 "So much nobility": Capellanus, p. 68.

125 "You are the cause": Capellanus, p. 45.

127 "Judge, can't you": Larry D. Benson, *Contradictions: From Beowulf to Chaucer: Selected Studies of Larry D. Benson,* eds. Theodore M. Andersson and Stephen A. Barney. (Brookfield, Vt.: Shocar Press, 1995).

128 "Whoever loves passionately": de Rougement, p. 281.

Chapter 6: The Courtier's Guide to How to Flatter

132 "the exigences of": Daniel Javitch, "Il Cortegiano and the Constraints of Despotism," in *Castiglione: The Ideal and the Real in Renaissance Culture,* ed. Robert W. Hanning and David Rosand (New Haven: Yale University Press, 1983), p. 17.

132 "Transactions with a despotic": Javitch, p. 25.

132 "Commonly the greater are": Frank Whigham, *Ambition and Privilege: The Social Tropes of Elizabethan Courtesy Literature* (Berkeley: University of California Press, 1984), p. 132.

133 "profession of a": Whigham, p. 100.

133 Flattery, Montaigne said: Burke notes that epideictic rhetoric, that is, rhetoric that is for show, becomes most common in periods of "rhetorical decay, as when the democratic functions of public debate were curtailed in Rome after the fall of the Republic." (Whigham, p. 186)

134 "the century of mobility": Whigham.

134 The pressure: Whigham, p. 7.

134 "Too many suitors": Whigham, p. 10.

135 Sir Thomas Wyatt condemned: Whigham, p. 23.

135 Everywhere, he says, he: Whigham, p. 24.

136 "a repertoire of strategies": Whigham, p. 5.

136 "it availeth not": Whigham, p. 124.

137 For 150 years: Woodhouse, p. 8.

137 *Il Cortegiano* was essential: Baldesar Castiglione, *The Book of the Courtier,* trans. and with an intro. by George Bull (Harmondsworth: Penguin Books, 1967).

138 "devote all his thought": Castiglione, p. 125.

138 "We would find": Ibid.

139 "the discretion to discern": Castiglione, pp. 125–26.

139 "So it seems": Castiglione, p. 127.

140 "I have a universal": Castiglione, p. 67.

140 "seem to be paying": Castiglione, p. 68.

141 "It was nothing": Whigham, p. 94.

141 "I will not see": Whigham, p. 92.

141 "Everyone," Castiglione says: Castiglione, p. 289.

141 "Even so," he says: Castiglione, p. 90–91.

142 "Let us leave these": Ibid.

142 "In this way": Castiglione, p. 286.

143 "Because men," Machiavelli writes: Niccolò Machiavelli, in *Great Books of the Western World,* vol. 21, ed. Mortimer J. Adler (Chicago: Encyclopedia Britannica Inc., 1994), *The Prince,* from the Everyman's Library, trans. W. K. Marriot (London: J. M. Dent & Sons; New York: E. P. Dutton & Co., n.d.) p. 16.

143 "Men who at the": Machiavelli, p. 31.

144 "because by arming:" Machiavelli, p. 30.

144 "a danger from which": Machiavelli, p. 33.

144 "is that of flatterers:" Ibid.

144 "Because there is no": Ibid.

146 Flattery is unnatural: The flatterer, he suggests, is a kind of pedant. Pedants,

he says, have knowledge, not wisdom. The flatterer is the kind of person, like the pedant, who knows the price of everything and the value of nothing. Montaigne says he dislikes men wise in words but base in deeds.

146   "I have an open way": Michel Euquem de Montaigne, *The Essays. Great Books of the Western World,* ed. Mortimer J. Adler, p. 423. Montaigne's essays from *The Complete Works of Montaigne,* ed. Donald M. Frame (Stanford: Stanford University Press, 1990).

146   "Every man likes": Montaigne, p. 492. He even cites a corollary that anticipates the Freudian idea of projection: "We . . . detest in others the defects that are more clearly in ourselves."

146   "Praise is always": Montaigne, p. 509.

146   "Benefits are agreeable": Montaigne, p. 497.

147   He cites the Pythagoreans: Montaigne, p. 63.

147   "The way of truth": You could argue that plain speech is immoderate in the sense that no one uses it. That people are so used to rhetorical flourishes and false praise that plain-spokenness is extreme. Montaigne does not, of course, make this argument. He does not even see it.

147   "I do not want": Montaigne, p. 425.

147   "inept for public": Montaigne, p. 165.

147   "so abject and servile": Ibid.

148   "uncivil by too": Montaigne, p. 69.

148   "There is nothing that": Montaigne, p. 341.

149   "maketh his train": Francis Bacon, "Of Followers and Friends," in Bacon, *The Essays,* ed. John Pitcher (London: Penguin Books, 1987), pp. 205–206.

149   "For there is no": Bacon, "Of Friendship," p. 142.

150   *"laudando praecipere" :* Pliny, *Letters,* III, 18.1–3.

150   "But if a man": Bacon, "Of Ceremonies and Respects," p. 98.

150   "For the common people": Bacon, "Of Praise," p. 215.

153   In some quarters: *Lord Chesterfield's Letters,* ed. and with an intro. by David Roberts (Oxford and New York: Oxford University Press, 1992), p. ix (hereafter, Chesterfield).

153   "to gain the approbation": Chesterfield, p. 13. Later, much later, Chesterfield confesses, "Call it vanity, if you please, and possibly it was so; but my great object was to make every man I met with like me, and every woman love me."

154   "is a very necessary": Chesterfield, p. 269.

154   The Art of Pleasing, he says: Chesterfield, p. 18.

154   "Have a real reserve": Chesterfield, p. 56.

154   "Do as you would": Chesterfield, p. 57.ß¡

154   "Observe the little habits": Chesterfield, p. 61.

155   "Cardinal Richelieu, who": Chesterfield, pp. 59–60.

155   "No flattery is either": Chesterfield, p. 92.

156   "If her face": Chesterfield, p. 60.

157   "Were you to converse": Chesterfield, p. 231.

157   "Whatever one ought": Chesterfield, p. 233.

157   "There is nothing that": Chesterfield, p. 47.

157   "Be convinced, that": Chesterfield, p. 85.

158   "Abhor a knave": Chesterfield, p. 125.

158   "Their enmity": Chesterfield, p. 55.

158   "This principle of vanity": Chesterfield, p. 104.

158   If a man has mind: Chesterfield, p. 61.

Chapter 7: American Transparency

161   Westward the course: And, a century and a half later, Bishop Berkeley had one of the West's fledgling university towns named after him.

162   "Let those flatter": Thomas Jefferson, "A Summary View of the Rights of British America," 1774.

163   "Let that alone": Perry Miller, *The New England Mind* (Cambridge, Mass.: Belknap Press of Harvard University Press, 1982), p. 46.

164   "fancy, fawning words": Miller, p. 304.

164   Obscure phrases and: Miller, p. 302.

164   "God's altar needs": Andrew Delbanco, *The Death of Satan* (New York: Farrar, Straus, and Giroux, 1995), p. 50.

165   "ambitious and deeply": Delbanco, *The Death of Satan,* p. 33.

166   "weaned affection": Miller, p. 42.

166   "A Puritan is": Andrew Delbanco, *The Puritan Ordeal* (Cambridge, Mass.: Harvard University Press, 1989), p. 66.

166   "ambidextrous theologians": Delbanco, *The Puritan Ordeal,* p. 67.

167   In 1791, Chateaubriand: Stephen Spender, *Love-Hate Relations* (New York: Random House, 1974), p. 39.

168   "There is not a king": George Washington, *Rules of Civility,* ed. and with commentary by Richard Brookhiser (New York: Free Press, 1997), p. 32.

168   "Cleanse not your teeth": Brookhiser, *Rules of Civility.* All quotes from actual rules taken from *Rules of Civility.*

168   A Virginia colonel: Catherine Drinker Bowen, *Miracle at Philadelphia* (Boston: Little Brown, 1986), p. 195.

168   "I have never seen": Bowen, p. 194.

169   "Do not think": Brookhiser, *Rules of Civility,* p. 36.

169   "You are wrong": Richard Brookhiser, *Founding Father* (New York: Free Press, 1996), p. 5.

170   "peculiarly conscious": Brookhiser, *Rules of Civility,* p. 46.

171   "In order to secure": Benjamin Franklin, *The Autobiography* (New York: Vintage Books, The Library of America, 1990), p. 65.

171   his reputation was greater: Bowen, p. 17.
172   "All Franklin's moral": Christopher Lasch, *The Culture of Narcissism* (New York: Norton, 1991), p. 55.
173   "I made it a Rule": Franklin, p. 89.
173   Franklin envies young Collins: Franklin, p. 15.
174   "My opposition," he writes: Franklin, pp. 99–100.
176   "the evils we experience": Bowen, p. 45.
176   "corrupted by flattery": For example, *The Federalist,* no. 63.
176   "A dangerous ambition": *The Federalist,* p. 30.
177   "does not require": *The Federalist.*
177   "An overscrupulous jealousy": *The Federalist,* p. 30.
178   sociologists call inner-directedness: This is David Riesman's term, and we will come back to it in the next chapter.
178   "Society's praise can": Ralph Waldo Emerson, *The Selected Writings of Ralph Waldo Emerson,* ed. Brooks Atkinson (New York: The Modern Library, Random House, 1992), p. 76.
179   "The soul that ascends": Emerson, "The Over-Soul," p. 250.
179   "Great is the soul": Ibid.
179   "Every natural process": Emerson, p. 21.
179   "the desire for riches": Emerson, pp. 15–16.
179   "The least admixture": Emerson, "The American Scholar," p. 65.
180   "Let [friendship] be": Emerson, "Friendship," pp. 210–11.
180   "this manlike love": Emerson, "New England Reformers," p. 415.
180   "Nothing shall warp me": Ibid.
180   "I shall hear without": Emerson, "Manners," p. 358.
180   He promptly sat: Robert D. Richardson, Jr., *Emerson: The Mind on Fire* (Berkeley: University of California Press, 1995), pp. 527–28.
181   Whitman's friend Horace: Richardson, p. 528.
182   "I know of no": Alexis de Tocqueville, *Democracy in America,* trans. George Lawrence (New York: Harper & Row, 1965), p. 25.
183   "There is not a crowned": Bowen, p. 46.
183   "I have derived": Spender, p. 58.
183   "There is indeed a": Tocqueville, p. 26.
184   "Each citizen of": Tocqueville, "Of Individualism in Democracies," p. 271.
184   "Aristocracy links everybody" Tocqueville, p. 272.
184   "They wonder how he": Tocqueville, p. 114.
184   "The least reproach": Tocqueville, p. 133.
185   In their relations: Tocqueville, p. 330.
185   "In absolute monarchies": Tocqueville, pp. 134–35.
186   "Democratic republics put": Tocqueville, p. 134.
186   "American moralists and": Tocqueville, pp. 134–35.
186   "Under the old monarchy": Tocqueville, p. 128.

187   "In America the majority": Tocqueville, p. 132.
187   "The inhabitants of democracies": Tocqueville, p. 330.
187   "If someone asks me": Tocqueville, p. 325.
187   "In Europe one has often": Tocqueville, p. 324.
188   "It is strange to see": Karen Halttunen, *Confidence Men and Painted Women: A Study of Middle-Class Culture in America, 1830–1870* (New Haven and London: Yale University Press, 1982), p. 191.
188   "With all the parts": Halttunen, p. 192.
189   The New York papers: Halttunen, p. 6.
190   "It's good to be shifty": Halttunen, p. 30.
190   In the early to middle: Halttunen, p. 34.
190   "a perfectly transparent": Halttunen, p. 52.
190   "hollow-hearted courtesy": Halttunen, p. 94.
191   They tended to be: Steven Starker, *Oracle at the Supermarket: The American Preoccupation with Self-Help Books* (New Brunswick, N.J.: Transaction Publishers, 1989) pp. 19–20.
191   It was only then: Richard M. Huber, *The American Idea of Success* (New York: McGraw-Hill, 1971).
191   He flatters his customers: Halttunen, pp. 199–202.
192   "a tinge of charlatanism": Halttunen, p. 205.

Chapter 8: How Flattery Won Friends and Influenced People

193   The Dale Carnegie course: Gail Thain Parker, "How to Win Friends and Influence People: Dale Carnegie and the Problem of Sincerity," *American Quarterly* 29, no. 5 (Winter 1977): 506.
195   "the management of interpersonal": Lasch, p. 58.
195   Young Dale yearned for: Parker, pp. 507–508.
196   "He is all things": Timothy B. Spears, " 'All Things to All Men:' The Commercial Traveler and the Rise of Modern Salesmanship," *American Quarterly* 45, no. 4 (December 1993): 527.
196   Even while acting: Huber, p. 233.
199   By the late 1950s: Richard Conniff, "The So-So Salesman Who Told Millions How to Make It Big," *Smithsonian,* 118 (October 1987).
199   It was the number-one: Starker, pp. 63ff.
200   "To whom it may": Dale Carnegie, *How to Win Friends and Influence People* (New York: Simon & Schuster, 1936), p. 19.
200   "The point of the story": *How to Win Friends,* p. 20. (1936)
200   "If Al Capone": *How to Win Friends,* pp. 20–21. (1936)
200   "Criticism is futile": *How to Win Friends,* p. 21. See also, "Ninety-nine

times out of a hundred, no man ever criticizes himself for anything, no matter how wrong he may be." Another way of looking at his philosophy is simply to reverse his equation about criticism and substitute the positive, flattery, for the negative, criticism. It would then read something like this: "Flattery is useful because it puts a man at his ease, and usually disarms him altogether. Flattery is safe because it salves a man's precious pride, inflates his sense of importance, and arouses his sympathy." Which is essentially what he counsels.

202 If you think: *How to Win Friends,* p. 58. (1937)

202 A person's toothache: *How to Win Friends,* p. 93. (1981)

202 Carnegie had been guided: Huber, p. 26.

203 "Say to yourself": *How to Win Friends,* p. xxi. (1937)

203 "Whenever you are confronted": *How to Win Friends,* p. xxiii. (1937)

202 Don't follow your instincts: To learn this skill, Carnegie even offers tips. At the end of chap. 1, he inserts a section called "Nine Suggestions on How to Get the Most Out of This Book." Among these are number 2, "Read each chapter twice"; number 5, "Review this book each month"; number 7, give a friend a "dime or a dollar every time he catches you violating one of these principles." This is behaviorism, Carnegie-style.

203 "I will speak ill": *How to Win Friends,* p. 41. (1937)

205 "There is only one": *How to Win Friends,* p. 43. (1937)

205 "hero bureaucrat": Donald Meyer, *The Positive Thinkers: Religion as Pop Psychology, from Mary Baker Eddy to Oral Roberts* (New York: Pantheon Books, 1980), p. 182.

205 "If I like anything": *How to Win Friends,* p. 34. (1937)

206 "Some readers" he writes: *How to Win Friends,* p. 36. (1937)

206 "One comes from": *How to Win Friends,* p. 37. (1937)

206 "Every act you have": *How to Win Friends,* p. 40. (1937)

207 "Everybody likes to be": *How to Win Friends,* p. 231. (1981)

207 "If all we had": *How to Win Friends,* p. 37. (1937)

208 "For years I have": *How to Win Friends,* p. 63. (1937)

209 "Remember," Carnegie says: *How to Win Friends,* p. 79. (1937)

212 "In earlier times": Haltunnen, p. 208.

214 "He has the right": Huber, p. 177.

214 Coué's spiritual philosophy: Huber, p. 194.

214 David Riesman called: David Riesman, with Nathan Glazer and Reuel Denncy, *The Lonely Crowd: A Study of the Changing American Character* (New Haven and London: Yale University Press, 1961; rev. ed., 1989), p. 149.

214 "a more popular, esteemed": Huber, p. 317.

216 "I believed that life was planless": Parker, pp. 151–52.

216 "You never read": *How to Win Friends,* pp. 57–58. (1937)

217 "the greatest winner": *How to Win Friends,* p. 57. (1937)

Chapter 9: The Science of Ingratiation

218 Goffman's theory: Goffman's subfield of sociology is often termed "symbolic interactionism."

218 He says that: Erving Goffman, *The Presentation of Self in Everyday Life* (New York: Anchor Books/Doubleday, 1959), p. 10.

218 *Ah, well:* Author's interview with Randall Gordon.

219 "harried fabricators of impressions": Goffman, p. 252.

219 Jones's own preoccupation: Edward E. Jones, *Interpersonal Perception* (New York: W. H. Freeman & Company, 1990), p. xii.

220 "the domain of systematic": Edward E. Jones, *Ingratiation: A Social Psychological Analysis* (New York: Appleton-Century-Crofts, 1964).

220 Every interpersonal encounter: In the preface to his groundbreaking work *Ingratiation,* he says that reserarchers on homosexuality, drug addiction, and schizophrenia are rarely asked why they became interested in what they're studying. But when you study ingratiation, he implied, everyone wants to know, are you a brownnose or something? Jones implied: Isn't it enough justification to study something that is absolutely ubiquitous in our society and that we all do knowingly or unknowingly every day of our lives?

220 "social rewards and punishments": Jones, *Interpersonal Perception,* p. 193.

221 "manipulative intent and": Jones, *Ingratiation,* p. 3.

221 Jones calls flattery: Jones, *Ingratiation,* p. 5.

221 "Ingratiation," he wrote: Jones, *Interpersonal Perception,* p. 177.

221 "non-normative behavior": Jones, *Ingratiation,* p. 5.

221 "The ingratiator," he says: Jones, *Ingratiation,* p. 7.

221 And as Jones notes: Jones, *Ingratiation,* p. 26.

222 "cognitively inaccessible": Jones, *Interpersonal Perception,* p. 178.

222 "distinguish between genuine": Jones, *Ingratiation,* p. vi.

222 "a class of strategic": Edward E. Jones and Camille Wortman, *Ingratiation: An Attributional Approach* (Morristown, N.J.: General Learning Press, 1973), p. 2. One thing to keep in mind is that every one of Jones's studies, and virtually all of the others cited by him, are of college students. Sociologists are academics and they experiment on their charges. These are not real-world situations, but the whole point of such social science is that the results can be extrapolated to everyone else, that they are testing profound and intrinsic human responses. But it's worth noting that, as the sociologist Marvin Bressler has pointed out, "Most of what we know about social psychology comes from captive audiences of college students."

224 "The communicator must": Jones, *Ingratiation,* p. 27.

224 *Don't give a compliment:* Jones and Wortman, p. 5.

225   "Every man willingly": Jones, *Ingratiation*, p. 378.

226   "uncertainty reduction principle": Jones, *Ingratiation*, p. 30.

227   "By and large": Jones and Wortman, p. 12.

230   Studies show that we don't: Jones and Wortman, p. 29.

230   Many studies show: Jones, *Ingratiation*, p. 41.

232   "We influence others": Jones, *Ingratiation*, p. 44.

233   "The trouble with favors": Jones and Wortman, p. 20.

234   "Opinion agreement": Jones, *Ingratiation*, p. 121.

234   "It is presumptuous": Jones, *Ingratiation*, p. 93.

234   "To evaluate someone": Jones, *Ingratiation*, p. 123.

235   Not a good: In *Ingratiation*, Jones cites a study he did of freshman and up-
      perclassman undergraduates in the Naval ROTC program at Duke Univer-
      sity. They were told that the navy was studying leadership potential and
      wanted to see if compatible groups provide a better setting in which to see
      leadership potential than do incompatible groups. They were tested in pairs,
      one high-status, an upperclassman, one low-status, a freshman. They were
      told to exchange information with each other. One group was told it was im-
      portant for them to be compatible. One group was told that it was important
      to be accurate. The duos in the compatibility groups conformed more than
      the people in the accurate duos. High-status conformed more on miscella-
      neous items that were not relevant to status differential; they were trying to
      show their approachability while maintaining power. Low-status subjects
      conformed more on items relevant to status differences than miscellaneous
      items. High-status subjects became more modest about important things.
      Low-status became more modest about the miscellaneous things; they didn't
      want to seem presumptuous about being modest about important things nor
      seem to be challenging the high-status colleague. The study showed that the
      low-status individuals flatttered their high-status mates, but that the high-
      status subjects were suspicious of the flattery.

235   "The trick": Jones, *Interpersonal Perception*, p. 181.

235   The researchers reasoned: Jones and Wortman, p. 28.

237   "Obsequious flatterers are often": Jones, *Ingratiation*, p. 166.

237   But this is actually: Jones and Wortman, p. 49.

238   In confirmation of: Randall Gordon, "Impact of Ingratiation on Judgments
      and Evaluations: A Meta-Analytic Investigation," *Journal of Personality and
      Social Psychology* 71, no. 1 (1996): 54–70.

239   "overlearned responses to": Jones and Wortman, p. 51.

239   "The benefits of information": Ibid.

240   "To charge all": Samuel Johnson, *Lives of the Poets*.

Chapter 10: The Capitals of Modern Flattery

243   found that handsome: Robert B. Cialdini, *Persuasion* (New York: William Morrow, 1993), pp. 171–72.

246   He got his "get": Both examples from Lawrence K. Grossman, "TV News: The Great Celebrity Chase," *Columbia Journalism Review,* July-August 1988, on-line.

262   "I know he's dying": Hadley Davis, *Development Girl: The Hollywood Virgin's Guide to Making It in the Movie Business* (New York: Doubleday, 1999), pp. 67–68, 88.

265   "Dave, I just": *Late Night with David Letterman,* CBS, November 13, 1997.

266   "loves the insults,": Don DeLillo, *Underworld* (New York: Scribner, 1997), p. 54.

Appendix

278   "a cajoling tongue": *OED,* "blarney."

278   It was also: *OED* on CD-ROM (Oxford: Oxford University Press, 1992.)

Acknowledgments

It's not flattery but a simple fact to say that without the following people this book would not have been possible: Marc Abraham, Kurt Andersen, James Basker, Marvin Bressler, Tricia Brock, Benedict Carton, Anita Dunn, Jake Gibbs, David Kuhn, Julian Levinson, Eugene Linden, David Michaelis, Tara McGann, Mary McGlynn, Adav Notia, Lawrence O'Donnell Jr., Dennis Ortiz, Pip Pfaff, Terron Schaefer, Gabriel Snyder, Chris and Priscilla Whittle, and Robert Wright. I want to thank Jim Kelly and Walter Isaacson for favors that I didn't even know about; Joanne Gruber, for her rigorous red pen; my agent, Joy Harris, for her support and unfailing good humor; Ana DeBevoise for always being a delight; and my editor, Alice Mayhew, for sticking with me and by me for longer than I deserved.

Index

Scribner

ONE GOOD TURN
A NATURAL HISTORY OF THE
SCREWDRIVER AND THE SCREW
Witold Rybczynski

'A perfectly turned little triumph'
THE TIMES

One Good Turn is a story of mechanical discovery
and genius that takes readers from Ancient
Greece to Victorian Glasgow, from weapons
design in the Italian Renaissance to car design
in the age of American industry. The screwdriver,
perhaps the last hand tool in a world gone cyber,
represents nothing less than the triumph of
precision.

One of our finest cultural and architectural historians,
Rybczynski renders a graceful, original, and engaging
portrait of the tool that changed the course of
civilisation.

PRICE £5.99
ISBN 0 7432 0850 1

**SIMON &
SCHUSTER**

MRS P's JOURNEY
The Remarkable Story of the Woman
Who Created the A-Z Map
Sarah Hartley

This is the story of Phyllis Pearsall: artist,
entrepreneur and creator of the *A-Z*. Frustrated by
the lack of proper maps of London in the '30s,
Phyllis took to the City's 23,000 streets – on foot.
She spent the next year tracing the streets from dawn
till dusk, painstakingly collating her work
in shoeboxes and finally delivering them to
WHSmith's in a wheelbarrow. And from this
laborious task the *A-Z* was born.

Mrs P's Journey is more than an account of this
remarkable feat, it is an amusing and beautifully
written tribute to this intriguing woman,
diminutive in size but renowned for her fractious
energy who has left a legacy for which every
Londoner is surely grateful. Indeed, where would
we be without the *A-Z*?

PRICE £15.99
ISBN 0 7432 0801 3

**SIMON &
SCHUSTER**

VANILLA BEANS &
BRODO

Real Life in the Hills of Tuscany

Isabella Dusi

Five years ago, Isabella Dusi and her husband left
their native Australia and settled in the close-knit
community of Montalcino, a beautiful mountain
eyrie and home to an eclectic tribe of Italians. In
Vanilla Beans & Brodo, Isabella writes an affectionate
and humorous account of a year in the Tuscan hills.
Following the Montalcinese through the seasons, she
captures the spirit of the place: the fierce rivalry
between the village neighbourhoods, the football
fever, the prestigious archery tournament, and the
delicious cuisine and much prized wine.

Vanilla Beans & Brodo is a warm and evocative portrait
of Montalcino, a village with a passionate and bloody
history and a wealth of traditions, that will surely
challenge the long held image that Tuscany moves at
a leisurely and docile pace.

PRICE £13.99
ISBN 0 7432 0934 6

POCKET
B O O K S

FUN RUN AND OTHER OXYMORONS

Singular Reflections of an Englishman Abroad

Joe Bennett

Have you ever wondered why baths are designed to grip nicely when dry but become hip-shatteringly slippery when wet or how you can be as rich as Bill Gates?

Joe Bennett explains all in his collection of exquisitely crafted pieces that explore some of the important questions in life and invariably find the funny side. These are the hilarious observations of an Englishman abroad, celebrating the joys of bachelorhood, attacking the pretensions of those purveyors of frothy cappuccinos, therapy, consultant speak and shining a sharp, new light on the absurdity of life.

PRICE £7.99
ISBN 0 684 86136 4

About the Author

Richard Stengel was most recently a senior editor at *Time* and has contributed to *The New Yorker, The New Republic, GQ,* and MSNBC.com. He is the author of *January Sun,* a book about life in a small South African town, and he collaborated with Nelson Mandela on *Long Walk to Freedom.* Stengel lives in New York City with his wife and son.